Winfried Heinemann
The GDR and Its Military

Winfried Heinemann

The GDR and Its Military

—

DE GRUYTER
OLDENBOURG

Bundeswehr Centre of Military History and Social Sciences, Publications Section (0655-01en)
Typesetting: Antje Lorenz
Copyediting: Philip Saunders, Berlin

ISBN 978-3-11-158752-3
e-ISBN (PDF) 978-3-11-158841-4
e-ISBN (EPUB) 978-3-11-158876-6

Library of Congress Control Number: 2025937616

Bibliographic information published by the Deutsche Nationalbibliothek
The Deutsche Nationalbibliothek lists this publication in the Deutsche Nationalbibliografie; detailed bibliographic data are available on the Internet at http://dnb.dnb.de.

© 2025 Walter de Gruyter GmbH, Berlin/Boston, Genthiner Straße 13, 10785 Berlin

Cover image: Parade in honor of the GDR's 40th anniversary. Alumni of the "Friedrich Engels" military academy march in front of the parade. BArch, Bild 183-1989-1007-038/Harmut Reiche

www.degruyterbrill.com
Questions about General Product Safety Regulation:
productsafety@degruyterbrill.com

Contents

Author's Note —— **VII**
Acknowledgements —— **VII**

State of the Art —— **1**
GDR Military History in the Historiography —— **1**
Questions of Security —— **2**
How German Was the NVA? —— **3**
Periods of GDR Military History —— **5**
General History of the GDR —— **6**
Memoirs and Early Scholarly Works —— **9**
Sources —— **11**
Scholarly Research —— **13**
Perspectives —— **14**

Chronological Overview —— **17**
Before 1956 —— **17**
Raising the NVA: 1956–1962 —— **24**
Consolidation: 1962–1970 —— **35**
Détente and Military Reform: 1971–1989 —— **41**
The GDR Military in the Peaceful Reform: 1989/90 —— **50**

The Armed Forces, Politics, and Society —— **55**
A "society dominated through and through": The Militarization of Everyday Life —— **55**
The Social Status of the Military —— **59**
The Military as an Instrument of Socialization —— **60**
The SED State Party and the NVA —— **64**
The Military and State Security ("Stasi") —— **68**
Women in the NVA —— **75**
Everyday Life, Culture, and Sports —— **77**
Soviet Idols and German Traditions —— **83**
The Enemy: The Bundeswehr, Desertion, and Opposition —— **85**

The Organization of the Armed Forces —— **90**
The Ministry of National Defense —— **90**
Ground Forces, Air Forces and Air Defense, the People's Navy —— **92**
A Special Case: The Border Troops —— **102**

The System of National Defense and the GDR's Other Armed Formations —— 106
Integration into the Warsaw Pact —— 116
A Militarized Security Policy —— 122

Recruiting —— 124
Conscripts, Reservists, and "Construction Soldiers" —— 124
Noncommissioned Officers —— 128
Officers —— 132
Training and Qualification —— 138

Armaments and Military Innovation —— 146
Methodological Problems —— 146
GDR Armaments Industry —— 147
Armaments Cooperation and Standardization within the Warsaw Pact —— 151
Uranium Exports —— 152
The Military and the Economy —— 155

Warfare, Operational Planning, and Military Thinking —— 160
Sources —— 160
Integration into the Warsaw Pact —— 161
Military Doctrines —— 164
The NVA during the Warsaw Pact Crises —— 167
The GDR in the "Third World" —— 170
West Berlin —— 173
"Policy of Peace" and Offensive Operational Planning —— 177
The New Soviet Military Doctrine of the 1980s —— 180

Appendix

Abbreviations —— 183

Rank equivalents —— 185

Bibliography —— 187

Texts —— 197

Tables —— 209

Index —— 215

Author's Note

This is the English edition of a paperback published in German in 2011. However, "English edition" means more than a mere translation – the translation of a book published a dozen years ago would hardly attract many readers.

Instead, this is also an updated version. During the last few of those twelve years, not much research has added to our knowledge, but during the 2010s, quite a number of books have contributed to a better understanding of GDR military history, eventually helping us to understand GDR history as a whole much better.

Obviously, a lot of the relevant research literature has been published only in German. The concept of this study book is to inform interested readers who are looking for a concise, yet complete and reliable source, while also enticing a few of them to conduct their own research into some of the as yet under-researched aspects. To achieve this, the book introduces the reader to the current state of the art, irrespective of whether publications are in German or English. An attempt has been made to include all relevant English-language books on the subject, while not omitting those German-language publications which helped research to move on and yielded new, sometimes even surprising, results.

The bibliography is somewhat unconventional in that it is not strictly alphabetical. Rather, the titles quoted are listed systematically by chapter to facilitate locating the relevant literature for any given subject. Each title has an identifying number referring to the literature list. Preference has been given to English-language titles, which are, however, thin on the ground in many aspects. The author and the series editors hope that this system most appropriately meets the needs of students and researchers trying to find their way into this fascinating topic.

Acknowledgements

German Democratic Republic (GDR) Military History is a vast subject. This volume contains a lot of information, and I generated only a small part of it myself. In many ways, it is the result of six years at the helm of a very active, innovative, and eventually highly productive research section on "GDR Military History" within what was then the Military History Research Office (MGFA) and is now the Bundeswehr Centre of Military History and Social Sciences (ZMSBw) in Potsdam.

I am eternally grateful to my colleagues, both civilian and in uniform, from this "Research Section IV." The first to name are Angelika Nawroth and Jutta Gierke, without whom I would have been bogged down by the jungle of defense bureaucracy. My academic colleagues I prefer to list in alphabetical order: Oliver Bange, Heiner Bröckermann, Torsten Diedrich, Matthias Rogg, Klaus Storkmann, and Rüdiger Wenzke. Armin Wagner, who had been part of this unit before my time, was a helpful and constructive partner in many dialogues. If the English version is more than just a translation of a twelve-year-old book, that is due to the continuing exchange with not only many of these colleagues but also scholars such as Hope Harrison (Elliott School of International Affairs, George Washington University) or Christian F. Ostermann, Director of the History and Public Policy Program at the Woodrow Wilson Center, both in Washington DC.

Manfred Wilke from the Institute of Contemporary History (Munich/Berlin) was another critical discussant. Sadly, he passed away before this book could be published. Our cooperation had its origins in a research project funded by the *Deutsche Forschungsgemeinschaft* (German Research Foundation). A special thanks is due in this context to Jochen Maurer, who, within this project, wrote his PhD thesis on the Border Troops, opening up new insights into the history and role of this formation. Two other names that deserve a mention in this context are those of Leo Schmidt and Axel Klausmeier, the former the chair of architectural conservation in the Cottbus University of Technology and the brain behind our Berlin Wall project, and the latter – like me – an honorary professor at that university, but also the director of the Berlin Wall Foundation; both contributed their knowledge to this book.

A manuscript requires a text editor to develop into a readable book. Michael Thomae patiently oversaw the growth of the original version, by correcting my German. Without Philip Saunders correcting my English, this book might have been in that language, but probably not all that readable. During his period as a reserve officer in the MGFA, Rouwen Wauschkies saw to the many attractive illustrations, while the maps appear thanks to the ZMSBw graphics section directed by Bernd Nogli.

Amélia Polónia, Professor of Early Modern History in the University of Porto, Portugal, lovingly accompanied me throughout all the stages of this book's development, both in German and in English.

This book is dedicated to my two sons and their families who made me a proud grandfather.

Winfried Heinemann

State of the Art

GDR Military History in the Historiography

Accounts of the history of the GDR are usually placed somewhere between two poles. Some answer the demand for an exact analysis of the political system ruling and controlling the GDR. The assumption is that the rule of the Socialist Unity Party (*Sozialistische Einheitspartei, SED*) needs to be understood and interpreted "from above." The other faction rejects just this approach and emphasizes the need for an "*Alltagsgeschichte*," a history of everyday life within the East German state.

What both perspectives have in common is that neither spends much time and effort looking at the GDR's military history. The "top-down" approach takes into consideration the mechanisms applied within the GDR to secure its political system against internal "enemies," applying today's distinction of "internal" and "external" security without questioning whether they are appropriate to the socialist bloc. The "bottom-up" approach, on the other hand, usually largely disregards to what extent everyday life in the GDR was subject to military patterns and forms, nor does it discuss how much the "system of socialist national defense" impacted on the citizens' lives. This is also relevant for the best-known English literature, such as the now-classic "Anatomy of a Dictatorship" by Fulbrook *1.14* and, for the more recent overview, "The German Democratic Republic" by Grieder *1.11*.

Yet, a general history of the GDR without taking into account the history of its hypertrophic security apparatus, omitting a comprehensive analysis of all its "armed organs," such as the military, the various police forces, the Working-Class Combat Groups, obviously the State Security Service (usually referred to here as the "Stasi") and many others, is, by definition, incomplete. According to its ideology, the GDR perceived itself as being in a continuous class struggle initiated by "the West." Situated on the "frontline" along the border between two antagonistic blocs, it had to maintain a continuous "combat readiness" – this characterized both the power structures of the SED state and the daily reality of its citizens.

For these reasons, a modern military history cannot limit itself to recounting the organization and equipment of the National People's Army (NVA) as the best-known and -equipped GDR military formation. Rather, all elements of the "system of socialist national defense" need to come into focus. This will have to include the GDR's security and defense policy in its most important framework of reference, i.e., the Warsaw Pact, as well as the economic and social costs of the state's "security precautions."

As there can be no doubt that the GDR forms part of German history, its military forces must undoubtedly be seen as part of German military history. In its outward appearance, such as its uniforms, the NVA was a military force which emphasized a continuity with former German and Prussian armed forces. (Stating this does not preempt an analysis of how independently national the GDR security apparatus was, or to what extent it was controlled from abroad – an analysis which will eventually contribute to an assessment of how sovereign or dependent the GDR was in its entirety.) No military history of Germany can, thus, afford not to take into account the NVA and the many other (para-)military units within the GDR.

Eventually, a deeper understanding of the GDR and its military will not be possible without placing it in the context of the Cold War in general, and the division of Germany in particular. While the Soviet hegemon in the East was the prime point of reference for the GDR political elites, many of its citizens compared their system more to the Federal Republic of Germany in the West; this was a unique feature of the East German state within the Soviet bloc. After all, West Germany was the core bogeyman of socialist propaganda; while positive references were emphatically discouraged, comparisons with "the West" were omnipresent in everyday discourse. In many ways, the NVA may have been the most potent army within the Warsaw Pact alongside the Soviet one; it was a relevant factor within the mutual threat scenarios between East and West, much as East Berlin was probably Moscow's most important partner politically. A history of the Cold War without reference to the GDR as the westernmost outpost of the socialist camp would be as incomplete as a history of the GDR overlooking its military, or any German military history without a chapter about the 40 years of GDR armed forces.

Questions of Security

Upon closer inspection, and in the light of its own self-perception at the time, there is little substance to the claim that the NVA served – exclusively or at least largely – purposes of external security. According to Marxist-Leninist doctrine, "Socialism" had to defend itself against the "counterrevolution," no matter whether the threat came from abroad or inside. On the contrary, a concept of "counterrevolution" as a more or less monolithic danger made it seem inconceivable that internal and external enemies would not be somehow linked to each other. According to this way of thinking, internal unrest, such as the traumatic uprising against SED rule of June 17, 1953, could only be explained away as being engineered from abroad. There was no need to prove in detail how that "revolt" had been initiated by the US or by West German "revanchists": that this was so was axiomatic within the ideology underpinning the GDR system.

All measures taken in East Berlin after the events of June 17, 1953, which aimed to protect the "socialist order", dispensed entirely with any differentiation between external and internal enemies. On the regional and the district level, contingency staffs *(Bezirkseinsatzleitung, Kreiseinsatzleitung)* were created to coordinate the protection of internal order, and it was a matter of course that the SED Party hierarchy took a leading role in them – the same way it did in the *Nationaler Verteidigungsrat* (NVR; National Defense Council of the GDR) which coordinated these preparations at the national level (*2.20* Bröckermann, Landesverteidigung, 142–185).

There is another indication that the NVA was expected to take an internal security role and its officers knew this very well, and that is the pride with which a number of them tirelessly emphasized that, after all, they had not fired on demonstrators during the heady months of the autumn and winter of 1989 – this pride only made sense if the underlying assumption was that they should have fired. Inversely, organs of internal security, such as the Riot Police *(Bereitschaftspolizei)*, had been trained and equipped to operate in "enemy" territory, and were scheduled to do so. It would be equally difficult to define the degree to which the Border Troops or the Working-Class Combat Groups were part of "internal" or "external" security. In view of this complexity, a history of the NVA alone would not do justice to the comprehensive "system of socialist national defense."

How German Was the NVA?

The popular uprising of June 17, 1953, was clear proof that the security of the SED Party regime relied on the presence of Soviet troops. The GDR had been a Soviet creation from its inception, and throughout its existence, its rulers were sitting on Soviet bayonets. For the Soviet Union, however, maintaining the GDR as its area of influence constituted a drain on its resources. The huge supplies of armaments, subsidized deliveries of weapons, raw materials, and energy served Soviet great power politics. Situated as it was on the borderline with the North Atlantic Treaty Organization (NATO), the GDR played a leading role in the Soviet game. Once post-World War II reparations had ceased, and the export of uranium ore from the GDR into the Soviet Union had lost its relevance, the GDR economy remained dependent on highly subsidized Soviet supplies of armaments and raw materials. In equal measure, it relied on the guaranteed sales of its own industrial products. Compared to what came from other member states of the Council for Mutual Economic Assistance (COMECON), GDR products were top standard and a fixture in the Soviet and other socialist economies, but on the world market, they were less and less competitive. On the other hand, exporting goods to "brother nations" meant that the revenue in convertible (i.e., Western) currency declined continuously, further hindering the modernization of the backward GDR industry.

For a long time, the West German federal government succeeded in precluding international diplomatic recognition of the GDR as a state, pointing at the SED system's lack of democratic credentials. The East German government's chief diplomatic aim was, therefore, to be recognized by Western nations as independent and sovereign – not least, so it could use such recognition to reinforce the political manipulation of its own citizens.

Throughout the 1950s, West German Chancellor Konrad Adenauer pursued a consistent policy of rearmament within the Western international framework; his critics feared this might perpetuate or, at least, increase the division of Germany. The Soviet Union, and in its wake, the GDR, knew how to put such national sentiments to good use. Their claims that they themselves were the true protagonists of German unity, whereas Adenauer was on the Americans' payroll and had pursued separatist ideas even before 1933 did not fall on deaf ears. It is to be read in this context that the armed forces created in the mid-1950s should have the word "national" in their very name. At the same time, the political and economic motto inside the GDR was "Learning from the Soviet Union means learning to win."

Even after the "Treaty concerning the basis of relations between the Federal Republic of Germany and the German Democratic Republic" had been signed in 1972, and both German states had finally joined the United Nations as members, the GDR's limited sovereignty remained obvious: After all, in the 1971 Four Power Agreement about Berlin, the Soviet Union had guaranteed the Allies' rights of access as well as certifying transit rights of West Berliners and West Germans – disposing of both GDR territory and air space without officially consulting the East Berlin government.

That the member states of the Eastern bloc should have only limited sovereignty was, of course, no secret. Following the Warsaw Pact's intervention in Czechoslovakia in 1968, crushing the "Prague Spring," it had been published more or less officially as the "Brezhnev Doctrine." Again, this demonstrates the interaction of internal and external security: The socialist regimes could only have their internal stability guaranteed by the threat of outside, i.e., Soviet, intervention, while their lack of fully sovereign statehood meant a degree of instability which required additional repression within. The GDR leadership, more than any other Warsaw Pact partner, urged Moscow to intervene militarily in case one of its allies seemed unstable at home; this resulted, of course, from the SED's admission that its own survival at the helm of GDR politics depended on the allies, above all, the Soviets' willingness to intervene in the case of unrest in the GDR.

All GDR policies had to maneuver between dependence on the Soviet Union and its allies, on the one hand, and the need to demonstrate national sovereignty, on the other. Just because the GDR's military history is an integral part of German military history generally, military historians have to ask to what degree the East German military was no more than a western outpost of the Soviet Army, and to what extent it differed from the other Warsaw Pact armed forces by showing distinctly specific German features.

A comparison with the West German *Bundeswehr* may be helpful here. Under the conditions of nuclear warfare in a supersonic age, traditional concepts of what national sovereignty was supposed to mean had been relativized anyway. Only a comparison can show whether such losses of sovereignty were inherent necessities of instrumental-rational warfare, or if they indicated politically motivated control by the hegemonial power. The question of how "German" the GDR – and its military – had been also needs to be answered in light of the experience that during the late 1980s, the Soviet Union and its East German "satellite" slowly drifted apart, a process which was halted only when both eventually ceased to exist. During the late 1980s, the slogan "Learning from the Soviet Union means learning to win" was hijacked by GDR civil rights activists who wanted Soviet Glasnost and Perestroika in their own country as well.

Periods of GDR Military History

The development of GDR security and defense policies was determined to such a degree by the Soviet Union and the course of international politics that the periodization normally applicable to GDR history is of little use in analyzing its military history (*2.6* Diedrich, Prägende Veränderungen, 120).

Even before the GDR was founded as a state on October 7, 1949, armed forces had been raised in the Soviet Occupation Zone of Germany. As of 1952, the *Kasernierte Volkspolizei* (KVP – literally translated as the "Barracked People's Police") began to form the nucleus for the build-up of regular military structures. They were eventually formed into the NVA (predominantly just a change of name), marking the first major caesura. The uprising of June 17, 1953, marking such a caesura for GDR general history, is less relevant for its specifically military history: It was the Soviet occupation regime which declared martial law; Soviet troops and tanks, not German forces, eventually put down the revolt. The KVP played no more than an auxiliary role.

Opposed to that, the sealing off of Berlin's previously open inner-city border in August 1961 was relevant for the East German military insofar as it allowed the GDR to introduce conscription the following year. That, in turn, changed the NVA: until then, its purpose had been largely to prepare for eventualities in internal or external security. Now, it also assumed the role of ensuring social discipline. Conscription meant that from then on, linking the "People's Army" with society and simultaneously socializing the conscripted recruits became a major task for the military.

Another caesura was the change from Walter Ulbricht to Erich Honecker at the helm of the GDR during 1970/1. While this change of leadership initially remained without major consequences for the NVA's structure and everyday life, it soon began to have long-term effects for the GDR "security architecture," i.e., the SED Party's policymaking apparatus in questions of security.

The early years of the Honecker era were characterized by the Conference on Security and Co-operation in Europe (CSCE) process. From the perspective of the GDR leadership, this meant a profoundly changed threat perception. This period was followed by the unruly years of 1980/1 and the need to meet the challenge of an "unstable" People's Republic of Poland in the GDR's immediate vicinity. The end of the decade saw the new Soviet military doctrine. While the changes brought about by the CSCE process during this period cannot be denied, most researchers tend to treat these years as a coherent phase. However, this period also saw cautious reform ideas, still basically loyal to the GDR's political system, and that included its military as well. The GDR's top brass was confronted with the 1987 revised Soviet military doctrine and, consequently, developed its own reform concepts. That, and the generals' attitude to the final crisis of their political system, are often treated as a distinct and separate period, and we will do so here as well.

It was by no means a given that there should have been substantial changes at all during the many years of GDR history and military history. While its official ideology claimed that the purpose of the "dictatorship of the proletariat" was to bring about the eventual development of a classless society, in practice, the regime – and particularly so during the Honecker years – increasingly rejected any notion of change or reform. There were practically no mechanisms which would have provided for a continuous development and improvement of political and ideological circumstances. On the contrary, the entire power apparatus was designed to maintain the SED rule, resulting in an essentially stagnant system. All the top SED and GDR functionaries were effectively appointed for life – or until they had to go under pressure from Moscow, as in the case of Walter Ulbricht. That prevented the rise of new brains and, consequently, new ideas. Even so, both the GDR and its military were, in fact, subject to change, and that in itself calls for a specific explanation.

General History of the GDR

Until 1989/90, West German historiography never comprehensively researched the GDR, its history, or its political, social, or economic realities. After the *détente* years of Chancellor Willy Brandt, critical analyses ran the risk of being labelled "anti-détente" or even "continuing the Cold War." East German secrecy in all walks of life did not entice historians to address GDR subjects. Hermann Weber, who had himself been a young Communist and, at the time, studied at the SED Party Academy "Karl Marx" *(SED-Parteihochschule)* in Kleinmachnow, conducted research into the history and political system of the GDR, but, in many ways, he was alone in doing so. In 1982, he published his standard work of reference (*1.7* Weber), "DDR," which he rewrote and republished after the GDR's collapse, subsequently based on a wealth of new sources (*1.8* Weber, Die DDR 2000). Other authors who had published in the West turned out to have collaborated with the Stasi, the GDR Ministry for State Security. Publications sponsored by the Federal Institute for International and Eastern Studies or by the Ministry for All-German Questions (later the "Ministry for Inner-German Relations") itself were perceived as being politically motivated and, therefore, not fit to be quoted in an academic context.

Sizable scholarly research into the history of the GDR only started after its demise. Initially, the focus was on those topics which had been designated by the GDR opposition and civil rights activists, i.e., the *"Aufarbeitung,"* coming to terms with GDR injustice. The first all-German Bundestag, elected in 1990 and serving until 1994, established a "Commission of Inquiry into the History and Consequences of the SED Dictatorship in Germany" *(Enquetekommission zur Aufarbeitung von Geschichte und Folgen der SED-Diktatur in Deutschland)*, which delivered its final report on May 31, 1994 (*1.12* Deutscher Bundestag: Materialien der Enquete-Kommission 1995). A second such commission during the next Bundestag term to analyze "Overcoming the Consequences of the SED Dictatorship in the Process of German Unity" *("Überwindung der Folgen der SED-Diktatur im Prozess der deutschen Einheit")* delivered its report on June 10, 1998 (*1.13* Deutscher Bundestag: Materialien der Enquete-Kommission 1999). Both commissions published their proceedings and the many documents used to come to their conclusions, creating a rich treasure trove for researching GDR history. However, the GDR's military history seems to have been little more than a sideshow for both commissions. The focus of GDR historiography only reluctantly moved away from highlighting the "injustice" of the entire system; and scholars were equally reluctant to attribute all the mechanisms of securing SED power to any other institution than the Stasi; the police forces, the military, and others disappeared for many years behind the overpowering "Stasi" topic. The process of historicizing the GDR was slow and took its time.

A new research institute *"Zeithistorische Studien"* ("Studies in Contemporary History") was created in Potsdam in the former GDR in 1992. Initially directed by none less than Jürgen Kocka, it continues to exist as the Leibniz Centre for Contemporary History (under that name since 1996). During the first ten years of its existence, its attention was clearly focused on researching the history of the GDR, and particularly its social structures. The Munich-based Institute of Contemporary History eventually opened a branch office in Berlin, which also concentrated on GDR history.

A collective volume (*1.17* Eppelmann/Faulenbach/Mählert, Bilanz und Perspektiven der DDR-Forschung) was published in honor of Hermann Weber's 75th birthday in 2003. The editors could report that there had been substantial progress in scholarly research into GDR history since the state's demise in 1990. On the other hand, Kocka claimed that there were still substantial gaps in knowledge. Until then, a lot of effort had gone into explaining why the GDR eventually failed in the late 1980s. The focus now shifted to explaining why it had continued to exist and remained rather stable, at least during the 1953–1988 period. How had the GDR's political system managed to achieve this degree of stability, what had been the economic reasons for it, and what had been the attitudes of large sections of GDR society toward the state in which they were living? Had the GDR been a "dictatorship by consent" ("*Zustimmungsdiktatur*," a term created by historians to explain Nazi rule in Germany), whose rule had been strengthened by the silent acceptance of broad sections of its society? Or had it been a "society dominated through and through," where all walks of life had been permeated by the "security organs" and their totalitarian control, so that – at least in theory – there had been no unsupervised spaces left? Opposed to that, the term "*Nischengesellschaft*" ("niche society") suggested that the GDR had remained a workable system because, notwithstanding all SED Party assertions that it alone controlled public discourse, the system left sufficient spaces of lesser state control, such as family, neighborhood, clubs, or churches.

Kocka was also somewhat critical of his own discipline, stating that it had become self-referenced and isolated from reality. The first overarching accounts which attempted to integrate the many source-based specialized studies into a coherent and comprehensive picture, aiming at a larger readership, were published only during the late 1990s and early 2000s. Foremost among them were publications by the research unit "The SED State," created within the Free University of Berlin in 1992, which explicitly concentrated on research into the history of the totalitarian GDR state Party. One of the first results was this kind of overview, "Der SED-Staat" by Schroeder published in 1998 *(1.6)*. That same year, Stefan Wolle collated what had been produced by research into the GDR's everyday life *(1.10* Wolle, Die heile Welt). At about the same time, the first English-language account of GDR society, Fulbrook's "Anatomy of a Dictatorship" *(1.14)*, became available (later to be succeeded by "Power and Society" *(1.15)*). A series of conferences held annually in the small town of Otzenhausen near the French border brought together almost everyone working in the field; the resulting acta volumes reflect the steady progress of historiographical research into GDR history (*1.1* Timmermann, Das war die DDR; *1.2* Timmernann, Die DDR in Deutschland).

Eventually, this led to calls for including the GDR into the context of a comprehensive history of Germany in the 20th century. When, in 2008, Hans-Ulrich Wehler published the fifth volume of his series on German social history during the 20th century, he offered a joint account of the GDR and the Federal Republic. Yet, this also met with criticism, as Wehler had treated the East German state as a "Soviet satrapy," largely disregarding it for being a foreign element in German history (*1.9* Wehler, Deutsche Gesellschaftsgeschichte, 5).

That, in turn, opened the way for compact, concise overviews, such as those published by Hedwig Richter (*1.4* Richter, Die DDR) or Ulrich Mählert (*1.3* Mählert, Kleine Geschichte der DDR). Similarly, authors such as Mary Fulbrook (*1.15* Fulbrook, Power and Society) or Andrew Port (*1.32* Port, Conflict and Stability) published English-language accounts of GDR history.

Since, there have been recurring complaints from the German public that the younger generations receive only rudimentary, if any, information about the history of the GDR, the result being that oral or media-based attitudes, such as those handed down in families, often rose-tinted, remain unquestioned and unreflected. One would hope that broader research in the field will, via a more thorough coverage in university teaching, eventually result in better and more balanced school education on the subject. This has not been helped by publications such as Hoyer, "Beyond the Wall" *1.16*, which has been criticized for a nostalgic view of the GDR. Yet, even the critics seem to have overlooked that the book hardly ever comments on the militarization of everyday life in the GDR; while the book's bibliography includes Adolf Hitler's *Mein Kampf*, there is no reference to the *Militärgeschichte der DDR* series (see chapter *1.8* below).

Memoirs and Early Scholarly Works

The GDR Institute of Military History (*Militärgeschichtliches Institut der DDR*, MGI) reported to the NVA Political Main Directorate (*Politische Hauptverwaltung*, PHV); its chief task was "partial," i.e., Party-controlled historiography. Most books written within this framework, and particularly those about the NVA's own history, should be used more as a source for the political thinking at the time they were created than as academic secondary literature. Even so, the standard publication *Armee für Frieden und Sozialismus* (Army for Peace and Socialism) *0.31* still has its uses today for factual information, time schedules or some select documents.

Some books on individual questions of GDR military history published soon after the 1990 developments were authored by officers or researchers who had had access to the documents held in the then Ministry for Disarmament and National Defense. Those files were, however, disjointed and largely uncatalogued; it seems likely that some of the material was purloined at that time. Other authors relied more on eyewitness interviews with those NVA officers who were willing to share information with the former "class enemy." The resulting publications, while, at first sight, based on sources, were, in fact, never founded on a systematic collation of archival material. On top of that, their interest was, at times, aimed largely at revealing "sensational" stories (*2.34* Koop, Abgewickelt?; *1.27* Koop/Schössler, Erbe NVA; *1.34* Wenzel, Kriegsbereit). Other publications were, instead "official" histories coordinated by high-ranking officers and civil servants; an example is *1.31* Naumann, NVA – Anspruch und Wirklichkeit (NVA – Claims and Reality), edited by a former Bundeswehr Chief of Staff, whose subtitle "based on documents" hints at a rather positivist recounting of recently discovered files rather than a thorough analysis, but may, at times, include material still valuable today.

It was not long before the first NVA officers wrote their memoirs. A notable example is the book by Admiral Theodor Hoffmann, Commander of the *Volksmarine*, for some time Minister of National Defense and finally NVA Chief of Staff (*1.26* Hoffmann, Das letzte Kommando; another example would be *1.30* Löffler, Soldat der NVA). Other memoirs appeared in politically biased publishing houses, or were distributed only in a very small, even intimate and politically "reliable" circle.

Some Bundeswehr officers, particularly those from branches which had been keeping a sharp eye on the GDR and the NVA even before 1989, saw their role in cooperating with former NVA officers with the aim of presenting a "more balanced" view of GDR military history – examples include *1.19* Backerra, *NVA*; or *2.32* Farwick, *Ein Staat – eine Armee*.

The *Deutscher Bundeswehr-Verband* is a sort of trade union for Bundeswehr military personnel. It soon formed a regional organization for East Germany which represented those members who had previously served in the GDR military. It instituted a "Working Group for the History of the NVA and the Integration of Former NVA Members into Society and the *Bundeswehr*," which published about NVA history, but based almost exclusively on the perspective of former GDR officers. Its authors also included some academics who had worked in the NVA's scholarly institutions, such as the Military Academy "Friedrich Engels" (*Militärakademie Friedrich Engels*, MAFE) in Dresden, the Academy for Military Politics "Wilhelm Pieck" (*Militärpolitische Hochschule*, MPH) in Berlin-Grünau, and the MGI in Potsdam. Three massive volumes were produced between 2001 and 2010, with a large number of very detailed articles, but which hardly reached a wider public (*1.23* Fischer/Usczeck/Knoll, Was war die NVA? Studien; *1.24* Fischer, Was war die NVA? Nachgetragen; *1.25* Fischer, Was war die NVA? Zapfenstreich).

Sources

The source basis available to GDR military history researchers is in many ways unique. Almost all documents of the former GDR became instantly available after its accession to the Federal Republic in October 1990. The only exception were the files produced by the GDR Ministry of Foreign Affairs, which are being held by the West German *Auswärtiges Amt* and subject to the thirty-year rule – seeing that those thirty years have since expired, this no longer constitutes a major problem. The limitations this would have imposed on research into GDR security policy or its role within the Warsaw Pact have effectively disappeared. The documents of all other GDR state agencies are being conserved in the Federal Archives *(Bundesarchiv)* in Berlin-Lichterfelde, with two major exceptions: The Ministry for State Security's holding, while now also part of the *Bundesarchiv*, is still located in separate premises in Berlin, while those of the Ministry of National Defense (MfNV) and of the NVA are part of the Federal Archive's military section *(Bundesarchiv Militärarchiv)* in Freiburg.

However, the ministries of the GDR government were not the place where political decisions were taken, nor would the *Volkskammer*, the GDR's parliament, have played that role. Decision-making happened within the SED Party structures, particularly through the departments of the Party's Central Committee and its Politburo. The vast SED holdings were taken over by a separate foundation *"Stiftung Archiv der Parteien und Massenorganisationen der DDR"* (SAPMO) after 1990, which, however, is collocated with the Federal Archives Berlin-Lichterfelde; the holdings can be consulted there.

The Ministry for State Security holdings are important for an analysis of that huge organization's operations, but they are relevant in another way as well: in some cases, they can serve as a backup for files destroyed or lost in the agency where they originated. However, using the former *Stasi*'s files can be a tedious process. Almost all documents contain references to identifiable individuals whose privacy the archive has to protect. As a result, readers will often be issued only with copies of the originals in which the names of individuals have been excised. In addition, no regular search aids exist; instead, readers have to present their queries to the (very helpful) archive staff, who will then consult the relevant databases. The latter, however, were originally conceived to facilitate the search for individuals; a systematic search is more complicated. The military historian's problem-oriented search is, therefore, often more complex and time-consuming than elsewhere, but for a solid source basis it is without alternative.

What is peculiar to all sources originating with GDR agencies is that decision-making processes are routinely camouflaged. Minutes of meetings will usually only reflect the results of such negotiating processes rather than highlight that process itself. According to Marxist-Leninist thought, as preached by the SED, there could only be one "correct" solution to a problem; obviously, that was the solution eventually arrived at. Anyone who might initially have argued along different lines would have been pursuing an "objectively wrong" course, and that could not be, thus, such diverging views were never represented in the documents.

There is yet another problem regarding the sources for operational planning. As a concession to Moscow security concerns, the democratically-elected Minister for Disarmament and Defense, Rainer Eppelmann, decided in the summer of 1990 that all documents relating to such planning were to be returned to Moscow prior to German unification. The result is that practically no such documents are now available. What is accessible, though, is a wealth of material relating to NVA and Warsaw Pact exercises. The methodological challenge here is that armies tend to train for the war they are planning, therefore, such files might well reflect at least part of the true plans. On the other hand, Warsaw Pact war plans were highly secret, and exercises were not supposed to permit any inferences regarding the actual war plans. We know today from Polish sources (where both exercises and actual plans have survived and been published; *7.10* Wenzke, Die Streitkräfte) that, in fact, exercises and actual war plans were rather close to each other, so that NVA exercise layouts allow at least a glimpse of what the real planning was about (for a mixture of eyewitness accounts and source-based analyses, see *1.28* Lautsch, Grundzüge).

As a consequence of all this, eyewitness accounts were an important source of information for many years. However, this required a different, though no less scrupulous, kind of source criticism. Numerous high-level GDR officials had to face professional disadvantages or even criminal prosecution after 1990, limiting their willingness to talk freely about what they had seen or done. Additionally, a strict "need-to-know" policy had applied, even at relatively high levels of responsibility, so that those willing to testify after the event had often only perceived a narrow aspect of the complex reality. The historian always has to keep in mind the risk that what the eyewitness was relating might have been "contaminated" by their need to exculpate themself, or by mixing personal experiences with what they have read or been told by others, *post festum*.

The heyday of eyewitness interviews is, naturally, over by now. Most major protagonists have either died, told their story, or are no longer in a condition to do so coherently, while others willing to come forward were, upon closer inspection, in such junior roles at the time that their testimony can only refer to relatively unimportant details.

What does survive, though, are the memoirs of major and minor protagonists, for which the same methodological considerations apply (see, to name only a few more recent examples, *1.20* Born, Es kommt alles ganz anders; *1.21* Brühl, Die Hoffnung bleibt; *1.30* Löffler, Soldat der NVA; *1.33* Stechbarth, Soldat im Osten).

Scholarly Research

Individual scholars in regular university posts would most probably be overtaxed with the task of single-handedly preparing a comprehensive, scholarly military history of the GDR. It will come as no surprise, then, that this came to be addressed by the Bundeswehr's Military History Office (*Militärgeschichtliches Forschungsamt*, MGFA), and its successor organization, the Center for Military History and Social Studies in Potsdam. Actually, such complex projects are its main purpose as a separate research institute outside regular university life.

The MGFA started with various introductory overviews, some of which are still worth citing today as they are more of a handbook than an analysis (*0.30* Diedrich/Ehlert/Wenzke, Im Dienste der Partei; *0.29* Froh/Wenzke, Die Generale und Admirale – both were sadly never translated into English). After that, the book series "Militärgeschichte der DDR" published by Christoph Links in Berlin became the major outlet for groundbreaking research in the field, both by MGFA/ZMSBw scholars and several outside authors.

The titles published in this series are in MGFA's tradition of a broad definition of military history. Firstly, there are publications about the very foundations of GDR military history, such as Torsten Dierich and Rüdiger Wenzke's volume on the *KVP* (*0.1* Diedrich/Wenzke, Die getarnte Armee) or Armin Wagner's analysis of the GDR's security policy (*0.4* Wagner, Walter Ulbricht during the Ulbricht era). Heiner Bröckermann's voluminous 2011 monograph (*0.20* Bröckermann, Landesverteidigung) about the GDR's security policies during the Honecker years brought this subject to a provisional conclusion.

Diedrich and Wenzke's volume on the *KVP* was also a history of the NVA's forerunner, covering aspects of the early GDR forces' internal structure, day-to-day barracks life, as well as their interaction with the emerging GDR state, its economy, political system, and society.

The same series, "*Militärgeschichte der DDR*," also included volumes with diachronic analyses of specific aspects, such as the noncommissioned officer (NCO) (*0.6* Müller, Tausend Tage) and the officer corps (*0.2* Fingerle, Waffen in Arbeiterhand?). Two books central for an understanding of the complex relations between the NVA and GDR society are the conference volume *0.8* Ehlert/Rogg, Militär, Staat und Gesellschaft (Military, State, and Society) and the monographic *0.15* Rogg, Armee des Volkes? (Army of the People?).

The uprising of June 17, 1953, has attracted the attention of a few English-language authors; an earlier (2001) but still relevant contribution is *2.5* Ostermann, Byrne, Uprising in East Germany 1953; for a more recent (2014) publication, see *2.4* Millington, State, Society and Memories. The standard work of reference specifically for the military context regarding both the origins and the consequences of the events is still *2.3* Diedrich, Waffen gegen das Volk (Arms against the People). Similarly, a lot has been written about the Prague Spring and the Warsaw Pact intervention that put an end to it, such as *2.18* Bischof/Karner/Ruggenthaler, The Prague Spring; *2.19* Gildea/Mark/Warring, Europe's 1968; *2.20* Tismaneanu, Promises of 1968, but the rather peculiar role (or non-role) of the GDR in this context is still best expounded in *2.21* Wenzke, Die NVA und der Prager Frühling (The NVA and the Prague Spring), a volume more recently supported by the same author's comparative approach of East and West German military reactions to the Warsaw Pact invasion (*0.26* Wenzke, Wo stehen unsere Truppen?).

There is a wealth of literature, both scholarly and for a more general readership, about the building of the "Berlin Wall" in August 1961 (*2.11* Henke, Die Mauer; *2.10* Harrison, Driving the Soviets up the Wall; *2.14* Taylor, The Berlin Wall). Yet again, works placing it in the context of Cold War East German military history have, so far, been published only in German (*2.9* Die Berliner Mauer; *0.11* Diedrich/Kowalczuk, Staatsgründung auf Raten?; *2.12* Maurer, Dienst an der Mauer). Similarly, a lot has been published about the suppression of the Polish Solidarność movement by imposing martial law, such as *2.27* Szporer, Solidarity; in German: *2.30* Olschowsky, Einvernehmen und Konflikt; also – slightly dated, but still good: *2.29* Wilke/Gutsche/Kubina, Die SED-Führung. But little attention is usually paid to the effects developments in Poland had on the security or threat perception of the political leaders in East Berlin.

Perspectives

Even after twelve years, the claim originally made in the German version of this book, that GDR military history had not yet been fully researched, is still valid. On the contrary, GDR history in general and its military aspects in particular still offer interesting challenges to future researchers. The diverse but also challenging source basis should not deter prospective researchers. After all, early modern, medieval or even classical historians have to deal with a much narrower source basis, calling for a more refined methodology and a decidedly careful evaluation of every individual document.

It is obviously unsatisfactory to be conducting research into an area where other and important sources are known to exist but are being withheld. In our case, this applies to the documents related to wartime operational planning. The sword of Damocles is hanging over everything, i.e., that a sudden liberalization of archival policy might suddenly render all previous findings obsolete. However, this would mean for GDR and Warsaw Pact military history that the Russian Federation made accessible its rather recent military archives, and, under the prevailing conditions, that seems highly unlikely. Therefore, for a long time to come, the community of international researchers will remain dependent on what documents are available in the satellite states and on other categories of sources.

It will be one thing to define specific areas in GDR military history which have not yet been sufficiently researched. The plurality of the state's "armed formations" *(bewaffnete Organe)* and their interaction to stabilize socialist party rule throughout 40 years of GDR history still offers substantial opportunities. Just one example may suffice: the Working-Class Combat Groups *(Kampfgruppen der Arbeiterklasse)* have been analyzed as part of the history of Communist and Socialist Parties' armed formations (*4.8* Siebeneichner, Proletarischer Mythos). However, their peculiar role in and contribution to GDR military history has still not been sufficiently analyzed. Public interest has traditionally been focused on the Ministry for State Security, including its armed formations, and on the Border Troops. But again, their multifaceted military roles are, as yet, under-researched. Aside from the "Stasi" and the "Border," the *Volkspolizei* ("People's Police" – the regular police force), the Transit Police *(Transportpolizei)*, the Combat Groups, and the NVA served to establish internal security as well, a fact that is often overlooked – opening up avenues for potential researchers.

More important still than select topics relating to GDR military history will be comparative analyses. These will serve to identify the specifically GDR way of guaranteeing Party rule, compared with that in other socialist nations. How much leeway did the Soviets allow national Party authorities in adapting the general model to their individual situations?

What is currently being undertaken, and with highly commendable results (see, e.g., the excellent study *1.29* Loch, Deutsche Generale, but also *1.22* Echternkamp, Militär und Gesellschaft), is the comparison between the Federal Republic and the GDR. The underlying question is how much standardization and unified command structures reflected hegemonial aspirations of the respective lead power, and to what extent they were due to the requirements of defense in a fast-moving war scenario dominated by missiles and supersonic jets (*0.18* Finke, Hüter des Luftraumes?). How much state sovereignty, in a traditional sense, had to be sacrificed to an alliance which was, in turn, the chief guarantor of such sovereignty?

Both the Federal Republic and the GDR had been founded by their respective occupying Allied Powers; both belonged to a political and military alliance, and were characterized by a very substantial military presence on their respective territories. In such respects, they have a lot in common, leaving the merits of comparative studies rather obvious. The two questions that have still not been sufficiently answered are in which ways the two states differed, and whether they managed to transfer national German traditions into their alliance contributions and, thus, their respective alliances as such.

Beyond that, international research has long begun to look at the second half of the Cold War, the period of arms control and arms reduction talks, *détente* in general, and the ensuing bilateral contacts between the two German states. As a result, it will become necessary to view East German military history not only by means of comparison with the West but also in the light of East-West interaction. If the GDR cannot be understood without its constituent rivalry and confrontation with the Federal Republic, then the NVA can only be adequately analyzed if its attitude toward the Bundeswehr is permanently kept in mind. When all is said and done, both states were related to each other, even if by an antagonism. The permanent hate propaganda against the "imperialist" West German military, which formed a constituent part of GDR political education, was also an indication that the GDR and its military could only justify themselves by recourse to the "other," i.e., the West.

A minimum of communication between the blocs, and between the two German states, was inevitable, even during the "hottest" phases of the Cold War. How this communication actually worked, what effects it had on the internal political life of each German state, whether the "change through rapprochement" that Egon Bahr had envisaged in the early 1960s really materialized – all this has already come into the focus of general historical research but, so far, not of military history.

Chronological Overview

Before 1956

Training Main Directorate *(Hauptverwaltung Ausbildung)*
The GDR came into existence as a successor of the Soviet Zone of Occupation, which, in turn, was a result of the Four Power administration of Germany after the end of World War II. The Soviet Zone, and later the GDR, was always dependent on the aims of Soviet policies regarding Germany, which, until the end of the second Berlin Crisis in 1961/2, were characterized by a peculiar duality. On the one hand, Moscow was determined not to give up its share of Germany, which the Soviets regarded as their fair spoil of the war; in that sense, Soviet policy had a static element. On the other hand, the Soviet Union, as one of the Four Powers, laid claim to having a say in the future of all of Germany, thus, questioning the status quo and giving it a dynamic element as well.

Even before the Western zones did so, the Soviet Zone began to reestablish German-staffed local and regional administrations, and allow the foundation of political parties. In this context, police forces were also created, firstly, within the framework of the states which had made up the system of the *Reich* until 1932, then been effectively disbanded by the Nazis, and reestablished by the Soviet Military Government. From the start, however, the Soviets systematically preferred the Communist Party *(Kommunistische Partei Deutschland*, KPD) as the main force designed to create the new state. Its functionaries assumed key positions, particularly within the police, soon to be called the "People's Police" *(Volkspolizei)*. The year 1946 saw the beginnings of the German Administration of the Interior *(Deutsche Verwaltung des Innern,* DVdI), which soon became responsible for all police forces within the Soviet Zone, gradually eroding *Länder* (state) competences. From the very beginning, the Soviet Military Administration in Germany *(Sowjetische Militäradministration in Deutschland,* SMAD) and the German Communist officials flown in from Moscow at the end of the war (Ulbricht Group) made sure that the command, control, and recruiting of the newly established police forces was under their exclusive control.

Acting upon Soviet instructions, the DVdI began in November 1946 to raise a border police which would not report to the constituent states but to the DVdI directly. For the time being, it was to have purely police functions and play no military role. However, during 1947, bloc rivalry between the East and West intensified, while, simultaneously, all walks of life were strictly aligned with the Soviet model (Stalinization). During the spring of 1948, preparations began to raise new, centrally controlled police forces. Company-sized units were to be referred to as *Bereitschaften* ("Readiness Units"), but that was a mere sop to the Allied Control Council, so as not to violate Four Power regulations prohibiting the creation of military forces. From the beginning, each unit was to have, apart from its commanding officer, a political officer as well, following the Soviet example, while indicating that the model was indeed military.

However, raising these units turned out to be more difficult than initially thought. At the beginning, the SED had planned to rely on former combatants from the red forces of the Spanish Civil War, and on members of the "National Committee for a Free Germany" *(Nationalkomitee Freies Deutschland)*, formed among German prisoners of war in Soviet camps after Stalingrad. Recruitment among other former Wehrmacht military personnel was to be as limited as possible. However, under these premises, it turned out to be impossible to achieve the intended strength of 10,000 men. The Soviet Union supported the East German effort by recruiting among the prisoners of war still in Soviet custody, promising an early release in return for signing up to the new police units. The recruitment drive yielded 5,000 recruits, but this did not make much difference: desertion into West Germany was rife, opening up vacancies in the 40 units which were supposed to have 250 men each.

Nor was it practicable not to employ former Wehrmacht officers and, above all, none of its generals. Without experienced organizers, trained leaders, and knowledgeable staff, the units raised would not be up to their prospective roles and tasks. In September 1948, the Soviet Union released five Wehrmacht generals and about a hundred other officers who were to serve within the DVdI as instructors and organizers.

As opposed to the border police, training and equipment in these "Readiness Units" were clearly military, even if no heavy weapons and no air or naval forces were initially envisaged. However, the issue of heavy machine guns made it clear that these units were to be the core elements of a future army.

Despite all the efforts of Political Commissars in the "police" units, discipline and internal cohesion remained major problems. Accommodation, equipment, and training were insufficient, leading to a high degree of dissatisfaction, and the number of desertions remained unbearably high. On top of that, the process of Stalinization continued unabated, claiming victims among recruits and instructors alike, filling everybody with fear and, thus, further reducing the units' readiness.

Even so, by the end of 1948, following the Soviet Military Administration's wishes, the SED had raised just over 20,000 men throughout the Soviet Zone in both the border police and the "Readiness Units"; the latter would certainly have represented a serious force in case of internal unrest or even civil war.

By the summer of 1949, *Generalinspekteur* ("Inspector General") Kurt Fischer had been appointed the president of the DVdI, making him effectively the Minister of the Interior for the entire Soviet Zone. Among his deputies was Heinz Hoffmann, also *Generalinspekteur*, who was in charge of "culture and politics" (i.e., the chief political officer). He was later to be the GDR's Minister of Defense. Other deputies were Wilhelm Zaisser and Erich Mielke; both eventually became Ministers of State Security. Apart from Mielke, they had all been German emigrants in Moscow during the war; Fischer and Zaisser had worked for the People's Commissariat for Internal Affairs *(Narodnyy Komissariat Vnutrennikh Del*, NKVD). Also in 1949, the first course was organized in the Soviet Union for "higher leaders," i.e., officers commanding regiment-sized units; its contents clearly betrayed the military character of the alleged police force.

When the GDR was founded on October 7, 1949, the DVdI was converted into the new state's Ministry of the Interior. The *Verwaltung für Schulung* (Education Directorate), which, in the DVdI, had been designed to command the "Readiness Units," was elevated to the status of *Hauptverwaltung für Ausbildung* (HVA; Training Main Directorate). This was a fitting name as the HVA's chief aim was not to raise units which would be ready quickly, but rather to form the cadre of a much larger army which was to be created at a later point in time – not unlike the *Führerheer* (Army of Leaders) during the *Reichswehr* period of the interwar years.

Generalinspekteur Wilhelm Zaisser was in command of the HVA until, in 1950, the State Security was reorganized into a separate ministry outside the Ministry of the Interior, and Zaisser became the GDR's first Minister of State Security. After a short period of transition, he was succeeded by *Generalinspekteur* Heinz Hoffmann. While all attempts failed at solving the staffing problems, the units were now beginning to be differentiated into specific branches, although with cover designations. By the end of 1949, some 30,000 men had been incorporated into the "Readiness Units" and the various schools. That, however, exacerbated the problems of housing, equipment, and supply, in turn increasing malcontent and desertion. The entire process had been closely monitored by the Soviets, whose "assistants" or "advisers," sometimes referred to unofficially as "Sovietniks," were omnipresent in all staffs, units, and schools.

Only when the 1950/1 training cycle had been concluded could the GDR leadership really count on the over 50,000 men in the "Readiness Units." They had been organized into units capable of combined-arms warfare and were both an efficient combat force and – as two-thirds of the personnel were made up of NCOs and officers – a cadre school for the leaders required in a much larger army. The GDR, thus, held a substantial military force at a time when, in the Federal Republic, no decision had even been taken on the founding of a Border Police.

Kasernierte Volkspolizei (KVP)

On March 10, 1952, Stalin attempted to prevent West German rearmament and integration into the West by purporting to offer reunification of a neutralized Germany ("Stalin Notes"). However, the West, including the Federal Chancellor Adenauer, took this as no more than an attempt to disrupt Western cohesion and gain hegemony over a nonaligned Germany. That Stalin's gambit had failed became clear when, at the end of May 1952, the treaties about the creation of a European Defense Community were signed.

At the end of March or in early April 1952, Stalin tasked the GDR with openly raising military forces, even if "without hue and cry." In July, the Second SED Party Conference adopted that position, and consequently, the HVA was converted into the KVP. While rearmament until the summer of 1952 had been covert, this was now to change.

Not only had ground forces been prepared and partly created, camouflaged as "police," but similar structures had also been prepared for air and naval units. They were now openly called *Volkspolizei-Luft* (Air) and *Volkspolizei-See* (Sea), respectively, and subordinated directly to the new Minister of the Interior, Willi Stoph. Stoph also created his own command organization and recruited former *Wehrmacht Generalleutnant* Vincenz Müller as his chief of staff. (GDR military ranks followed the Soviet model and should not be confounded with their Anglo-American homonyms; they were: *Generalmajor, Generalleutnant, Generaloberst, Armeegeneral,* and will be rendered here in German; the naval equivalents were *Konteradmiral, Vizeadmiral,* and *Admiral,* respectively; while, in principle, there was the rank of *Flottenadmiral,* nobody was ever promoted to it.) As Commander in Chief of the *Wehrmacht's* 4th Army, Müller had gone into Soviet captivity in July 1944 and then been actively involved in the National Committee "Free Germany" and the corresponding League of German Officers *(Bund Deutscher Offiziere).* He now became the First Deputy of the Minister, and Chief of Staff of the Ministry of the Interior, where Heinz Hoffmann, until then the commander of the HVA, was relegated to the Directorate for Training. However, both Müller and Hoffmann were given military ranks in October 1952, each now being a *Generalleutnant* (the second general's rank, equivalent to a Western Major General).

The SED proclaimed the intention to "build up socialism" at its Second Party Conference, and that would include the armed forces. Consequently, military ranks within the entire KVP took the place of the police ranks awarded so far during the autumn of 1952. Simultaneously, Soviet-style uniforms were issued. That, however, did not sit well with the general population, who were reluctant to identify with the new formation, anyway. Soon, they were secretly referred to as "copy-cat Russians."

see page 21

Territorialverwaltungen (Territorial Administrations, TVs) were created as the basis of the new organization, each the equivalent of an army corps. While TV

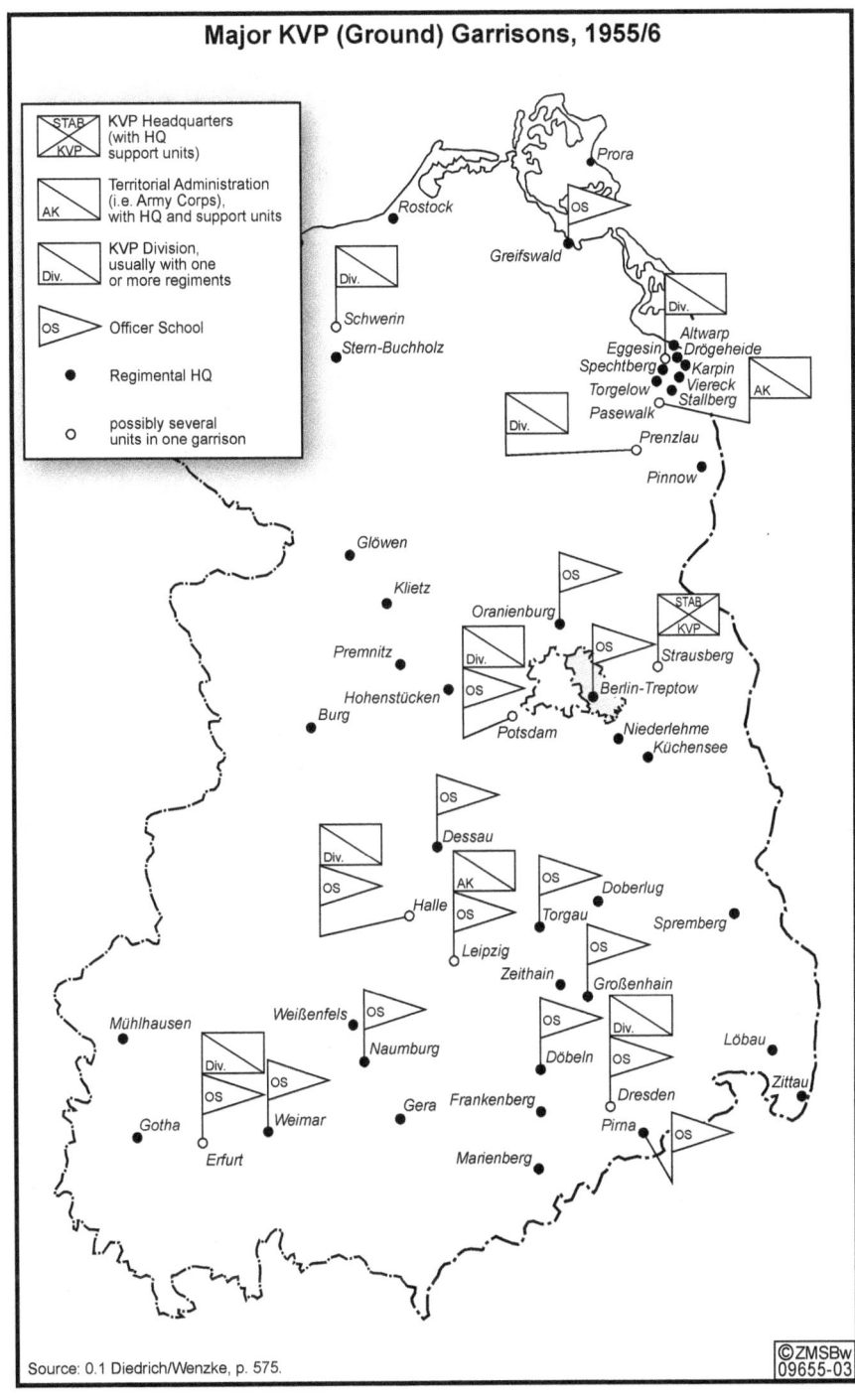

Pasewalk in the North soon commanded one mechanized and two infantry divisions, the three TVs in the South (Dresden, Dessau, and Leipzig) remained skeleton organizations for a long time. The divisions, in turn, consisted of regiments and battalions, but at these levels, camouflage designations (*A-Kommando* for an infantry regiment, or *D2 Section* for an engineer battalion) were selected to cover up the true nature of the various components.

The KVP training was concentrated on attacking in open terrain. This corresponded to Soviet doctrine, which envisaged an immediate push into enemy territory in case of war, an obvious consequence of the Soviet experience of the summer of 1941. Other kinds of combat, such as defense or fighting in built-up areas, were largely neglected in the new "police" force training.

see table page 209

The surviving documents show that a force of some 160,000 men was envisaged (*2.1* Diedrich, Die Kasernierte Volkspolizei, 342; *0.1* Diedrich/Wenzke, Die getarnte Armee, 169–180).

Soviet armaments deliveries, 1949–1953

Weapons system	Quantity	Unit price, in rubels	Total price, in millions of rubels
Heavy tank, IS-2	47	307,445	14.5
Medium tank, T-34/85	361	174,570	63.0
Tank, T-34-76	19	163,520	3.1
Self-propelled gun SU-100	23	217,900	5.0
Self-propelled gun SU-85	46	155,400	7.1
Self-propelled gun SU-76	59	60,812	3.6
Jak-11 Training aircraft	35	108,000	3.8
Jak-18 Training aircraft	35	40,000	1.4
BTR-152 Armored personnel carrier	268	86,485	23.2
BA-64 Armored scout car	238	17,668	4.2
152 mm Howitzer	6	56,696	0.4
85 mm Cannon "90-K"	6	153,497	.9
25 mm Cannon "84-K"	24	92,285	2.2
Cannon IS II	2	64,054	.1
Cannon T-24/85	11	23,470	.3

Source: *0.1* Diedrich/Wenzke, Die getarnte Armee, 283-4, based on BArch, AZN Strausberg, 29909, unnumbered. According to the GDR Statistical Yearbook (Statistisches Jahrbuch DDR 1957, 514), at the time, 120 rubels officially equaled 100 DM, but these conversion rates are highly doubtful.

The problems encountered when raising the HVA resurfaced on an even larger scale due to the repeated numerical expansion. What added to the difficulties was that many junior officers had undergone insufficient selection and training, and turned out to be incapable of doing their jobs properly. By the end of 1952, the targets set for training (rather unambitious as they had looked from the start) had not been met practically anywhere. A steady improvement of training standards was only achieved after 1954/5. One of the reasons was that not even a minimum of accommodation, clothing, and equipment was provided. At the same time, motivation within the units gave reason for concern once more. Desertion rates were again noticeably up, with many of those disappearing ending up in the Federal Republic, providing Western intelligence services with valuable and highly classified data. The KVP leadership reacted by instituting a separate KVP justice system, precursor of what was to become the NVA courts-martial.

Raising such extensive forces and equipping them with everything they needed to fulfil their tasks massively overtaxed the weak GDR economy – something the ambitious Soviet targets had not taken into account. During 1952, production in all branches of industry was realigned according to the Soviet example. The Soviet Union continued to exact reparations from their zone of occupation. Adding to that, agriculture was collectivized in the same year, resulting in a major supply crisis toward the end of the year, and exacerbated during the spring of 1953. The only response the SED could come up with was reducing their people's living standards further. However, it was not an extravagant lifestyle of GDR citizens that caused the widespread misery, but rather the cost of rearmament and general social militarization (*0.1* Diedrich/Wenzke, Die getarnte Armee, 313).

see table page 22

June 17, 1953

In mid-June 1953, the population began to rise up in protest almost everywhere in the country. The SED regime was caught entirely unprepared for the situation. Its eventual survival was due not to popular support but to the bayonets of the Soviet army of occupation. The course of events also highlighted the Party's inability to respond quickly to an emergency or to take decisions independently of Moscow.

The GDR Ministry of the Interior permitted only a very limited deployment of armed KVP units; the literature assumes a figure of less than 10,000 men. The Soviet Control Commission *(Sowjetische Kontrollkommission)*, which succeeded the Soviet Military Administration, had to be consulted first in each and every instance.

Wherever KVP units were actually deployed, they did not succeed in putting down the uprising. It turned out that Soviet combat units were required to curtail the revolt. As for the KVP, when faced with vastly superior numbers of protesters, they repeatedly found themselves in precarious situations. It was only when the Chief Political Commissar, *Generalmajor* Rudolf Dölling, allowed the KVP to make use of their weapons and delegated decision-making to commanders on the spot that the situation could gradually be brought under control.

The KVP had proven itself to be reliable politically. Fraternization with the workers on strike, refusal to follow orders, or desertion had been the exception. Yet, the entire event had starkly revealed the KVP's deficiencies in terms of training and equipment. The same was true for command and control as well as logistics; another severely limiting factor was the lack of motorization.

The events of June 1953 were traumatic for the SED, and the Party never succeeded in living that trauma down. State and Party leadership took a series of measures with the aim of preparing the next deployment of the "camouflaged army" for purposes of internal security much more thoroughly. The most important organizational change was that emergency staffs were created in all districts, led by the Party's District Secretary. In the case of internal unrest, these staffs were to coordinate and command all available armed forces so as to provide a unified response. These were the precursors of what was later to be styled the *Bezirkseinsatzleitungen* (Regional Operation Commands). Apart from the SED Party, stakeholders included the KVP, the Ministry for State Security (MfS), and the regular police *(Volkspolizei)*.

Another consequence was the reorganization of the top military leadership. The post of "Deputy Minister of the Interior and Chief of the KVP" reverted to a Party cadre, namely, *Generalleutnant* Heinz Hoffmann. *Generalleutnant* Vincenz Müller served under him as his Chief of Staff. Moreover, the KVP headquarters were moved from Berlin to Strausberg, more than 30 kms east of the center of Berlin, probably so that it would not be immediately threatened in case of internal unrest.

The political leadership also reduced the exaggerated target figures for rearmament, reduced troop strengths by about 24,000 men, and merged the three AVs in the south of the country into one army corps headquartered in Leipzig. Rather than increase the quantity, the idea was now to consolidate the existing elements. Hoffmann expressly prioritized the creation of a combat-ready cadre army – even if this was not yet to be made public as long as Soviet approval was still being withheld ("camouflaged army"). Converting the combat units raised in every enterprise into coherent Working-Class Combat Groups was another consequence of the events of June 1953.

Raising the NVA: 1956–1962

Soviet Policies for Germany and the Aims of the SED
All decisions concerning GDR security polices at the time were taken in Moscow, and that also applied to the decision to openly convert the KVP into a regular military force. The chief Soviet aim was to prevent the full alignment of West Germany

with the West, as propagated by Chancellor Konrad Adenauer. By the mid-1950s, that meant stopping West German rearmament, which would go hand in hand with the Federal Republic's membership of NATO. Once the Paris Agreements had been signed in the autumn of 1954, this had clearly failed. It was in response to this failure that the Soviet leadership finally agreed to the overt rearmament of its German satellite state. In December 1954, Walter Ulbricht quoted the "new political situation" as the reason for the shift toward publicly admitting rearmament (*0.22 Wenzke, Ulbrichts Soldaten*, 35).

This suited the East German Party leadership. In March 1952, Stalin, in his two notes to the Western Powers, had put into question the sheer existence of the GDR, indicating openly that the GDR government was in no position to even decide about the continued existence of its own state. The events of June 1953 had demonstrated publicly the SED state's lack of both democratic legitimation and national sovereignty, showing clearly their dependence on the "Russians." The SED would be able to interpret the creation of its own "national" army as an expression of GDR sovereignty.

West German Chancellor Konrad Adenauer visited Moscow in September 1955. Soon after, an "agreement" *(Staatsvertrag)* was concluded between the Soviet Union and the GDR, the term itself indicating that this was not an international treaty between two sovereign nations. The agreement authorized the GDR to raise its own military forces, while simultaneously providing for the permanent stationing of up to 500,000 Soviet military in the GDR. Until the very end of the Cold War, the Soviets would have more than twice as many troops in East Germany as the GDR itself.

The same month, the GDR *Volkskammer* (parliament) passed the necessary changes to the country's constitution. Again following Moscow guidelines, the new forces were to be called the "National People's Army" *(Nationale Volksarmee)*. After all, communist propaganda was based on the notion that Adenauer's policy of integration into the West was the root cause for the increasing division of Germany. Along those lines, the GDR media would systematically refer to the West German *Bundeswehr* as the *Spalterarmee* (divisive army) in the pay of the US. The GDR laid claim to being the real and sole representative of the German nation, starting with its national anthem calling for *"Deutschland, einig Vaterland"* ("Germany, United Fatherland"). On a more concrete level, "all-German conferences of officers" in East Berlin in January and June 1955 were organized, whose participants loudly denounced West German rearmament (*2.7 Helfert, Gesamtdeutsche Offiziertagung*).

Membership of the Warsaw Pact

The GDR was a founding member of the Warsaw Pact. When the Soviet leadership decided to supersede the network of bilateral alliances between Moscow and its satellites by creating a multilateral alliance, this also has to be seen in the context of West German integration into NATO starting in May 1955. Upon close inspection, the new, multilateral treaty signed in Warsaw on May 14, 1955, did not bring about any substantial additional obligations, nor did it have military results during the first years of its existence. For those reasons, researchers nowadays assume that its true role was that of a "bargaining chip," offering its dissolution to the West in return for a parallel abolition of NATO (for a documentation of the various viewpoints, see *0.16* Diedrich/Heinemann/Ostermann, Der Warschauer Pakt).

The NVA existed as a coalition army from its very inception, in that respect, not unlike the Bundeswehr (*0.22* Wenzke, Ulbrichts Soldaten). Its development throughout its history was strictly along the lines laid down by the alliance, with the Soviet hegemon de facto in control throughout. On the other hand, the GDR was always eager for the East German military forces to be the most important, qualitatively excellent alliance partner. Regarding the Warsaw Pact, this meant creating security "alongside Germany" without losing sight of security "against Germany" – again, much the same as in NATO (*2.8* Mastny/Byrne, A Cardboard Castle?, 1–28; *2.22* Bange, The German Problem).

In January 1956, the Warsaw Pact's Political Consultative Committee (which included the Party Chairmen, heads of government, and foreign ministers of all member states) decided to place the NVA under the command of the Combined Command of the alliance's armed forces. The practical consequences were rather limited: The NVA was still in its formative phase; it would be unable to contribute significantly to the pact's force dispositions for quite some time. However, the GDR Minister of National Defense, therefore, became a member of the committee of defense ministers, putting him on a par with the other Warsaw Pact ministers and, thus, enhancing the GDR's international standing.

Founding the NVA
By the end of 1954, *Generalleutnant* Heinz Hoffmann had already ordered plans to be elaborated to "prepare the conversion of the KVP into a cadre army" (*2.1* Diedrich, Die Kasernierte Volkspolizei, 358). On January 18, 1956, the *Volkskammer* passed the "Law concerning the creation of the NVA and the Ministry of National Defense" – that this was the anniversary of the founding of the Kingdom of Prussia in 1701 and of the Second German Empire in 1871 seems to have gone unnoticed, and January 18 became the official commemoration date for the founding of the NVA.

Ranking *Generaloberst* (three-star general), Willi Stoph became the first GDR Minister of Defense. Here, too, the GDR followed the Soviet example of appointing a serving officer as minister, whereas the primacy of politics is usually cited as a reason for not entrusting the defense ministry to anyone in uniform in Western states.

Generalmajor Friedrich Dickel was appointed Deputy Minister and Head of the Political Division, and *Generalleutnant* Vincenz Müller also became Deputy Minister and served as Chief of the Main Staff. *Generalleutnant* Hoffmann was among the first to be sent to the Military Academy of the General Staff of the Armed Forces of the USSR in Moscow. Most of the comrades who went with him also later returned to serve in key positions.

Structure

The newly created ministry was also located in Strausberg. This helped to maintain the illusion of a demilitarized Berlin, as laid down by the Four Powers, since Strausberg is just outside Berlin proper. Therefore, the new ministry was not within reach of the three Western Powers who were entitled to move freely within all of Berlin, while also remaining at a distance from protesters, such as those who had disrupted the workings of government on June 17, 1953.

The same year, the Central Committee created a Security Commission, chaired by Walter Ulbricht, with a young up-and-coming cadre by the name of Erich Honecker as its secretary. From 1958 to 1971, Honecker also served on the Politburo as the Central Committee secretary for security questions, making him responsible for most military and political decision-making processes within the GDR.

Below the MfNV came two Military Districts, in Leipzig and Pasewalk (as of November 1956: Neubrandenburg – MB-V). This remained the NVA's basic territorial structure until 1990. The first units reported ready for combat by March 1, 1956, thus, March 1 was celebrated annually as the "Day of the People's Army" *(Tag der Volksarmee)* from then on.

Six divisions, designated motorized rifle *(mot-Schützen-Division* – MSD) and Panzer divisions (PDs), had been raised by the end of 1956.

Initially, separate branches had been created for the air force *(Luftstreitkräfte,* LSK) and air defense *(Luftverteidigung,* LV). However, they were combined under a unified LSK/LV command in Eggersdorf, near Strausberg, as early as 1957. What had been camouflaged as the KVP's "aero clubs" was now officially unveiled as regular squadrons, initially based as far east as possible.

The *Volkspolizei-See* was converted into the GDR Naval Command *(Kommando der DDR-Seestreitkräfte)* in Rostock; it was renamed the *Volksmarine* ("People's Navy") in 1960, in memory of the sailors who, at the end of the First World War in 1918, had started the German revolution and toppled the monarchy. However, the naval forces remained limited to the role of a purely coastal navy for a long time. In the early 1950s the GDR had begun to develop its own U-boats in the early 1950s and had also prepared for the creation of submarine squadrons, but the Soviets put an end to all that after the events of June 17, 1953.

The KVP had ceased to exist by the end of 1956. Its personnel and equipment had laid the foundations for the new NVA.

Personnel

The GDR had perforce to rely on volunteers to recruit sufficient numbers of soldiers, sailors, and airmen. The Federal Republic had introduced conscription as of 1957, but that was no viable option for the East German state – as yet. The SED leadership was intent on appearing different from the West German state, but the GDR was suffering a substantial human drain, particularly of highly qualified young men who made for the West. Almost three million people had left the GDR before the Berlin Wall was built in August 1961; introducing conscription would have seriously reinforced this trend.

The situation was made worse by the fact that many KVP recruits had signed up in 1954 for a three-year period, which was now coming to an end. Despite all efforts, new recruits would not sign up in even remotely sufficient numbers. As a result, recruiting targets had to be lowered to raising an army of 90,000 men – actually fewer than had served in the KVP. On the other hand, this reduction in numbers helped alleviate some of the problems of accommodation, equipment, and supply. It also allowed GDR propaganda to present its state as the "peaceful Germany."

Just over 85,000 men were on active duty by the end of 1956, among them 17,800 officers (twenty percent) and 24,800 NCOs (just under thirty percent). About half of the entire force consisted of leaders – a clear indication that the NVA as it then existed was an army of cadres, ready to expand into a much larger force at short notice. The NCOs and men would serve for four years with the welcome result that after the end of their term, they would make a substantial reserve. Other GDR citizens had volunteered for courses lasting a few weeks; between them, they numbered about 300,000 reservists in the early 1960s.

The lack of experienced personnel, and particularly of higher commanders, forced the NVA to continue employing former Wehrmacht officers, including four generals. However, from this point onward, former Wehrmacht generals would only serve in staff functions and no longer be employed as commanding officers. A first wave of dismissals was targeted at this group in 1957, probably also due to the events of 1956 in Hungary, where large parts of the officer corps had supported the "counterrevolutionary putsch." *Generalleutnant* Vincenz Müller had to go in 1958; he committed suicide in 1961.

The SED continued to ensure tight political control of the new armed forces. All key leadership functions were held by SED Party members, several generals and admirals belonged to the Party's Central Committee, and Defense Minister Stoph was even a Politburo member. Even at this point, some eighty percent of all officers were Party members; by the end of 1959, that figure had risen to ninety percent. However, the 30th meeting of the SED Central Committee in January and February 1957 substantially tightened ideological premises. Quite a number of officers were sanctioned by the Party, often for "violating socialist morality." In the interest of an undisturbed NVA buildup, the respective SED Control Commissions were quietly ordered to be more lenient in such cases. In the beginning, most officers came from (industrial) working-class backgrounds, but the percentage of workers' offspring among the officers decreased continuously throughout the 1960s.

As we have seen, former Wehrmacht officers would only be employed in administrative functions. The downside of that was that all NVA leadership jobs were being held by generals and admirals without any experience of commanding larger units in combat. Even those who had fought in the Spanish Civil War would not normally have served in higher command positions. This required extensive additional training and education. Officers who, like Heinz Hoffmann, were slated for higher command positions were detached to the Military Academy of the General Staff of the Armed Forces of the USSR in Moscow. Even in the early 1950s, HVA or KVP officers had attended courses in the Soviet Union for technical or specialist staff, often linked to the introduction of Soviet equipment into the GDR armed forces.

New Arms and Equipment
The Soviet Union provided the GDR's initial issue of arms and equipment. The NVA had to initially put up with the enormous variety of KVP materiel, but soon the "submachine gun K" (i.e., the Kalashnikov AK-47) was being introduced. The motorized rifle units received the SPW-152 troop carrier, which GDR soldiers soon termed the *Eisenschwein* ("iron pig"), and the wheeled recce vehicle BRDM (known in the NVA as the "SPW-40"). Some of the armored forces had to make do, for the time being, with the World War II veteran T-34; only the two tank divisions were gradually issued with the more modern T-54.

The LSK could now replace its outdated models of "aero club" vintage with jet-propelled fighter planes. These would initially be MiG-15 interceptors, to be followed in June 1957 by the first MiG-17 interceptors, a model the NVA was to use, in various versions, as its standard aircraft. This gave the LSK/LV their first all-weather capable jet plane.

The *Volksmarine* received Soviet-made frigates and antisubmarine warfare craft; the production of naval vessels in East German shipyards was slow to start.

Throughout the Cold War, the West perceived unified and standardized equipment and weaponry as a major industrial and logistical Eastern Bloc advantage, especially when compared with the vast array of different types and models employed in NATO forces. This, however, tended to overlook the multitude of different versions and modifications within each Warsaw Pact model, such as the MiG-17. Moreover, relying on equipment provided by the Soviet Union further reinforced the structural dependency of all satellite states. They had to rely on the hegemon to obtain further arms, equipment, and spare parts. What was more, the allies' combat readiness also depended on Soviet willingness to sell the most modern, technologically advanced, equipment to their partners.

Internal Problems

The SED was very keen on reducing the influence of former Wehrmacht officers further so as to ensure political control by the Party. However, that overlooked to what extent the NVA had been led by former Wehrmacht NCOs since its inception. The generation succeeding the Moscow-trained "founding fathers" included many officers, such as *Generaloberst* Erich Peter (in charge of the Border Troops from 1961–1972), *Generaloberst* Wolfgang Reinhold (who assumed command of the LSK/LV in 1972), or Admiral Wilhelm Ehm, (commander of the *Volksmarine* from 1972–1987) – all of whom had served as Wehrmacht corporals or sergeants. It was this generation which left its mark on everyday life in the units and barracks, especially as the NVA never attempted a dedicated reform of its internal structures, such as the Bundeswehr's *Innere Führung* concept. Not only did the NVA wear uniforms and a steel helmet resembling the Wehrmacht's, but the tone was also rude and aggressive, and senseless drill and bullying was the norm. Insufficiently trained officers and NCOs without proper supervision would organize inadequate activism and random abuse instead of proper training and education. All attempts, driven by ideology (including the GDR's temporary tendency to lean toward Chinese practices), to replace traditional military discipline with something more adequate to a classless society eventually failed utterly.

Aside from a stringent "cadre policy" (i.e., a politically driven selection process), the GDR leadership adopted the Soviet example of political officers to ensure that the NVA would toe the Party line unconditionally. During the years until about 1961, the change from the ideologically preferred "collective leadership" toward single-person leadership was very slow to take effect. The political officer would initially have to countersign all military decisions and ensuing orders, but gradually the exigencies of an efficient, combat-capable army resulted in the decisive role being assigned to the military commander. New NVA regulations for discipline in 1959 laid down that the political officer could issue orders only within his own area of responsibility; he ceased to be able to issue orders to all soldiers, as had been the case until then. Of course, there was criticism by some Party functionaries that the military commanders were "mere military experts," without sufficient party-political awareness. Any problems or failures were quickly attributed to a "lack of solid political-ideological attitude" – a charge which could lead to serious consequences

Fig. 1:
On October 11, 1949, General Vasily Ivanovich Chuikov (center), Chief of the newly appointed Soviet Control Commission, hands over administrative functions of the Soviet Military Administration to the respective authorities of the provisional GDR government. GDR Prime Minister Otto Grotewohl is on the right.
BArch, Bild 183-S89744 / Erich Zühlsdorf

Fig. 2:
Potsdamer Platz, Berlin, June 17, 1953: In the immediate vicinity of the border between the Soviet and the British sectors, demonstrators attack Soviet tanks – in this case, a T 34/85.
BArch, B 145 Bild-F065142-0004/o.Ang.

Fig. 3:
Founding the NVA: On April 30, 1956, the Minister of National Defense, Generaloberst Willi Stoph, hands over the regimental colors to the first regiment of the 1st NVA Division.
BArch, Bild 183-37818-0004/ Heilig

Fig. 4:
August 1961: Passersby watch border troops building the Berlin Wall in Zimmerstraße (West-Berlin).
BArch, Bild B 145 Bild-00048794/ Klaus Lehnartz

Fig. 5:
On November 11, 1989, thousands of Berliners from East and West congregate on top of the Wall in front of Brandenburg Gate, with Border Troops forming a protective ring.
BArch, Bild B 145 Bild-00010488/ Klaus Lehnartz

Fig. 6:
On September 24, 1990, after signing, the Warsaw Pact Commander-in-Chief, Army General Pyotr Georgievich Lushev, and GDR Minister of Disarmament and Defense, Rainer Eppelmann, exchange copies of the document regulating the country's withdrawal from the Warsaw Pact.
picture-alliance/dpa | Wolfgang Kumm

for the respective officers (*0.5* Hagemann, Parteiherrschaft, 64). The Party leadership repeatedly deplored the commanding officers' tendency to leave ideological education to the political officers alone and concentrate instead on the "real" military subjects. Erich Honecker, in an article in the journal *"Militärwesen"* in 1957, pointed at the Hungarian example and expressly demanded a "unified political and military education and training."

The dilemma between ideological indoctrination of the new units and the requirements of sound military training were to haunt the early years of the NVA in yet another way. The Politburo decided in January 1959 that all officers, including generals and admirals, would have to serve as simple privates for one month every year. In this way, the SED meant to follow a Chinese example at a time when its relationship with the Maoist Communist Party of China was still undisturbed. A lot of officers, especially high-ranking ones, managed to escape this new demand from the Party from day one. One admiral actually allowed himself to undertake this effort, but not a single general. The "Chinese Principle" experiment was officially discontinued in 1961 because the hoped-for political and educational advantages had not materialized, whereas the damage had been equally heavy for training and discipline. The units still being formed lacked officers, anyway, and relations with the People's Republic of China were souring after the slow estrangement between Moscow and Beijing (*2.16* Storkmann, Das chinesische Prinzip).

Discipline generally remained a major concern for the NVA commanders. The ever-increasing number of desertions, usually into the West, was the gravest problem by far. Until the building of the Berlin Wall in August 1961, statistics prepared by the NVA itself gave an annual figure of between 110 and 240 desertions, ten percent of them officers (*0.5* Hagemann, Parteiherrschaft, 115). Suicide rates also remained high.

The Hungarian Crisis/The Berlin Wall

Soviet troops invaded Hungary in the autumn of 1956. Unlike the invasion of Czechoslovakia by Warsaw Pact troops in 1968, however, Hungary in 1956 was not a multilateral operation undertaken by the entire alliance, so that participation of the nascent NVA was out of the question, irrespective of how far its creation had progressed.

Soviet Party leader Nikita Sergeyevich Khrushchev escalated the situation in and around Berlin by issuing the Western Allies an ultimatum in November 1958 if they refused to sign a peace treaty giving the GDR the full sovereignty over its territory and airspace. This was obviously unacceptable as this would have meant GDR control over the Western Powers' access routes into West Berlin. A peace treaty would have solved another problem for the GDR even if the Western Powers had remained in West Berlin for the time being: Once the GDR controlled all the access routes, any of its citizens who had made it into West Berlin could no longer be evacuated to the Federal Republic, and faced with being flooded by refugees from East Berlin, West Berlin would soon have no other choice than to refuse to take in more of them. By that time, the exponentially increasing numbers of GDR citizens fleeing into the west were becoming East Berlin's most urgent political and economic problem.

The Soviet ultimatum grew into what became known as the Second Berlin Crisis (after the blockade and airlift of 1948/9), which peaked with the building of the Berlin Wall on August 13, 1961. The GDR decided to seal off the border between East and West Berlin which had, by then, become the last major loophole through which East Germans could reach the "free world" (the border between the GDR and the Federal Republic as well as that between the GDR and West Berlin had been fortified increasingly, starting in 1952).

What was built in August 1961 was initially not even a "wall," but barbed wire was laid as a more or less provisional measure along most parts of the inner-city border. The aim was obviously not to divide the city of Berlin permanently but to force the Western Allies out of its Western half, allowing the GDR to eventually take over the entire former German capital. It was only when the Western Powers' steadfastness doomed this plan that the GDR saw a need to replace these makeshift barriers with a more solid "wall." A particular reason was that manpower requirements to control a makeshift obstacle by far exceeded the GDR's military resources, while a more structured and in-depth "border system" would be much easier to patrol and guard (*2.13* Schmidt, The Architecture and Message; *2.12* Maurer, Dienst an der Mauer, 21–27; for an English language account see *2.14* Taylor, The Berlin Wall).

On August 13, 1961, and during the weeks that followed, the NVA remained quite literally in the background. Instead, various other armed formations, such as the Border Police, Riot Police *(Bereitschaftspolizei)*, and regular policemen, served on the borderline proper, reinforced by the Working-Class Combat Groups. As Berlin was still officially demilitarized, the absence of regular military forces was also designed not to provide the Western Powers with a pretext for armed intervention. However, the NVA was by no means sitting on its hands. Two MSDs had been mobilized and deployed out of immediate sight of the West in the eastern districts of Berlin. Representatives of the GDR MfNV, the city commandant, and the Soviet forces in Germany had set up a joint command post in Karlshorst, where the Soviet headquarters were stationed, the location alone indicating again who was really in charge of the operation. Part of their purview was to be able to react should the West threaten to intervene by force. More NVA units were standing by further afield.

Consolidation: 1962–1970

Standardizing Warsaw Pact Mobilization Systems

The Warsaw pact Political Consultative Committee, which included both Khrushchev and Ulbricht, agreed in March 1961 to standardize the pact's various national mobilization systems (*2.6* Diedrich, Prägende Veränderungen, 133). The agreement was binding for the GDR and imposed substantial demands. The first consequence was that the *Volkskammer* passed the "Law Concerning the Defense of the GDR" *(Gesetz zur Verteidigung der DDR)* on September 20, 1961. It provided the legal basis for tapping all national resources for the purposes of national defense. Its Paragraph 2 stated: "The protection of the German Democratic Republic and the fulfilment of its alliance obligations require special measures in all areas of state economic and social life to strengthen defense capabilities." The NVR was created to coordinate all ensuing efforts and measures; all state institutions were subject to its directives (*0.4* Wagner, Walter Ulbricht). There was an express provision stating that, even in peacetime, all planning of the national economy had to take into account the country's needs in case of war. Seizing equipment or land for defense purposes in wartime as well as a general labor conscription were also to be prepared in advance.

The Warsaw Pact gradually turned into a transmission device for Soviet military demands addressed to the GDR and the other allies. The East German territory was systematically prepared for its role as the concentration area for Soviet troops in a European war. The Cuban Missile Crisis had marked the end of a security policy based exclusively on nuclear weapons for both sides. This led to an increased role for conventional forces, which, in turn, meant that the Soviet Union's allies gained in importance – after all it was them who provided a substantial part of those conventional troops. Only now did the Warsaw Pact command structure come into its own, as Moscow used it to maintain control over all its satellites' defense efforts.

For the GDR, this meant a thorough militarization of its society. The further expansion of its rail and motorway network as well as its waterways was largely subject to the Soviet Union's strategic needs. In a country with a predominantly north-south extension, and with ports in the north and major industrial assets in the south, this now meant the reinforcement of its east-west lines of communication. Further Soviet requirements were designed to ensure logistical and medical support for the masses of troops expected to traverse the country in wartime.

National Defense Council (NVR)

The NVR was created by a *Volkskammer* law dated February 10, 1961, to coordinate GDR preparations for a possible war, as well as to better protect the SED Party's regime against internal troubles. When the first president of the GDR, Wilhelm

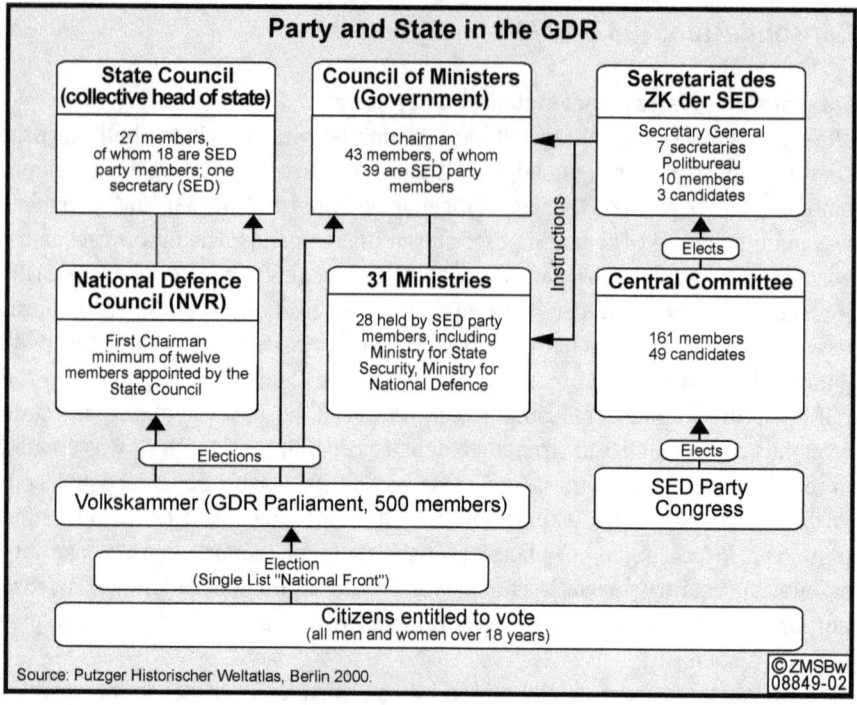

Source: Putzger Historischer Weltatlas, Berlin 2000.

Pieck, died on September 7, 1960, this allowed Ulbricht to become both state and Party leader under the new title of "Chairman of the State Council." During the entire Ulbricht era, the NVR served as the forum for all questions of mobilization and preparing for it, as well as those affecting military policies in general. The minutes of its proceedings are now publicly available on the internet (www.nationalerverteidigungsrat.de); for the time up to 1971, they are the single most important source for the military history of the GDR, and are of great importance for the Honecker era as well.

The NVR as a state institution succeeded the SED Politburo's Security Commission *(Sicherheitskommission beim Politbüro der SED)*, which had been set up after the uprising of June 17, 1953. The members of the NVR were, by and large, the same as those of the now defunct Security Commission. Moving responsibilities into the state as opposed to the Party sector did not mean, however, a relaxation of Party control – all NVR decisions had to be submitted to the Party Central Committee for approval.

The NVR was presided over by the First Party Secretary, Walter Ulbricht. From the first meeting, Erich Honecker served as its secretary. Its *modus operandi* was analogous to that of other bodies within the socialist states system: Proper debates were the exception; in most cases, the decision-making process had been concluded prior to the meeting, so that the proposals submitted by the chairman would normally be passed unanimously. However, the submissions would also include voluminous and very detailed enclosures, thus, the NVR also facilitated an exchange of information between all actors involved in security policies.

Conscription, Conscientious Objectors, and Construction Soldiers
The GDR constitution had undergone major amendments in 1955 to create the basis for more detailed legislation to facilitate "socialist defense." In particular, the *Volkskammer* passed the *Gesetz zur Verteidigung der Deutschen Demokratischen Republik* (Defense Law) on September 20, 1961 (i.e., immediately after the building of the Berlin Wall), which provided the legal basis for the systematic preparation of all subsystems in the state and society for mobilization and war, and which stipulated the all-encompassing competencies of the NVR.

The *Volkskammer* passed a *Gesetz über die allgemeine Wehrpflicht* (Law about General Conscription) on January 24, 1962, and, the same year, the first conscripts were mustered and drafted. All men aged between 18 and 50 were now subject to national service, with the age limit extended to 60 in time of war. This opened a vast human potential for the NVA, even though there was no disguising the fact that the young men forced to serve in the military were lacking elsewhere in a country plagued by a chronic lack of labor (see The Military in the Economy).

The GDR, more than any other Warsaw Pact member state, was characterized by having a Western counterpart, the Federal Republic, which was its chief ideological competitor. Very soon, therefore, the GDR was faced with demands to permit conscientious objectors to refuse serving under arms, much as the West German constitution, the *Grundgesetz*, has allowed to this day. The GDR solution consisted of the introduction of a separate service within the NVA but without weapons. *Bausoldaten* ("Construction Soldiers") were regular conscripts but wore a spade on their epaulettes and served in separate units called "Building Battalions." This made the GDR the first country in the Soviet orbit which provided for an unarmed service (*0.9* Wenzke, Staatsfeinde in Uniform?, 162–172).

What was not accepted, on the other hand, was a "total refusal," i.e., rejecting any state service at all, such as that practiced by Jehovah's Witnesses out of religious beliefs, or the refusal to serve within the NVA at all as the consequence of a fundamental rejection of the GDR's political system in general, which occurred more frequently during the 1980s. Such a total refusal was usually met with prison terms which would not be suspended. Those refusing for political reasons could, however, hope to be "bought out" by the West German government. That way, they might even be allowed to go into the West faster than if they had applied for a visa in the normal way. This made those practicing "total refusal" into a welcome source of hard currency for the GDR (*3.9* Rehlinger, Freikauf).

The Army as a Means of Socialization

Conscription was not only a means of raising a sufficient number of recruits for the NVA. Through registration, muster, and eventual drafting, a large section of the population could be registered not only organizationally but also structurally, subjecting them to discipline and closely-knit social control. That is why the young men subject to conscription could also choose to serve with the Riot Police, the Ministry for State Security Guard Regiment (but only as a three-year volunteer), or the Border Troops, as all these would achieve the same purpose. By sealing off the last escape route into the West, the Berlin Wall created "a qualitatively new point of departure" (*2.2* Diedrich, Herrschaftssicherung, 273). The SED leadership hoped that stopping the exodus of its citizens would result in an economic improvement, which would, in turn, make it easier for citizens to identify with "their" political system. On the other hand, the Party expected the NVA and the other armed formations to function as a "school of the nation" (*2.6* Diedrich, Prägende Veränderungen, 134). In reality, though, national service caused many a young man to be alienated from the SED state and its armed forces.

Integrating the Border Guards into the System of Socialist National Defense

Securing the borders of the GDR, whether the inner-German border with the Federal Republic, the border around West Berlin, or the international borders with Poland and Czechoslovakia, had been the responsibility of the Ministry of the Interior until 1961. In September 1961, however, most of what had until then been the "German Border Police" *(Deutsche Grenzpolizei* – DGP) came under the control of the MfNV. (Those elements of the border police stationed around West Berlin came under MfNV control only during the summer of 1962.) For the Border Troops, this opened up the prospect of tapping into the manpower resources created by the introduction of conscription. The former Border Police differed quite substantially from the NVA: firstly, the officer-men ratio was less top-heavy than in the military, as there had been no need to provide for a major expansion at a later date. Secondly, and this comes as a surprise, only about a third of officers were Party members; obviously, the Party's efforts to enforce its primacy had been focused on the "real" officers, due possibly to Party functionaries' underlying distrust of any kind of military officers.

By the end of 1963, the NVA had grown to include 26,000 officers, 29,000 NCOs, and 92,000 men, altogether some 147,000 military personnel. What seems striking is not only the numerical increase as such, which can be explained, to some extent, by the transfer of almost 40,000 Border Police, but the fact that by then, privates made up almost two-thirds of the overall force. What had been an army of cadres had now, as originally envisaged, used conscription to expand into a structurally balanced force. By the end of the 1960s, the NVA had reached a strength of about 131,000 officers and men.

Modernizing the Equipment

Regarding procurement and equipment, the 1960s were marked by the introduction of missile systems in all services. The NVA land forces received their first nuclear delivery systems, Scud-A and Scud-B. The warheads, however, obviously remained in Soviet custody. This gave the GDR a tactical nuclear system as well as one at the operational level, with a range of up to 300 km.

The motorized rifle units were issued with the first RPG-7 anti-tank systems, while the tank units were now all updated to T-55 tanks.

Integration within the alliance was particularly advanced in the air and air defense forces (LSK/LV) due to the threat posed by supersonic aircraft and missiles. To bring the GDR military up to its allies' standards, its air defense units were equipped with the latest in surface-to-air missiles (S-75 Volkhov, NATO codename SA-2 "Guideline"). It had been a Soviet missile of this type which, on May 1, 1960, had shot down a US "U-2" reconnaissance aircraft over Sverdlovsk. At the same time, the air force began introducing the versatile and highly successful MiG-21 jet fighters; this type would remain the NVA's standard fighter plane until well into the 1970s.

The *Volksmarine*, in turn, received with its first missile-equipped fast patrol boats, carrying the P-15 ship-to-ship missile, which NATO would refer to as "Styx." The GDR navy also built its first limited amphibious capacities; for the first time, its potential expanded beyond securing its own shores.

The Prague Spring

How closely internal and external security were linked in the Soviet satellite states, and the SED state in particular, was highlighted again poignantly during the "Prague Spring" of 1968. The Czechoslovak communists' reform ideas during the spring and summer of that year soon resulted in similar demands being made in the GDR, whose citizens could travel to Czechoslovakia without major hindrance. The SED was among the first to call for a swift end to all these reform concepts; as early as March, the SED leadership warned against a "system change" in Prague, and used the term "counterrevolution" while referring to what was going on in its neighbor state – one of the harshest words in the socialist parties' vocabulary.

The SED played a driving role in the decision-making process which resulted in the invasion of Warsaw Pact troops into Czechoslovakia in August 1968. From its point of view, this was not about occupying a sovereign neighboring state by military means but about securing the stability of all socialist regimes. This, however, made for difficult arguments: in its rivalry with the Federal Republic, which claimed to be speaking for all of Germany, the GDR government had forever condemned any intervention in the affairs of neighboring states, insisting on the national sovereignty of every country – a claim which might now come to haunt East Berlin.

Even so, the GDR had to insist on being treated as an equal partner within the Warsaw Pact alliance, and perceived as such. That explains why Ulbricht never stopped calling for the NVA to play a role in the military intervention in Czechoslovakia.

To make things worse, the timing was highly inappropriate: the end of September would see the 30th anniversary of the Munich Agreement, in which Britain, France, and Italy had allowed Nazi Germany to militarily occupy large parts of Czechoslovakia. Soviet and Czechoslovak propaganda had been looking forward to drawing on this example of Western capitalist perfidy. Both the Soviets and particularly their collaborators in Prague were now keen on escaping that historical parallel; obviously not involving (East) German troops in the planned operation would help in this.

By the end of July 1968, the NVA's 7th PD (Dresden) and 11th MSD (Halle) had been earmarked to participate in operation "Danube." Both divisions had deployed to their staging areas in the days immediately preceding August 20, 1968, and stood ready to move. In the end, it was a last-minute Soviet decision to leave both divisions inside the borders of the GDR and hold them in reserve. Apart from a few liaison elements, mostly signals units *(Nachrichtentruppen)*, no NVA military personnel took part in operations on Czechoslovak territory.

The legend, however, was ineradicable: for decades to come, most observers and historians were convinced the GDR military had been directly involved in putting an end to the "Prague Spring." In some ways, this was not entirely wrong, either: The GDR had allowed its territory to be used as the chief staging area for the allied troops, it had provided the logistical support which had been planned in advance, and, by keeping two divisions in reserve, it had freed other allied units to actually invade Czechoslovak territory. However, the fact remains that the two NVA divisions which had long prepared to take part in that invasion never left GDR territory.

The GDR leadership, in turn, never did anything to dispel the myth. That no NVA combat units had taken part could, in itself, lead to troublesome questions about the country's role within the alliance. More than that, the fact that the decision to exclude them had been taken without even consulting the SED leadership could be construed as proof of the still limited sovereignty of the East German regime. For all of these reasons, the GDR political and military leadership could have no interest in seeing their nonparticipation publicized.

There was considerable unrest among the GDR population in view of the brutal clampdown on the reforming communist Czechoslovak experiment. A lot of people saw their hopes for a "socialism with a human face" in their own country cruelly disappointed. In spite of all attempts to isolate the military, this disappointment also spread through the NVA, even if only in numerically few cases. Even so, the Party perceived the need to expel a number of officers, which meant that they also had to leave the armed forces (*0.9* Wenzke, Staatsfeinde in Uniform?, 199–240).

That the NVA should only play a limited role in the events of the summer of 1968 was a clear indication that it was still very much a junior partner of the Soviet Union. While it had been equipped with more modern weapons systems and had undergone much better training, and although the GDR as a state had largely consolidated at home, the SED state continued to be in a peculiar situation: It was still obviously without democratic legitimacy, enjoyed very limited sovereignty, and existed on the very boundary of the two antagonistic blocs, so that its political weight was still not great.

Détente and Military Reform: 1971–1989

Waffenbrüderschaft

The NVA could see its efforts to create a modern, efficient, and combat-capable army validated when the Warsaw Pact decided to hold its largest 1970 exercise in the GDR and entrust the NVA with preparing it. Designated *Waffenbrüderschaft* ("Brotherhood in Arms"), it was to be the first Warsaw Pact exercise involving all three services under the command of the GDR Defense Minister, *Armeegeneral* Heinz Hoffmann, while also constituting the largest Warsaw Pact exercise so far. Units from all Warsaw Pact member states deployed in the area of responsibility of Military District V (MB-V), practically the northern half of the GDR, as well as on the shores of the Baltic. The GDR, as the host nation, seized the opportunity to display what the raising and training of the NVA had achieved so far, and that the GDR military was now a force to be reckoned with. The NVA put amphibious and airborne forces on display and operated with large units of land forces, fitting in smoothly with the entire alliance's combined-arms operations. In addition, the SED leadership took the opportunity to proudly show how far the nonmilitary aspects of preparing for war progressed. Altogether, the 1970 *Waffenbrüderschaft* maneuver stood for the end of the NVA's preparatory phase: it had become a fully qualified member of the Warsaw Pact alliance.

From Ulbricht to Honecker

The beginning of the 1970s also brought a change in leadership for the GDR. Walter Ulbricht resigned under pressure from Moscow on May 3, 1971, and was replaced by Erich Honecker. The change also marked the end of Ulbricht's attempt at a more independent German policy on the frontier between the two blocs. Erecting the Berlin Wall had consolidated the GDR internally as well as economically, and based on that success, Ulbricht had never lost sight of his eventual aim of a reunited Germany under socialist rule. Instead, the new Soviet leadership under Leonid Ilyich Brezhnev was working toward an arrangement with the United States and, as a consequence, West Germany, to maintain the *status quo*.

One of the changes in the wake of Honecker's takeover was the modified "security architecture" of the GDR. As a matter of course, the new Party chief also assumed control of the NVR, but it soon became obvious that this body would be allotted a different role under Honecker. Honecker had been its secretary until 1971, but that job now went to a military officer, *Generalleutnant* (after 1979 *Generaloberst*) Fritz Streletz, with the result that the real political decision-making reverted to the Party's Central Committee and its Politburo, while the NVR degenerated into a body that merely rubber-stamped decisions taken elsewhere.

Four Power Agreement on Berlin, Basic Treaty

The GDR never lost sight of its chief aim, namely, to be accepted internationally as a sovereign state on an equal footing with the Federal Republic. Ever since the 1950s, the Soviet Union had proposed a pan-European security conference, and while Moscow hoped it would keep the US out of European security structures, East Berlin saw this as an opportunity to obtain the international recognition it craved. Conversely, the West would refuse to take part in such a conference as long as the German question was unresolved. The deadlock only began to be overcome once, in 1969, the Federal Republic had elected a new, Social Democrat chancellor, after twenty years of Christian Democrat rule: Willy Brandt. Together with the Liberal foreign minister, Walter Scheel, the new coalition sought novel approaches to reduce international tensions – the period of *détente* had begun.

The new federal government signed a treaty with the Soviet Union in August 1970, to be followed by Brandt's visit to Warsaw and the signature of another treaty there in December of the same year. In both treaties, the Federal Republic accepted the western border of Poland as it had emerged after World War II (the "Oder–Neisse line"). What was more, it declared that the border between East and West Germany was to be "inviolable," not "immutable," but at least the wording ruled out any change by military aggression. The Bonn government, however, was forced to declare unilaterally that this was not in contravention of its constitutional duty to do everything in its power to bring about German reunification. This, in turn, opened the way for the Four Power Agreement of the United States, Britain, France, and the Soviet Union over Berlin, which was signed on September 3, 1971.

The Four Power Agreement was the most problematic of all these international arrangements for the GDR. For the first time, the Soviet Union guaranteed the Allied access rights by land, waterway and air to and from West Berlin, and promised improved rights of transit for West Germans and West Berliners. Based on its rights as one of the four victorious powers of the Second World War, the Soviet Union unilaterally disposed of the allegedly "sovereign" GDR's rights to its territory and airspace, highlighting again the limitations of GDR sovereignty for all to see. It was not made better by the fact that the details of the use of transit routes were to be hammered out in a direct agreement between East and West Germany, putting Bonn and East Berlin on an equal footing (*0.20* Bröckermann, Landesverteidigung, 184–473).

In a way, the change from Ulbricht to Honecker had facilitated this development: Honecker was willing to follow instructions from Moscow and acknowledge the *status quo* in order to obtain *de facto* recognition by the Federal Republic. The two German states concluded a Basic Treaty *(Grundlagenvertrag)* on December 21, 1972. It provided for an exchange of special representations (short of full embassies), and both German states became members of the United Nations on September 18, 1973. The times when both antagonist German states had denied each other's right to exist at all were over.

Creating the *Kommando Landstreitkräfte*
It is in this context that the *Kommando Landstreitkräfte* (Army Command – LaSK) was created in Potsdam. The post of Deputy Minister for Training was abolished to allow for a separate Army Commander. At first sight, it does not seem particularly relevant that, after the *Volksmarine* and the LSK/LV, the ground forces should now also be controlled by a separate, specific service command. On closer inspection, however, it should be noted that this structural change was closely connected with a new task which had been allotted to the NVA: it was to prepare for the seizure of West Berlin in case of a European war. It is, at times, alleged that LaSK was to assume a territorial role in wartime, commanding the two military districts. Rather, the LaSK staff was to regroup in a crisis, assume command of a "Special Grouping" *(Besondere Gruppierung)*, and conduct this only major operation only under national GDR command.

What led Moscow to decide this, and when exactly it was decided, will remain unclear as long as the formerly Soviet material is being refused to researchers in Russian archives. However, all organizational measures taken in this context seem to indicate rather clearly that this transfer of responsibility must have happened in the very early 1970s. This may have been due to the increased fighting power of the NVA; the East German army may have been deemed "adult" enough to conduct this operation. Or else this was an attempt to respond to the new realities around West Berlin – we do not know.

Crises in the Middle East

The GDR military took detailed note of the outcome of the two wars in the Middle East in 1967 and 1973. Both times, Israeli troops with mostly Western weapons systems had overwhelmed Arab armies predominantly equipped with Eastern Bloc systems. In particular, the Israeli *Blitz*, which in 1967 had largely destroyed the Arab air forces while still on the ground, led the NVA generals to rethink. More powerful radar systems to give early warning of a surprise air attack would not be forthcoming anytime soon, so that the solution seemed to lie in protection and dispersal. During the subsequent years, all LSK air bases were fitted with concrete shelters. In the Yom Kippur war of 1973, on the other hand, numerically superior armored Arab troops had been bested by more flexibly commanded Israeli units; the lessons to be learned from that concerned largely tank design and, thus, the Soviet armaments industry. In any case, that Soviet-built weapons systems should twice have proven inferior to Western designs resulted in doubts among NVA officers regarding the quality and operational value of their own equipment when facing Western enemies (*0.4* Wagner, Walter Ulbricht, 499).

The CSCE Process

Ever since the 1950s, the Soviet Union had pushed for a European security conference. The GDR had two good reasons to pursue this goal: having a seat at the table alongside all other European nations would indicate its status as a sovereign state, and the conference was expected to guarantee the existing borders, thus, legitimizing the division of Germany and the sheer existence of the East German state (*2.24* Morgan, The Final Act; *2.28* Villaume/Bange, The Long Détente). For the Soviets, it also seemed possible to render both the Warsaw Pact and NATO superfluous as the result of the hoped-for conference – a goal Moscow probably pursued even at the time the Warsaw Pact was founded in 1955. Seen from that perspective, NATO's Harmel Report of 1967 (named after the Belgian Prime Minister at that time, Pierre Harmel) was a major setback for the Soviet position, as it converted the Western alliance into the core coordinator for a common *détente* policy.

The West was basically willing to join the conference, but made its actual participation dependent on the discussion of human rights questions as part of its agenda. The socialist camp eventually found itself faced with the choice of either accepting such talks, even if they resented any such topics as unwarranted "interference in sovereign states' internal affairs" and understood their potential for the destabilization of their rule – or else allow the entire project to come to naught. Eventually, and especially after the experience of Prague in 1968, the Soviet leadership decided that its satellite regimes were sufficiently stable at home to warrant the internal risks in the hope of obtaining diplomatic gains. The CSCE was to be launched in Helsinki in July 1973; it was to comprise three "baskets": renunciation of the use of force and inviolability of existing borders, cooperation between European nations, and human rights. Researchers largely agree today that taking part in the CSCE marked, in a way, the apogee of GDR foreign policy, but that the continuing complaints about human rights' violations constituted a very high price the SED had to pay (*2.26* Selvage/Süß, Staatssicherheit und KSZE-Prozess; *1.5* Scholtyseck, Die Außenpolitik der DDR, 114).

The CSCE also enabled the GDR to unobtrusively establish closer links with the Federal Republic, always under Moscow's watchful eyes. Honecker had decided to secure his regime against the possible wrath of its population by offering a wide range of social benefits – although these manifold benefits could soon only be financed by borrowing money from "capitalist" countries. This increased the GDR's economic dependency on the West without, in the final reckoning, greatly contributing to its internal stability.

Equipment and Structure

The Honecker era did not only bring about another, substantially modified constitution, passed in 1974 and overtaking the preceding version from 1968. It also saw a substantially redrafted legal framework for the military and its needs. A new Defense Law was passed on October 13, 1978, increasing yet again the military's options for utilizing all state, social, and economic resources. For the first time, the Conscription Law of March 25, 1982, opened careers in the forces for women – not least, because volunteer recruitment figures among men persistently remained below expectations.

During the Honecker years, the NVA basically maintained its structure, but continuously improved its equipment and armament, deploying modern technology. The land forces (LaSK) continued to be organized into two Military Districts and six divisions, but during the 1980s, they received their first attack helicopters, enabling them to conduct three-dimensional combat. Guided missiles were introduced, greatly improving the NVA's antitank capabilities. During the 1970s, the BMP-1 armored fighting vehicle was issued, and the units received the more modern BMP-2 in the subsequent decade. Starting in the mid-1970s, T-72 main battle tanks brought the NVA roughly up to the standard of the Bundeswehr Leopard 1 tanks, replacing the ageing T-55 models, at least in the tank divisions.

Similarly, developments in the air and air defense force (LSK/LV) were characterized by the introduction of more modern weapons systems. The focus so far had been on fighter planes to gain air superiority; now, fighter-bombers were added to conduct air-to-ground operations and support combat troops on the battlefield itself. The standard type in this role was the Su-22, known in NATO as the "Fitter-F," which became available in 1984.

In May 1989, LSK/LV was issued the first MiG-29 fighter planes, which again marked a substantial qualitative leap forward. The ground-based air defense systems were equipped with missiles throughout; they were all now integral parts of the Warsaw Pact's integrated air defense system *(Diensthabendes System der Luftverteidigung)* (0.18 Finke, Hüter des Luftraumes?).

Until then, the *Volksmarine* had maintained separate brigades for missile and torpedo patrol boats. In 1971/2, these were restructured into three mixed brigades, each incorporating both missile and torpedo boats. This matched the structure of such brigades both in the Red-Banner Baltic Fleet and the Polish Navy. In the mid-1980s, the LSK/LV founded its first naval aviation fighter-bomber squadron (*Marinefliegergeschwader* 28) in Rostock-Laage, equipped with Su-22 fighter-bombers. It remained under LSK/LV control until the end of the GDR, but was supposed to fly air-to-surface missions in support of the *Volksmarine* in time of war.

Altogether, the NVA grew to include some 170,000 men and women during the 1980s, of whom roughly 106,000 served in the LaSK, 35,000 in the LSK/LV, and about 15,000 in the *Volksmarine*. The remaining 14,000 military personnel were attached to the Ministry of Defense and other central agencies.

Confidence-building Measures

The CSCE Final Act also provided for "Confidence-building measures" in European security policies. As a consequence, a Conference on Security and Confidence-Building Measures and Disarmament in Europe was created. In 1986, agreement was reached regarding the exchange of information, particularly about the stationing of troops and the exchange of observers for major troop exercises. However, the negotiations about Mutual Balanced Force Reductions, which had started in Vienna in 1973, never reached an agreement on the reduction of conventional forces. In view of the marked Eastern preponderance in such conventional capabilities, there was not even a common understanding of what the term "balanced" should mean. The Soviet Union proposed proportionate reductions (by a fixed percentage), but from a Western perspective, that would have perpetuated the unequal force ratios indefinitely.

Out of the panoply of confidence-building measures, the exchange of maneuver observers and inspection teams affected the GDR security concepts in several ways. Closed societies, such as those of the Eastern Bloc, obviously had more to lose by the openness which had been agreed upon as they had classified far more information. The GDR leadership looked at Western military observers with a degree of skepticism, and the State Security treated them as legalized spies. However, this also meant that, due to these confidence-building measures, East and West German officers officially came into contact with each other in 1987, the first time since the two armies had been created.

Observers were to be invited to any maneuvers which comprised more than 25,000 military personnel. The Warsaw Pact states attempted to limit this kind of exchange to a minimum, largely by reducing troop strengths in exercises; full-scale maneuvers of this size became an exception (*2.22* Bange, The German Problem).

Poland

Starting in the mid-1960s, relationships with Poland developed into a latent security concern for GDR policymakers. The East Berlin government watched the nascent reconciliation between Bonn and Warsaw skeptically. The starting point was the exchange of letters between the Polish and German Catholic bishops, who had come to know each other during the Second Vatican Council (1962–1965); a leading role in this process was played, on the Polish side, by the young archbishop of Cracow, Karol Cardinal Woytiła. The development culminated in December 1970 when Chancellor Brandt fell on his knees in front of the memorial for those killed in the Warsaw Ghetto. In 1978, Woytiła was elected Pope John Paul II, inciting the Catholic-national opposition, grouped around the independent trade union Solidarność, to call for radical reforms. That was the point where the SED began to worry about being encircled by the counterrevolution in the East as well as the West. During the 1960s, the SED had never failed to point out that the GDR was the "better Germany" which had recognized Poland's western borders as established after 1945, while the Federal Republic refused to do so until a peace treaty was signed – an argument which lost most of its point once Brandt had signed the treaty between the Federal Republic and Poland.

The insecurity surrounding Poland's role led to additional challenges for the GDR and its economy. From a Soviet perspective, the Polish opposition threatened to disrupt the rear lines of communication of Soviet troops deployed in the Central European theater which linked them with the mother country. Securing these strategic lines of communication through Poland and the GDR would require Soviet troops which could then not be sent into the frontline and would have to be replaced by East German units. To make up for this, a ferry line was built, linking Mukran on the German island of Rügen with Klaipeda in the Soviet Union (now Lithuania). A large share of the expense, plus the infrastructure on GDR soil, had to be paid for by East Berlin.

Militarization of Society

The European and German *détente*, so the SED regime feared, could well result in a decreased "vigilance." The "enemy" might seem more difficult to define, resulting in a lessened "defense spirit." The GDR leadership decided to expatriate critics, most notably the singer and songwriter Wolf Biermann, who was not allowed back into the country after touring West German cities in 1976. This, in turn, was followed by an exodus of a lot more artists and intellectuals, further alienating large sections of the population. The socialist ideology taught by the Party was increasingly perceived as hollow, and the ideological bankruptcy required disciplining the people by other means.

One of those was introducing "Defense Education" into GDR schools; the subject became obligatory in all Polytechnical Schools for 15- and 16-year-olds after 1978. The state callously disregarded vehement Protestant church objections, but, as a consequence, the nascent GDR peace movement often crystallized around Protestant churches which served as sanctuaries for meetings.

Here, too, the GDR had a multifaceted problem. The official line was to support the growing peace movement in West Germany which objected to the deployment of intermediate-range nuclear forces (Pershing II ballistic missiles and Tomahawk cruise missiles). At the same time, the authoritarian regime swiftly repressed any analog calls for disarmament within the GDR. The Soviet Union had donated a sculpture to the United Nations in 1959 depicting the biblical image of "Swords into Ploughshares"; its reproductions soon became the symbol of the West German and the GDR peace movement, but sewing it onto garments and displaying it in public was usually sanctioned in the East (*2.23* Geiger, Der NATO-Doppelbeschluss; *2.25* Ploetz/Müller, Ferngelenkte Friedensbewegung?).

Social militarization was also pursued by other means: Until then, emergency services, such as the many volunteer fire brigades, had been under civilian control – now they were placed at least under military coordination. The NVR placed the Civil Defense Command *(Zivilverteidigung)* under the MfNV in the mid-1970s. Its new director was *Generalleutnant* Fritz Peter, who had previously served as the Chief of the Army Staff. Again, the aim was not only to improve the efficiency of the overall System of National Defense, it was also to introduce military forms (e.g., parades, saluting) and discipline to shape wider sections of the population again according to the regime's wishes (*0.12* Heitmann, Schützen und Helfen?).

Reform Movements

There is still no comprehensive academic analysis of a phenomenon which came to the fore during the late, agonal phase of the GDR. Within the socialist state and the GDR in particular, individuals loyal to the socialist state and military began to conceive of reforms to maintain both viable in the long term.

The GDR had ceased to make "proletarian ancestors" the prime criterium for recruiting officers for its military in the late 1960s. An advanced education was now the paramount criterium, marking a trend toward a growing "professionalization" of the officer corps (*1.29* Loch, Deutsche Generale, 220–279). Consequently, a new generation of officers was promoted to senior ranks, many of whom eventually reached an age at which they could have assumed key decision-making positions.

While there were still a large number of officers in this generation with limited intellect, quite a few were sufficiently independently minded.

This generation would possibly have had the potential to modernize the NVA without putting it – or the political system it served – into question in a general sense. Among the ideas which were now being vented within the NVA among its more independently minded officers was a radical modernization of its internal life: the housing conditions, daily routines, and working conditions. Above all, the role of the SED and the Stasi was to be curtailed. Such innovative concepts were developed, above all, in the NVA's academic institutions, such as the MAFE in Dresden, the MPH in Berlin-Grünau, and the MGI in Potsdam.

Yet, none of these groups managed to have any noticeable impact on the NVA's development prior to the upheavals of 1989/90. In this, they shared the same fate as similar ambitions in industry or the economy. There, too, there would have been the potential for a thorough evolutionary modernization, but it was utilized no more than in the military. A major cause for this was probably that the system, as such, was not designed to encourage change, nor to promote representatives of such change into responsible positions. On the contrary, Walter Ulbricht had remained at the head of the Party until he had been deposed for political reasons, and the same was to happen his successor, Erich Honecker. Minister of National Defense *Armeegeneral* Heinz Hoffmann died in harness in 1985, aged 75; he had been in command of the HVA in 1950 and had been defense minister since 1960 – for no less than 25 years.

The reform-minded groups received a special impetus as soon as the new Soviet military doctrine became known. When the Warsaw Pact Political Consultative Committee met in May 1987 in East Berlin, the Soviet Communist Party General Secretary, Mikhail Sergeyevich Gorbachev, made it plain that for him, "New Thinking" would not exclude the common defense of the socialist nations. Until then, the member states had taken the forces needed for a sweeping offensive as their yardstick. Now, they only talked about "reasonable sufficiency." Should war break out, the fighting was not to be taken onto the enemy's territory immediately, but the initial phase would be marked by defending "in-country."

"In-country" meant, of course, largely the GDR, which would have become the central European battleground. This change in Soviet planning might mean, in the extreme, the physical annihilation of wide swathes of the GDR; this would have demanded imperatively a general conceptual reaction from the very top of the GDR apparatus. But that obviously exceeded the gerontocratic system's abilities, which turned out to be unable to formulate any kind of response to any of the many Gorbachev reforms. In some sections of the potentially succeeding generation of functional elites, this failure of the state and military leadership to rethink military policies when faced with a changing world provided the impetus to think about a possible military reform.

<small>see page 197</small>

The GDR leadership was unwilling to adopt Gorbachev's ideas and the developments in the Soviet Union in general. When asked whether there would be Perestroika in the GDR, the chief SED ideologue, Kurt Hager, had replied in the spring of 1987 that "if your neighbor renovates his house, you are not under an obligation to renovate your own four walls." In refusing to follow Moscow's example, East Berlin was alienating itself from the very foundation of its existence. Gorbachev is supposed to have told the GDR leadership in October 1989 that "life punishes those who come too late" – the remark is a plain indication of the rift between the GDR and its hegemon.

That was at a time when the GDR authorities had begun to markedly downsize the NVA, anyway. Without consulting the top brass in advance, Honecker publicly announced ten-percent troop reductions. The effect was that the NVA's four MSDs lost their tank regiments. This unilateral disarmament was, however, not due to considerations of *détente* or strategic insights, but rather to economic and demographic necessities as well as the wish to pander to Western public opinion. The GDR's inability to reform itself, or its military, eventually resulted in a generation of disillusioned potential leaders. It was not enough to turn them into an active opposition – there was never a "Stauffenberg in Strausberg" – but it did suffice to make them indifferent toward the state and political systems which they had sworn to defend when they chose their profession.

The GDR Military in the Peaceful Reform: 1989/90

<small>see page 197 f.</small>

For many years after the peaceful end of the GDR, former NVA officers would claim in public debates to their "merit" that, at least, "their" army had remained quiet and inactive, and had not fired upon the peaceful demonstrators during the heady autumn days of 1989. This throws an interesting light on a military which habitually referred to itself as the "Army of the People." After all, it implies that in its own definition of the role it was to play, it would have been the normal thing for the "Army of the People" to open fire on the people.

As a matter of fact, since the 1960s, the NVA had been trained and equipped predominantly as a tool of classic security politics, and only in an emergency was it to be deployed for purposes of GDR internal security. Even so, it was the NVR, with the Party chief as its nominal chair but an NVA general as its secretary, which was responsible for the entire system of maintaining the Socialist Party regime within the GDR. Similarly, the NVA sat on the regional contingency staffs *(Bezirkseinsatz-*

leitungen) as well as their subordinate commands at district level *(Kreiseinsatzleitungen)*.

Still, when the GDR population began to take to the streets in greater numbers during 1989, it was initially the police (the Riot Police units above all) and then the Ministry for State Security (whose "Felix Dzerzhinsky" Guard Regiment had by now grown to 11,000 men, effectively equaling an NVA division) who were supposed to stem the ever-rising tide. Only when even those forces no longer sufficed did the NVA concentrate NCO and officer cadets under the command of regular officers and NCOs into units of about 100 men each, totaling about 20,000, which were held in readiness to quash the demonstrations, largely around Leipzig (*0.23* Wenzke, Damit hatten wir). The hasty change away from regular units toward improvised formations has, at times, been attributed to the Party chiefs growing mistrust of the many conscripts who formed the core of the regular units, and whose political reliability might well be questionable. However, even those NVA officers and men from elite units, such as the *Luftsturmregiment*-40 (Airborne Regiment) who had been moved to barracks in Leipzig in readiness for putting down further demonstrations, began to question their orders once they realized that they were not to combat evil counterrevolutionaries in the pay of the West but their own countrymen chanting for nonviolence (*0.28* Niemetz, Staatsmacht am Ende, 103–136; see also the wealth of sources published in that volume).

In the event, these ad hoc units were never called to intervene. Honecker had been sick for a long time, then he was replaced by Egon Krenz, an apparatchik who was anything but charismatic, rendering the ossified SED Party hierarchy largely unable to take decisions and keep abreast of events. Nothing indicated this more than its complete inability to respond to the surprise opening of the Berlin Wall on November 9, 1989. In addition, dependency on the Soviet "friends" was still so great that without "guidance" from them, no decision to intervene was to be expected. Gorbachev, however, had publicly renounced the Brezhnev Doctrine the year before, and the meeting of the Warsaw Pact Political Consultative Committee in July 1989 had officially stated it no longer applied. Gorbachev visited the GDR as part of the commemorations of the East German state's fortieth anniversary in October 1989; he had taken the opportunity to let the SED leadership know without a doubt that the Soviet Union was no longer prepared to pay the price of military intervention to maintain the GDR's political existence. The GDR had lost not only its economic and ecological basis, and it had never had the "support of the masses"; now, it had also lost its international power basis.

That the Soviet troops in the GDR remained in barracks during the autumn of 1989 constituted an important prerequisite for what became known as the GDR "peaceful revolution". This revolutionary process culminated in the first free elections on March 18, 1990, which resulted in an overwhelming majority for those parties which had called for the accession of the GDR to the Federal Republic and its constitution, the *Grundgesetz*. A grand coalition was formed, and on July 1, 1990, the GDR introduced the West German mark as its official currency. Once economic unity had been achieved, political unification would have to follow swiftly. Even so, a number of East German politicians continued to believe, at least for some time, that they would have roughly two years to prepare their country – and its military – for German unity. Still, the democratic government under Prime Minister Lothar de Maizière continued to downsize the NVA. From 170,000 men at the height of the Cold War, the GDR military was reduced to about 90,000. This was achieved, to some extent, by pensioning off more senior and more elderly officers, but largely by drafting far fewer conscripts than would have been normal. As a result, about 50,000 out of the remaining 90,000 military personnel were longer-serving volunteers which had become career officers and NCOs.

In November 1989, the last GDR government led by the SED (which had renamed itself the Partei des demokratischen Sozialismus – Party of Democratic Socialism, PDS) had replaced the 69-year-old defense minister, *Armeegeneral* Heinz Kessler, with one of the cautious reformers, *Volksmarine* Admiral Theodor Hoffmann. The new NVA leadership set out to implement many of the reforms conceived much earlier, expecting to have several years during which the East German forces might be brought up to modern, Western standards.

Even when it became clear in the autumn of 1990 that the GDR would accede to the Federal Republic and, therefore, cease to exist, for a while, there was still talk of two armies in one single state. One would be the West German Bundeswehr, under NATO control, and the other would be the East German NVA, which would not form part of the alliance. This both met the wishful thinking of many NVA officers and corresponded to the refusal of the Polish government of the day to countenance the permanent stationing of NATO forces on its border. Yet, within a short period of time, Warsaw thought better about this and withdrew its objections. Polish politicians had realized that this solution would mean national German military forces right on its own border, without any kind of international command or control – the last thing Poland could wish for at a time when Germany still had not fully recognized Poland's western border as it had been determined in 1945 *(Oder-Neiße-Linie)*.

The elections of March 18, 1990, had brought to power a democratically legitimized administration, led by Minister President Lothar de Maizière (whose uncle Ulrich de Maizière had been the Bundeswehr *Generalinspekteur* during the late 1960s and early 1970s); the new Minister for Disarmament and Defense (the new designation) was a pacifist Protestant pastor, Rainer Eppelmann. His aim was the dissolution of both Cold War alliances. For a while, he led the NVA top brass to believe that even the West had agreed to maintain two military forces post-reunification, one in the West and one in the East. On July 20, 1990, he made the entire NVA swear a new oath, without reference to socialism, the rule of the Party, or the Soviet Union. It was no coincidence that the date was the anniversary of the failed 1944 coup d'état against Hitler which had been part of Bundeswehr tradition ever since the 1950s – the new NVA was beginning to adopt Western sets of values and, therefore, Western traditions.

Yet, by mid-July 1990, Soviet Party General Secretary Gorbachev had already agreed to NATO membership of a reunited Germany, rendering all speculations about the further existence of a separate East German army superfluous. According to the disarmament ceilings agreed in the arms reduction talks, the all-German military forces would be no more than 370,000 strong, as compared to 495,000 West German and 170,000 East German men and women in uniform only about two years before. The Soviet troops were to leave the country no later than 1994.

see page 198 f.

The NVA officers began to realize that they would soon be facing an existence outside the military. What made things worse for them was that in their plight, they had hardly any political support. The GDR was now governed by former dissidents for whom the army had always represented the oppressive system. The former SED, now the Party of Democratic Socialism, was eagerly preparing a role for itself in a reunited Germany – a role which included a radically pacifist posture and a call for general disarmament, both were hardly compatible with public support for former NVA officers.

While there were occasional instances of substantial malcontent, the NVA (or what was left of it) remained remarkably disciplined and quiet. Even when many officers had understood there was no future for them in the armed forces of a united Germany, they continued to serve loyally. In particular, they took it upon themselves to collect the enormous masses of weaponry and equipment which had to be stored safely so as to prevent embezzlement or theft.

When, on October 3, 1990, the East German state acceded to the Federal Republic by adhering to its constitution, not only did this state but also the armed forces it had created cease to exist. This automatically terminated all rights and claims deriving from employment by these forces; this was also because the GDR had never created specific conditions of service for its military personnel (as was the case in the Federal Republic); technically, they had been employees like all others. Individual former NVA personnel could, if they wished, apply for a posting in the Bundeswehr. In a process involving several steps over a few years, applicants were vetted, selected, and some eventually retained.

No one who had in any way collaborated with the Ministry for State Security (Stasi) could be accepted into the Bundeswehr. With hindsight, this was a harsh criterium which led to cases of obvious injustice. Individuals who, as a 16-year-old, had signed an undertaking to inform the Stasi but had never actually given substantial information or harmed anyone, were sent packing within hours once their involvement became known. For many years, there were instances where former NVA personnel suddenly had to go, making personnel planning and human resource development difficult, and, what was more, leading to a general distrust of former East German personnel.

Here, the Stasi continued to serve the Party's interest, even after the demise of both: after all, the Stasi had been "the shield and sword of the Party" – the Stasi had served the Party, not the other way around. Many Party members, police officers, or other agents of the SED state had helped to arrest people trying to flee the GDR, ratted on colleagues or contributed in other ways to the stabilization of the GDR system. No one came into focus half as much as former Stasi agents and informers.

Nevertheless, one also has to admit that this decision was taken in respect of a broad democratic consensus among GDR citizens. In the heady days of 1989/90, it would have been inconceivable to suggest a differentiated view of former Stasi personnel. There was a sweeping majority in favor of removing all of them from the corridors of power (*2.33* Heinemann, East German Army Personnel; see also *2.32* Farwick, Ein Staat – eine Armee).

These were the first steps toward a military history of a reunited Germany – the military history of the GDR, however, had come to a conclusion on October 2, 1990.

The Armed Forces, Politics, and Society

A "society dominated through and through": The Militarization of Everyday Life

Which mechanisms the GDR employed to successfully secure its rule is one of the central questions whenever academics attempt to understand the SED state. The term coined by Jürgen Kocka in 1994, *"durchherrschte Gesellschaft"* ("society dominated through and through" – *1.18* Kocka, Eine durchherrschte Gesellschaft), still seems useful to denote the omnipresence of the state and its security organs, despite all the niches GDR citizens found for themselves. Regarding a military history of the GDR, this leads to a follow-up question: What was the contribution of the "armed organs" *(bewaffnete Organe)* in all this, particularly the NVA? Our knowledge about these mechanisms are largely due to the exhaustive study by Matthias Rogg (*0.15* Rogg, Armee des Volkes?).

It seems useful to start with a definition of terminology. A distinction is required between "militarism" and "militarization." In our sense, "militarism" refers to a political system in which the military as an organization or military officers have an undue influence on the formulation of policies; the example usually quoted for this is Imperial Germany (1871–1918). "Militarization," however, is understood here as "ongoing changes or empirically quantifiable tendencies of the military's social status" (*3.11* Seubert, Zum Legitimitätsverfall, 88–89), in other words, the transfer of military or paramilitary habits and norms into civil society's everyday life.

In this sense, the degree of military and paramilitary mobilization within the GDR clearly exceeded that of any other Warsaw Pact state, including the Soviet Union. If, apart from the NVA, all the other armed formations of the GDR are taken into account, such as the Ministry of the Interior, Ministry for State Security, Border Troops, the "Sport and Technology Association" *(Gesellschaft für Sport und Technik – GST)*, Riot Police, Working-Class Combat Groups, Civil Defense Command, and voluntary collectives of reservists, they comprised roughly two million GDR citizens. And this is without counting all those who acted as "voluntary assistants" *(freiwillige Helfer)* of the police, Border Troops, or the Stasi, as many of those would then be counted twice as they are already included in the first count. Altogether, some twenty percent of the ten million GDR citizens of working age were involved, one way or the other, in one of the military or paramilitary organizations.

As the account of events in 1953, 1961, and 1968 had shown, and as the salvoes fired along the inner-German border continuously proved as well, the GDR regime had no qualms about using violence, at home and abroad, in order to ensure its survival. The high degree of militarization of GDR society, however, ensured conformity with the Party's guidelines even without actually resorting to violence. Instead, the general knowledge that the regime was prepared to use such force sufficed to make citizens conform to the norms. To use but one example: the actual Border Troops had a rather small share in the total figure of foiled "escapes" from the GDR; most attempts to flee were stopped by the overarching system of repression and surveillance by regular police and the Stasi. That was not to say that the Border Troops and their extensive border regime were pointless: they were a highly visible symbol of the regime's willingness to use lethal force against its citizens and, thus, contributed to what Matthias Rogg (*0.15* Rogg, Armee des Volkes?, 10–12) calls a "structural standardization." Even those subjects who would never have dreamt of leaving the GDR knew about their limited scope of action even in their daily lives and conformed accordingly.

A further indication of the high degree of militarization is the extent to which the education system was geared toward the needs of the armed forces. Even in nursery schools, which some eighty percent of all GDR children below the age of three attended, the teachers were to celebrate the "Day of the National People's Army" with their little ones. Once they had reached the age of three, children would attend kindergarten, where military subjects were to be introduced in all contexts. It is safe to assume that almost all teachers would follow the respective guidelines in this respect. Childrens' journals, such as "Bummi," "ABC-Zeitung," or "Frösi," regularly included articles which painted a rosy picture both of the NVA and the Soviet Army. During the 1960s, the NVA and the MfNV even subsidized the production of war toys, as true to the original as possible, in state-owned enterprises.

see table page 209

The close combination of social, political, and military education then continued in school. From the first year, "defense education" (*"Wehrerziehung"*) was supposed to be taught in all subjects at school. The Ministries of National Defense and Education concluded a detailed agreement on the modes of cooperation in 1966. The idea was to include military-political topics more regularly in classroom teaching. Schools and the armed forces were to stay in close contact through mutual exchanges or jointly organized events. As a matter of course, school textbooks for all subjects would include military topics, and physical education was declared to serve the aim of "creating the preconditions for national defense."

There was a noticeable overlap of activities between schools, the Free German Youth (*Freie Deutsche Jugend* – FDJ), and the GST (see above). The FDJ suborganization looking after younger children, called the "Ernst Thälmann Pioneers," held annual "Thälmann Maneuvers," which set the groups military tasks and trained them in designated sports. The children and youngsters would take part not so much because they were being coerced, but because the "Pioneers" pandered to their expectations of adventure, comradeship, and a desire to travel. Military sports were also the subject of the "Hans Beimler Games," organized by the FDJ annually from 1967; aiming and throwing hand grenades, cross-country runs, and live shooting were included, as were scouting games with predominantly military elements.

When, in 1978, the GDR made "Military Education" a regular subject for all 9th and 10th classes (ages 15–17), this was no more than just following the example of all other Warsaw Pact countries. However, it was also part of the increased internal repression and ideological tightening, once the CSCE process and inner-German rapprochement had begun to result in "instances of [ideological] softening," especially among the young. As the international political developments could not be reversed, a combination of reinforced repression and increased ideological indoctrination was expected to bring about the much-needed stabilization of the political system. However, this goal was only partially achieved, as the introduction of "Military Education" in schools resulted in massive protests, widely supported by the churches, so that eventually the Protestant church (by far the single largest denomination among remaining GDR Christians) developed into a catalyst for oppositional movements.

The inclusion of military elements continued even in tertiary education, both in its professional and academic form. Even before nationwide conscription had been introduced, the SED Security Commission had, in 1955, made military training obligatory for all university students. The actual amount of time spent in these courses varied throughout the history of the SED state, but they remained an obligation until the very end of the GDR. Both male and female students attended, but often rather listlessly; the male students had already done their military service in the NVA as conscripts or as three-year "volunteers."

Twinning arrangements, which linked schools or enterprises with NVA units or with reservist organizations, were another form of military publicity. Such twinning arrangements, repeatedly encouraged by the MfNV, could be quite an onus on NVA units stationed in larger, more populated garrisons. They obliged military personnel to be present regularly at a variety of events organized by "their" twinning partner – all that, of course, without regard for the units' regular military duties. On the other hand, enterprises and schools seem to have had no more than a lukewarm interest either; the twinning events were often perceived as sterile, labored, and constrained.

As opposed to that, public military events, such as swearing-in ceremonies, parades, or concerts by NVA military bands, attracted large audiences. Such events were regular parts of the annual "Brotherhood-in-Arms Week," which ended on March 1, the "Day of the NVA." New recruits would be sworn in publicly, following the rhythm of their drafting, this would usually be in May or November. As a rule, there was no need to put pressure on people to attend so as to achieve an impressive audience; the interest of GDR citizens seems to have been quite genuine.

Still, they were probably more interested in the folkloristic elements or in the fascinating military technology on exhibit. If the military and the Party expected to be able to use such events to put across military-political or ideological messages, this seems to have been achieved only in a minority of instances.

The NVA was never shy of public appearances. Any major exercise would end with a parade, allowing the units involved to display themselves and, thus, boost their morale. However, the public parades were often performed by units with heavy equipment which had not themselves taken part in the actual exercise, not least, so they could thoroughly prepare their vehicles and weapons systems for the great day, avoiding breakdowns under the eyes of a large public audience.

The NVA also insisted on being appropriately represented in the state-owned mass media. Here, however, limitations were due to the demands of military secrecy. Programs about the military and defense politics were not uncommon on GDR television; on average, they would cover about 20 minutes per day. Added to that was the military presence in TV feature films and soap operas, right down to the popular children's programs. Even the best-known of the latter, *"Sandmännchen"* ("Sandman"), featured episodes with military content at least twice. As opposed to that, the NVA hardly ever made an appearance in cinema movies produced in the famous DEFA studios in Potsdam-Babelsberg. On the other hand, the NVA had its own professional film studio *(Armeefilmstudio)* in Berlin-Biesdorf. It served not only to shoot instruction films for internal army use, but its productions were also meant for the GDR public. For this purpose, the *Armeefilmstudio* made some 600 "documentaries," which were used as propaganda material in educational institutions, or occasionally as trailers in GDR cinemas preceding the main feature film.

The NVA leadership insisted to a surprisingly high degree on the representation of the military in art. Yet, artistic creativity had its limits: the motives were usually rather stereotypical, even wooden. In a similar vein, the propaganda literature, written at the instigation of the NVA, even if it claimed to be belletristic, was usually plain propaganda so that it never reached more than a very limited readership.

When all was said and done, that was the dilemma of the state-controlled interaction between the "People's Army" and the people: the paranoid attempt to keep all and everything secret and shape day-to-day life according to ideological norms doomed all attempts at an exchange from the very beginning, not to mention the true integration of the forces into society. In truth, a real exchange was not what the NVA leadership was hoping for, anyway: their aim was to subject civil society to military concepts and norms – what we call militarization.

The Social Status of the Military

It is difficult to give precise figures for the GDR citizens' attitudes to any question related to the military. There was no real public in a society controlled by Party ideology and, therefore, no public opinion in the common sense of the word. All attempts by the GDR regime to use public opinion research and polling campaigns to ascertain their subjects' real thoughts remained without success. There was no way one could tell how frankly the citizens questioned would give true answers about their innermost political attitudes to a dictatorship which tried to curb any oppositional thinking.

As the public discourse was heavily controlled and censored, individual GDR citizens had only limited means of obtaining information about their country's armed forces. The state-controlled channels of mass communications spread the official propaganda, but almost every male adult had had first-hand experience of life in the ranks and could tell the difference. In the long term, conscription, including the drafting of reservists, turned out to be the most efficient medium for spreading information about and attitudes to the military within GDR society.

Most young men would leave barracks life with rather critical judgments about the military. From their point of view, everyday life in the forces had been marked by slackness and idleness, mindless repetitions and unnecessary chicanery. That the NVA had recruited officers for their working-class background but without proper education, had long meant that many conscripts had every reason to feel intellectually superior to their officers – who, in turn, realized their shortcomings and often tried to make up for them by sheer bullying.

Throughout its existence, the NVA never managed to solve the problem that not enough highly qualified young men would apply for a career in the army after leaving school. Subtle pressure was often not enough, therefore, the military resorted to promising a university education to such potential cadets who would not otherwise have qualified for it in civil life – thus, continuing the qualitative downward trend of officer cadets.

This offer of additional academic education or professional training was perceived by GDR society as an unfair and unjustified privilege. In general, for lack of more precise information, GDR citizens tended to believe that NVA military personnel enjoyed a plethora of advantages and privileges. Upon closer inspection, this was not necessarily so. One example of this is the provision of accommodation in the state-controlled housing market. As time went on, the blocks of housing built specifically for NVA personnel, and permanently administered by the armed forces, continued to be inhabited by retired soldiers or their surviving families, who had the right to continue in their apartments even after leaving active service. There was a Military Shopping Organization *(Militärische Handelsorganisation),* but again, the range of items on offer usually fell far below what young men had been led to expect when they had been recruited. Similarly, the chances of obtaining one of the much sought-after slots in nice hotels for a summer holiday were often disappointing.

The real world of the professional military remained largely hidden from the eyes of GDR society at large. The exaggerated culture of secrecy prevented any conversation about job-related topics, while the many transfers including the need to relocate elsewhere, combined with the ghetto-like housing areas for the military, stood in the way of any social integration. Here, the intention to present itself as the "Army of the People" was also in sharp contrast with the perceived need to insulate the forces against civilian influences. Military and civic societies became increasingly estranged. While in Poland, the army was perceived as an element of national integration (*0.16* Diedrich/Heinemann/Ostermann, Der Warschauer Pakt, 149–174), in the GDR, there was more skepticism and even resentment – particularly among those who had themselves experienced the NVA firsthand. The GDR's claim that large sections of the population identified with the NVA remained a myth.

The Military as an Instrument of Socialization

During the 1950s, and even into the 1960s, many living in the GDR had felt that the socialist system was on its way into a new, better world. The 1970s, however, brought about an ideological disillusionment. The last great attempt at creating a "Socialism with a human face" had been the Prague Spring of 1968; once it had been crushed by the Warsaw Pact invasion of Czechoslovakia in August of the same year, this stagnancy was felt more poignantly. Seeing that the SED's ideology was increasingly perceived as bankrupt, other means of disciplining the population were required. The military seemed to be able to make a major contribution to that.

Until 1990, GDR conscripts served for eighteen months; this was reduced to twelve months only during the final stage. However, there was substantial pressure on young men to sign up for a total of three years and serve as a junior NCO (corporal/lance corporal). Thus, for a period from one-and-a-half to three years, the young male GDR citizen would be subjected to the "total institution" of the NVA – a unique opportunity for the state and military to shape and transform him according to the norms and standards of the regime.

Similar to probably all armies worldwide, deindividualization started with the issue of uniforms to the newly drafted recruits. What was different from other armies, including the Bundeswehr, however, was that civilian clothes then had to be packed and sent home. Storing civilian clothing was not permitted in barracks, so that even if the conscript soldier was granted leave or furlough, he had to wear uniform during his free time in the garrison, or on the way home and back again if he was lucky enough to be able to stay away long enough for a trip to his family. In a similar fashion, the military haircut served both utility and sanitary purposes, but also helped deindividualize and standardize the young soldier.

The NVA was required to maintain a continuously high standard of readiness *(ständige Gefechtsbereitschaft)*. To achieve that, eighty-five percent of all personnel had to be present in their unit's barracks (the "object") at any given time. Conscripts were entitled to eighteen days of leave throughout their term of service; they had no right, however, to dispose of these free days according to their own wishes. Instead, they were usually ordered when to take their leave. Short-term furlough or weekend leave were the exception, and, therefore, coveted; granting or withholding leave was a probate means of disciplining conscripts. What little free time left apart from the strenuous military duties had to be spent, therefore, largely inside the barracks. Even here, the NVA intervened and controlled. Most companies or similar-sized units would have a "club" where privates could spend their leisure time. However, the "programmatic connection between individual leisure and collective political indoctrination" (*0.15* Rogg, Armee des Volkes?, 311) was undeniable. The PHV explicitly referred to the company clubs as "political establishments." That was why the clubs usually provided German and Soviet war literature and World War II memoirs; the young soldiers, however, much preferred to read easy and apolitical books. Diverse other leisure facilities on offer, including musical and sports events, would also combine aspects of relaxation and political education. As with the literature, the result was not always what the political officers had been hoping for; from their perspective, participation in the discussion circles and other more political events continuously left a lot to be desired.

The soldiers' attire, haircut, and outward appearance in general were all strictly regulated. Even the design of their immediate environment was controlled: introducing individualist elements into barracks rooms required special permission. While "order" is a category most would take as being inherent to the military, "order" in the NVA came as part of the "socialist order" of state and society. Order and security were "inherent to the order of socialist society, and reflected a state of social relations continuously being realized," as the *Kleines Politisches Wörterbuch* (Small Political Dictionary) formulated it in its third edition in 1978 (*3.10* Schütz et al., Kleines politisches Wörterbuch).

The paranoid secrecy within the GDR military not only affected free time inside the barracks but also communication with family and friends in civilian life. No details should be related about the true living and housing conditions; the exact character of the soldier's tasks and job and certainly any problems and difficulties in the unit's performance were to be kept secret. This spirit of secrecy added to the strict separation between the military and civilian spheres, eventually creating a parallel military society subject to very different norms from those of life outside the barracks walls. Conversely, the restrictive norms for leave and furlough were also meant to reduce the influx of "unwholesome" information from the unofficial GDR public. Officers repeatedly complained that soldiers just returned from leave gave their friends and comrades harmful and disquieting accounts of life outside the barracks walls. In turn, this seemed a good enough reason to be even more restrictive when it came to giving permits for soldiers to spend their uncontrolled leisure "out there."

Apart from the regular superiors, officers and NCOs, the other authority which laid down norms of barracks life were those "comrades" who had already served longer. This meant, above all, conscripts during the third and last semester of their term of duty, and those junior NCOs who had agreed to serve for three years and were now looking forward to their "freedom." These "candidates for discharge" (*Entlassungskandidaten* – EKs) held an unofficial but very pronounced position of power, and they knew how to use and abuse it. This would often turn against the official hierarchy and respect for the state and the army, as demanded by the Party, but the "EK Movement" was another link in the chain which deprived the young conscript of his freedom and individuality. There were even cases where fathers told their sons about to be drafted that, once inside barracks, they would have to follow the instructions issued by their elders. These cases illustrate the expectation in civil society that the military would, at least, teach the young man "orderliness and cleanliness."

Service in the NVA was praised in the official GDR propaganda as an "honorable duty." This did not mean, however, that the SED state would have trusted its military. On the contrary, no other part of the GDR was subject to such tight and intense controls as the various military and paramilitary formations, with a special focus on the Border Troops. At least one out of every fourteen privates there was a Stasi informer; among the officers, the ratio was one in five (*2.12* Maurer, Dienst an der Mauer, 127–131). An additional burden for many career soldiers was the prohibition on contacts with "the West," which effectively meant that, unlike many GDR citizens, they could not profit from the material benefits of having family or friends in the Federal Republic. Here, too, the NVA was in no way willing to place a modicum of trust in those who were willing to serve for an entire lifetime.

Under the circumstances, it was absurd to expect a "Stauffenberg in Strausberg" to arise. There was never an organized political or military alternative, let alone an opposition movement, within the NVA. Even petty deviations from the norms of conduct or minimal criticism of Party or state policies could have severe consequences. The catalogue of possible sanctions started with everyday mobbing; it included a refusal or even revocation of leave or furlough, the threat of having to serve longer, and ended with the military justice system and the infamous military jail in Schwedt on the river Oder (*3.13* Wenzke, Ab nach Schwedt!).

The military justice system had originated after 1956, initially as a prosecutor's office which had already existed within the KVP. The chief military prosecutor *(Militäroberstaatsanwalt)* was subject to the MfNV, but also belonged, since he was part of the GDR "justice" system, to the hierarchy of the GDR's judiciary. Military prosecutors operated under him, usually responsible for specific major military units. Military courts were created only in 1963, i.e., after the introduction of conscription. Their structure consisted of three distinct levels, following the Soviet example. The Military College of the GDR's Supreme Court was at the top of the system, under which three Superior Military Courts and then the Military Courts pronounced sentences (*0.5* Hagemann, Parteiherrschaft, 31–32; *3.13* Wenzke, Ab nach Schwedt!, 81–90). Similar to all other judicial personnel in the GDR, the military judges were also subject to explicit guidance and instructions; there was no such thing as an independent legal system.

Yet another element of political indoctrination of all young men drafted into the armed forces was the manifold and extensive political instruction – and this is not identical to the Party's influence over the military, as discussed below. Regarding conscript privates, 14 hours of political instruction per month were the norm, and, as a rule, they were actually taught as well. However, most soldiers seem to have responded to this challenge with the same skepsis and reluctance with which they also accepted the limits on their personal freedom; it seems safe to assume that most of them had also lived through political instruction in the GDR schools before. The conscripted young men had an acute sense that at least the junior officers no longer seemed to believe in what they were teaching in the classroom. Every GDR citizen and, therefore, every GDR conscript had "two opinions" anyway: one was the official version which was required to be reeled off in the classroom, and the other, private, which was often the exact opposite of the first. In a similar vein, many superior officers seemed to just reel off what was expected of them, in as soulless a fashion as possible so as not to have to take a personal position. The "red light irradiation" to which NVA soldiers of all ranks were subjected was hardly credible and, therefore, seldom believed. This, in turn, opens up the more general question of how well the SED state used the opportunity to educate and indoctrinate the young men which the introduction of conscription had created in 1962.

Matthias Rogg subsumes the GDR's expectations toward the political education of young men in the forces:

"Under the hermetic conditions of the barracks, and under the pressure of the Party apparatus, the young soldier was not only to be trained to defend the fatherland, with criteria of efficiency applied. At the same time, judged by moral criteria, he was to be refined and elevated into a better socialist person. Making him face the example of socialist military personalities, and letting him experience socialist principles in organizing barracks life, while at the same time making him part of an efficient military apparatus using supreme armaments technologies, the State expected to also convincingly prove the superiority of the socialist system.

In this sense, the NVA contributed to a stabilization of the SED-controlled political system in two separate ways: It provided the military means to use force if necessary, but also served as a permanent institution of socialization. However, Rogg also concludes: 'All these goals were clearly never achieved'" (*0.15* Rogg, Armee des Volkes?, 401).

The SED State Party and the NVA

The SED, almost from its very inception, saw itself as a "new type of party," as defined by Lenin, and claimed for itself the "leading role" in all walks of life. In 1968, the Party's role as the leading political force was even formally written into the constitution. This claim covered all elements of the state, obviously including the military.

However, within the military, this "domination through and through" *(Durchherrschung)* met with two distinct obstructions. The first was that, while the NVA tried to present itself as the "Army of the People," it simultaneously insulated itself from civilian society as much as possible. The other impediment was that the inherent rules of efficient military leadership, necessary to win battles and wars, were in obvious conflict with the Party's ideological claim to control all and everything (*0.5* Hagemann, Parteiherrschaft; *3.3* Giese, Die NVA als Parteiarmee). This latter *aporia* was flatly denied in the official doctrine: the Party operated on the premise of the "unity of political and military education and training." In this sense, the officer with a trained class mentality who actively supported Marxism-Leninism would be the optimum defender of the state order of the classless state.

While Willi Stoph was Minister of the Interior of the GDR, and later Minister of Defense, from 1953–1960, the armed forces were actually represented in the Politburo. As of 1958, the SED Central Committee had its own Secretary for Questions of Security, the young Erich Honecker. Until then, Ulbricht himself had personally "guided" the creation of the new armed forces.

see page 200

Under the impression of the 1953 uprising, the Party created a "Security Commission" in 1954 to both instruct and control the armed forces; the commission's remit included both internal and external security, as the SED believed in an ultimately monolithic class enemy – any unrest at home had to have been instigated from abroad. The Party's Security Commission was abolished in 1960, and its tasks were assumed by the NVR, with Erich Honecker again as its secretary. This gave

Honecker a key position, as the always unanimous votes in the Politburo served to hide the fact that all relevant questions had been decided in advance between the respective Central Committee member (in this case, Honecker) and the Party's First Secretary (Ulbricht). Stoph's successor as Minister of Defense, Heinz Hoffmann, had to accept that his role was curtailed accordingly. Hoffmann rose to the Politburo only during Honecker's term as Party chief, after trying, in vain, several times to realize his own ideas in direct contact with Ulbricht, bypassing Honecker. This reflects what we know about the GDR political power system in general: the state government and its ministries did not serve for political decision-making; instead, their job was to convert party political decisions into concrete government actions and laws.

A further element of SED control over the military was the Party's Central Control Commission *(Zentrale Partei-Kontroll-Kommission)*, with its subordinate Party Control Commissions, particularly within the Political Main Directorate of the MfNV. As of the 1960s, practically all officers had to be Party members. As a consequence, all disciplinary punishment doled out by military institutions would also lead to Party measures, while conversely, exclusion from the SED routinely led to an officer's discharge from the NVA as well.

The Soviet example had generally dominated the creation of the NVA after 1956, thus, the same applied to the influence of the Party over the military. After 1941, the Soviet Army had operated on a pattern where the "Commissar," who had once been on an equal footing with the military commander (and often been the decisive man, which is why the Wehrmacht in its infamous *Kommissarbefehl* had ordered all political commissars to be shot), had been replaced by a "Political Officer," who was part of the military hierarchy, making him effectively one out of several department heads in any command staff. What set him off from the other heads of department, however, was that he reported both to the military commander and the next level of the Party's political hierarchy. In this way, NVA political officers served both the MfNV and the SED's Central Committee. This opened up a second, highly influential chain of command and communication, giving the political officers a far more independent role than that of the "mere" military officers. Frank Hagemann, in his seminal book on Party rule in the NVA, calls this a "hybrid position both as a Party organ and as a military head of department" (*0.5 Hagemann, Parteiherrschaft, 45*).

At the top of the Party apparatus was the PHV ("Political Main Directorate"; until 1961, it had rated only as the *Politische Verwaltung* – "Political Directorate," the difference being largely semiotic). Following the dual structure introduced above, it served both as a department within the SED Central Committee and a District Administration (all SED members in the NVA forming a "Party district," again emphasizing how distinct the military was from the rest of society). While the head of this administration was also "Deputy Minister for Political Work," as a leading Party official, he was solely responsible to the Party hierarchy. This allowed the SED Central Committee a separate channel of information about what was happening inside the forces, and also – to a certain degree – political influence over the military. The political officers and their staffs were, therefore, responsible primarily for political education, but they also helped supervise the military officers' political reliability, and, not least, played a role in the selection of future military elites (*1.29* Loch, Deutsche Generale, 382–406). As the ideology eroded during the 1980s, many political officers began to play a role in caring for the emotional and physical needs of military personnel, not unlike military chaplaincies in Western armies.

In 1957, *Generalmajor* Rudolf Dölling had just returned from a two-year course in Moscow (where he had resided during the war); he was appointed head of the Political Directorate. He had already served as the chief political officer of the HVA and then the KVP from 1949–1955. He rose to be deputy minister and was admitted to the Central Committee in 1958, but performed his duties rather haplessly, so that in the summer of 1959, he was appointed ambassador to Moscow – certainly the GDR's most important ambassadorial post, but even so, many felt it was a demotion. His successor *Vizeadmiral* Waldemar Verner, who was to command the Political Main Directorate until 1978, had until then been the head of the naval forces; he joined the Central Committee in 1963. In 1957, some fifteen percent of all NVA officers had been political commissars, a percentage which went down slightly to 12.5 percent in 1971.

Apart from the political officers, there were the SED Party structures within the military. Basically, they worked along the lines of "democratic centralism" that applied to all SED cells. The Party members would normally meet at battalion level (at company level in the Border Troops) and elect a Party secretary for their respective grouping *(Grundorganisation)*; however, the candidate elected would need to be confirmed by the political officer responsible, thus, the selection of potential leaders in higher echelons was still tightly controlled by the SED leadership.

The result was a permanent jostling for influence between the military commander, his political officer, and the Party chairman, who was, however, subordinate to both. The military commanders were, therefore, at times, derided in Party circles and publications as "mere specialists" who preferred to deal with the "real" topics and would leave political education to their respective deputy for political work, disregarding the stipulation that ideological and military-technical training were to be integrated. Other military commanders tasked their political officers with seeing to morale, i.e., the discipline and good conduct of the soldiers, thus, contributing to battle-readiness. Some political officers refused to see themselves in that role. When reporting to the higher Party echelons, they would point at real or alleged mistakes and shortcomings which they would routinely attribute to a lack of "political-ideological awareness" of the soldiers and their superior officers. At the other end of the spectrum were those political officers who saw their chief task as maintaining morale, but who, thus, risked minimizing themselves in their own role and competences.

The conflict between military commanders and political officers was not new. Marshal of the Soviet Union Georgy Konstantinovich Zhukov, hero of World War II fame, had been made Soviet Minister of Defense in 1955. He insisted on clearly subordinating the political officers to the military commanders, thus, limiting the Communist Party's influence over the military. That was why Communist Party Chairman Khrushchev, who had himself served as a political commissar, dismissed Zhukov, although the latter had helped Khrushchev during the power struggle following Stalin's death. The SED leadership keenly observed this and was prompted to increase the role of the Party apparatus within the NVA. Early in 1958, the political officers were given the right to criticize a commander's purely military decisions in Party meetings. The political officer had to be present in all military deliberations. The institution of the "Chinese Principle" (whereby all officers were to serve as privates for one month every year) has to be seen in this context (*2.16* Storkmann, Das chinesische Prinzip).

These measures showed a degree of Party mistrust in the military officers, even though the latter had all been selected by the Party apparatus. It became obvious that the Party's "cadre work" (personnel recruitment) had not yet borne the hoped-for fruits. Again and again, political officers reported up their chain of command that the military commanders were lacking political enthusiasm, and failed to support the political education activities sufficiently – but then, we can also interpret these complaints as attempts by the political officers to explain away the poor results of their indoctrination attempts among the young soldiers.

In the GDR, it was not so much the highly indoctrinated army leadership which objected to such politicization of the military as the Soviet "advisers." During the winter of 1958/9, the Commander of the Soviet forces in the GDR, Marshal of the Soviet Union Ivan Stepanovich Konev, gave voice to his concerns that this tendency might jeopardize the further build-up of the nascent NVA. Another aspect, not mentioned that clearly, was the increasing rivalry between Moscow and Beijing, which militated against a continuation of "Chinese" revolutionary policies. All these experiments came to an inglorious end, indicating that military efficiency and combat power was indeed more relevant than toeing ideological lines.

The Party perceived the NVA's severe problems as a challenge to its own work. Desertions, suicides, lack of discipline, alcohol – all these were understood as indicating a lack of socialist education. Party members were exhorted to put in extra efforts to remedy that, but also intensify the supervision of their comrades to perceive potential problems as early as possible. Aside from the control by their superiors and the Stasi, there was the mutual control of the soldiers – this represented a conscious and intended break with the phenomena of "false comradeship" denounced as being "reactionary."

Only the building of the Berlin wall allowed the NVA to stabilize its internal order. Political guidance by the Party was never questioned in principle, but opportunities for the Party apparatus to influence genuinely military decisions and, thus, to obstruct military training, were curtailed again in the mid-1960s. Similarly, the recruitment of officers emphasized more and more the potential cadets' intellectual abilities, and their "proletarian credentials" became a far less relevant criterium in the selection process. This is probably an important reason for the increasing professionalization of the GDR military during the 1970s and 1980s (*1.29* Loch, Deutsche Generale, 459–473).

When all was said and done, however, the fact remained that "the priority of political over military strategies in solving problems resulted in profound dysfunctionalities" (*3.3* Giese, Die NVA als Parteiarmee, 293) in the NVA, as in all other Warsaw Pact armies.

The Military and State Security ("Stasi")

In a way similar to that of what eventually became the NVA, the Ministry for State Security had also gradually developed in a process of differentiation out of the Ministry of the Interior (*3.5* Gieseke, The History of the Stasi; *3.4* Gieseke, Mielke-Konzern; *3.14* Wolf, Das Ministerium für Staatssicherheit). One of its chief tasks from the start had been controlling and supervising the HVA, later the KVP, and eventually the NVA as well as all the other armed formations, and particularly the Border Troops.

The primary task of the Stasi was to prevent Western spies and saboteurs from infiltrating the various elements of GDR national defense. However, since there was only one omnipresent enemy in the SED ideology, vigilance against the class enemy from outside necessitated vigilance against the counterrevolutionary from within. The Stasi saw itself as the "Shield and Sword of the Party," and that included nipping in the bud any tendencies within the military to emancipate itself from its political control. To do so, the Stasi would investigate any unusual occurrences within the armed forces, particularly desertion, suicide, any other suspicious fatalities, allegations of treason, or loss of sensitive equipment, especially weapons. The Stasi was both a secret police and an intelligence agency; therefore, its remit also included espionage and, more particularly, military espionage in the countries of the West.

The NVA also had its own Military Intelligence service which, however, had to leave investigations into military personnel to the Stasi, and was, instead, strictly

Fig. 7:
Soldiers of the Friedrich Engels Guard Regiment visit a crèche for the "Day of the Child," 1983.
MHM Dresden/BAAO4896

Fig. 8:
"Thälmann Maneuvers" at the Tank School Site in the "Pioneer Park," Wuhlheide, Berlin. Both Young and Thälmann Pioneers preparing for the winter exercise "Maneuver Snowflake II."
BArch, Bild 183-H0124-0032-001/ Klaus Franke

Fig. 9:
NVA Entlassungskandidaten (EKs: "candidates for discharge") proudly present the measuring tapes indicating the days of their remaining service (1980s).
Museum für Alltagskultur der Griesen Gegend, Hagenow

limited to intelligence activities abroad. What was more, the Military Intelligence service was, in turn, heavily infiltrated by Stasi informers. Military Intelligence depended on Stasi communications to contact its agents in "enemy" countries, consequently, the Stasi was well-informed about anything that the Military Intelligence service managed to obtain (*3.12* Wegmann, Die Militäraufklärung der NVA).

For some time, the Ministry for State Security was also responsible for "border reconnaissance," i.e., operating outside the border fortifications, at times even on West German territory. Those officers in the official border control posts who had immediate contact with Westerners, while wearing Border Troops uniforms, were, in fact, working for the Stasi.

As early as 1949, the "Main Administration for the Protection of the National Economy" *(Hauptverwaltung zum Schutz der Volkswirtschaft)* within the Ministry of the Interior included a branch (VII a) responsible for "safeguarding" *(Absicherung)* the HVA. It was soon joined by branches VII b and VII c, responsible for doing the same for the aero clubs and the maritime police *(Volkspolizei See)*.

A main department *(Hauptabteilung* I – HA I) was created during 1951, commanded by *Inspekteur* (equal to a one-star general) Heinz Gronau, whose job was to coordinate the work of the three branches (VII a, VII b, and VII c). By 1952, these three had effectively ceased to exist as separate entities and become part of HA I. In the spring of 1953, Gronau was dismissed and replaced by *Generalmajor* Ottomar Pech, who until then had commanded branch VII g, responsible for the Border Police – a responsibility he brought with him into the orbit of HA I. At the same time, military instead of police ranks were introduced.

After the uprising of June 17, 1953, the State Security was temporarily demoted again to a State Secretariat within the Ministry of the Interior; what had been "*Hauptabteilung I*" (i.e., the "Main Department") now became a mere department *(Abteilung)*, without, however, losing any of its tasks or having to give up resources.

During the 1950s, the GDR's concern with being infiltrated by Western spies was by no means without foundation in fact. Apart from the US intelligence services, the *Organisation Gehlen*, forerunner of what was later to be the Federal Intelligence Service *(Bundesnachrichtendienst* – BND), had cast a tight and very efficient espionage net over the GDR, largely to have advance warning of any Soviet or GDR preparations for a military offensive. The Stasi counterintelligence could claim a number of spectacular successes which resulted in quite a few death sentences, but the State Secretariat for State Security, later again the Ministry, never managed to put a definitive stop to West German espionage in the GDR and its military (*0.14* Wagner/Uhl, BND contra Sowjetarmee).

Analyzing the lack of discipline, the high rates of desertion, and the cases of espionage, the SED did not see the unqualified officer corps as a cause or the disastrous conditions in some of the more remote garrisons, particularly in the northern

GDR, but again attributed any shortcomings to deficiencies in ideological education and an alleged lack of covert surveillance. And, indeed, HA I had to admit that it often had insufficient contact with the rank and file, and operated in a vacuum. The solution consisted in yet another change at the top: Colonel (later *Generalleutnant*) Karl Kleinjung succeeded Pech on July 1, 1955. Kleinjung had fought in the Spanish Civil War, served as an intelligence specialist with Soviet partisans during World War II, and held elevated posts in both the KVP and the Ministry for State Security.

The field of responsibility of HA I had for a time also included the Riot Police units under the command of the Ministry of the Interior, and the Transit Police. The Secretariat of State again became a fully-fledged Ministry in November 1955, and in November 1957, Minister Ernst Wollweber was succeeded by Erich Mielke, who remained at the helm of the Stasi until the autumn of 1989.

In the years to follow, thwarting attempts at desertion remained the chief task of the Stasi. Desertion usually entailed escape to the West, the assumption being that the deserters would have shared any confidential NVA information they might have obtained with their interrogators working for Western intelligence services. This hit the Stasi's HA I particularly badly if there were some of their own informers, who would have been in a position to betray details of the Stasi's underground conspiratorial methods, among the deserters gone West. That desertions could be stopped almost completely (down from 621 in 1961 to less than twenty per year during the 1980s) is due to not only the improved border regime, but also the more efficient work of HA I within the NVA (*0.9* Wenzke, Staatsfeinde in Uniform?, 429–464).

HA I cooperated closely with the HVA to bring back those who had actually made it into West Germany. Escapees would usually be promised that they would not be punished, but if they did return, the moment they set foot on GDR soil, they were invariably arrested and tried for desertion and espionage or treason, resulting in long prison sentences.

In some cases of those who were unwilling to return, the Stasi went so far as to attempt murder, even on West German soil (*3.2* Buchbender/Rothe, Hilfe).

The maneuver *Oktobersturm* ("October Storm") in October 1965 was to demonstrate the successful integration of the NVA into the First Strategic Echelon of Warsaw Pact forces. Polish, Czechoslovak, and Soviet forces, alongside the NVA, were to take part in the first large-scale exercise to be conducted in the GDR outside the defined training areas. This meant a challenging practical test for the Stasi and also its HA I. The evaluation after the event, however, laid bare enormous problems in the cooperation between the secret police and the regular military, as well as between the "Chekists" of the various nations involved; "Cheka" was the original name of the NKVD, and the term "Chekist," referring to individuals working for it, had been introduced into the use of secret police agents in all other states in the Soviet orbit. For an example well-documented in published sources, see the *Report about Maneuver Oktobersturm*, October 19, 1965. BA, BStU, MfS, ZAIG 31074, ff. 44–51 (online at https://www.ddr-im-blick.de/jahrgaenge/jahrgang-1965/report/4-bericht-ueber-das-manoever-oktobersturm/).

The Stasi was also obliged to cooperate closely with its Soviet sister, or rather parent organization, the KGB (Committee for State Security). Over and above that, the Soviet troops stationed in the GDR ran their own Military Intelligence network which the Stasi was not allowed to penetrate. On the other hand, it was never fully clarified who, Soviets or Germans, were responsible for "securing" these Soviet troops. In the end, the Soviet "organs" were the ultimate deciders. In an agreement concluded in December 1973, the GDR Ministry for State Security assured the KGB that it and its Stasi would offer "operational assistance," while the KGB retained the right to "draw on GDR citizens for covert intelligence if present security interests warranted it" (*3.1* Borchert, Die Zusammenarbeit, 66).

The Ministry for State Security had its own armed forces in the form of the "Feliks Dzierzynski" Guard Regiment, named after the founder of the Soviet Cheka. However, it remained dependent on the NVA for logistical support. The HA I had also disposed of a separate company-sized unit since 1968. In the summer of 1976, it lured the former GDR citizen Michael Gartenschläger into a trap and shot him dead, after he had approached the inner-German border from the West, hoping to dismantle one of the new SM-70 horizontal mines ("spring guns").

The *détente* policies of the 1970s posed a special challenge for the Ministry for State Security. On the one hand, they brought with them just that international recognition which the GDR had hoped for over such a long period of time. On the other hand, the agreements about humanitarian relief, largely visits of West Germans to the GDR, resulted in more contacts between GDR citizens and the "class enemy." This also affected the NVA indirectly, whose personnel continued to be strictly forbidden to have any such contacts – making military service even less appealing.

The situation became even more complex for HA I once the agreements concluded in 1986 as part of the CSCE process allowed for unannounced inspections as part of confidence-building measures. Such inspections would not only be aimed at the NVA, but also at the Soviet troops stationed in the GDR. That Western observers and inspectors should roam the country was bound to give the secret police headaches. HA I created an "operative group," which was available at short notice to intervene in case of surprise inspections and to safeguard the interests of the GDR.

HA I was placed under *Generalleutnant* Gerhard Neiber, the Deputy Minister for State Security for the operational military sector, in 1980. In 1981, *Generalleutnant* Kleinjung retired and handed over command of HA I to *Generalleutnant* Manfred Dietze, who served at the head of the organization until 1989. During the

Fig. 10:
The "Chinese Principle" in the NVA: In 1959, SED Chief Walter Ulbricht visits the naval forces; second from the right is Vizeadmiral Waldemar Verner during his one month as a simple sailor.
MHM Dresden/BAAD4968

Fig. 11:
Minister for State Security Erich Mielke (in uniform) with Erich Honecker (center) and Walter Ulbricht (right), end of the 1960s.
BArch, MfS, HA XX, Fo, 1701

Fig. 12:
The Conscription Law of March 25, 1982, allowed women to serve in the NVA. Female alumni of the "Franz Mehring" Officer School are being promoted to officers, August 1988.
MHM Dresden/MB014888

upheavals of 1990, HA I attempted to save its existence by placing itself under the MfNV, but to no avail.

The staff of HA I were in no way subordinate to NVA officers and would not take orders from them. The NVA (and the Border Troops) were obliged, on the other hand, to give logistical support to the Stasi operating within the military. This included offices and other space within military barracks, so that in many cases, the intelligence character of a given institution would not be readily apparent to the outsider. HA I would routinely be referred to as "Administration 2000" *(Verwaltung 2000)* within the NVA as a matter of camouflage.

HA I differed from all the other branches of the Ministry for State Security in one way: it did not have corresponding offices at the regional and district level as all the others had (the "Line"). Instead, HA I structure mirrored that of the military, and every NVA command authority had a corresponding HA I office assigned to it. After 1956, those offices were no longer designated by numbers but by the military authorities to which they were "attached."

In 1954, HA I was comprised of 565 full-time staff; by 1987, this had risen fourfold to 2,509, while the number of military personnel to be supervised ("secured") had only doubled. By 1960, one in seventeen NVA, Riot Police, or "Feliks Dzierzynski" Guard Regiment men was a Stasi informer, with most of them recruited among the career soldiers or the three-year volunteers. Recruiting conscripts for the Stasi was considered rather inefficient as they would only be available as informers for a limited time. The exception from this rule were the Border Troops. Stasi officers needed complex military knowledge and abilities to be able to serve within the NVA command staffs, which is why some attended military training establishments right up to the "Friedrich Engels" Military Academy in Dresden. In the final phase of the NVA and HA I, the full-time staff coordinated and controlled about 12,500 informers (IM's), plus about 9,500 other covert personnel of various categories who were, however, recruited among not only the uniformed soldiers but also the civilian NVA employees. Apart from HA I, other branches of the Ministry for State Security were involved in surveilling military and paramilitary formations, such as Civil Defense or the GST.

A core job of the Stasi was to contribute to human resources selection processes. A Stasi operative would be present quite openly, starting at the medical examination of potential recruits. As the risk of desertion was greatest among the Border Troops, even the decision to assign a conscript to this specific service required the consent of HA I. No one was admitted to duty on the actual border without clearance by the secret intelligence service. The Ministry for State Security had to give an assessment of the candidate's political and ideological reliability in all decision-making processes regarding the recruiting, advancement, and promotion of officer cadets and officers; thus, the Stasi had an enormous impact on the armed forces' personnel management.

The Ministry for State Security and its HA I also had to consider how to bring their work to a war footing. It is still not entirely clear whether, in time of war, HA I was to come under the command of the MfNV; there are good indicators that their affiliation would have remained with the Ministry for State Security even during a crisis or a "hot" war. That, however, raised a number of specific problems. The offices assigned to military command staffs would have to be able to move with those command elements, but would also require separate safe communication links with the Ministry for State Security. Moreover, cooperation with the Warsaw Pact partner services had to be prepared in ways to ensure that they would remain workable in case of a military conflict. These processes were repeatedly tested during Warsaw Pact maneuvers or war games, but the outcome, even in the final phase of the GDR, was that there was still substantial "friction" in that cooperation.

Apart from the NVA, the Ministry for State Security was among the most important "armed organs" of the GDR; during the Honecker years, not only the Minister of National Defense but also the Minister for State Security belonged to both the NVR and the SED Politburo. Yet, relations between the two ministers, Heinz Hoffmann and Erich Mielke, were tense, and both saw the other as a rival – a tension which poisoned relations between the two organizations on all levels. The primacy of politics, i.e., the primacy of the SED state Party, resulted in a climate of perpetual mistrust by the leading figures of the Party and state toward those who were supposed and expected to defend this system. Those concerned could not help perceiving this mistrust as offensive; it stifled any independent initiative and, thus, reduced military efficiency. The GDR political leadership, however, had decided long ago to accept these friction losses; the seamless surveillance of all its citizens seemed all the more important where those citizens had access to instruments of great power. Controlling those was determined to be essential to effectively securing the system's very existence.

Women in the NVA

Contrary to popular belief, women in the GDR were not in a better position than those in the Federal Republic (*3.7* Kaminsky, Frauen in der DDR). As a rule, they would fulfil a dual role as both housewife and worker. They were noticeably underrepresented in the upper echelons of the state economy, industry, and the state. No woman was ever a member of the Politburo, and only a very few state combines were under female leadership. Just about a third of the SED members was female

(*1.4* Richter, Die DDR, 29). On average, GDR women earned two-thirds of what men would bring home (*3.7* Kaminsky, Frauen in der DDR).

It may be surprising that during the 1950s, there had been sporadic instances of women in the KVP and then the early NVA, including some who piloted aircraft, but by the early 1960s, the People's Army was an all-male business. In peacetime, conscription only applied to men; in case of mobilization, it could also be extended to cover women. Women and men who had not served in the NVA could also be drafted into the Civil Defense forces.

Women had, in fact, been employed as secretaries, later also as medical doctors, but it was only the Conscription Law of March 25, 1982, that opened the door for them serve as volunteers – without specifying in which positions exactly they might operate.

As it turned out, the opportunities for "female citizens" were largely reduced to "Rear Services" (logistics), signals, and posts as political officers. In any case, women were rarely employed in command positions – which was also due to the short time span before the NVA came to an end – but more often as long-serving specialists, with the rank of *Fähnrich*, which did not denote, as in the Bundeswehr or the Wehrmacht, an officer cadet but, instead, a kind of warrant officer. The acceptance of women into the military was also possibly related to the increasing unwillingness of young men to enroll for three years or even longer.

Entering a world that had until then been entirely male was not easy for women, as occasional eyewitness accounts attest. Nothing is known about centrally initiated campaigns to integrate women smoothly and without harassment, in all likelihood, there never were any. Again, we see a lofty unconcern of the NVA top brass regarding real life in barracks.

That opening careers as officers to women was due more to the shortage of "man"-power, and far less to any concept of equal rights, became obvious toward the end of the decade, but significantly so before the major changes during the autumn of 1989. In view of the planned troop reductions, the remaining posts for officers could be filled with male candidates. Therefore, no more female cadets were recruited, and out of the 190 female officers and more than 400 female cadets, the first were transferred to civilian life.

Effective as of September 30, 1990, all women in uniform were discharged, the only exception being those in the medical services. As the Bundeswehr, at that time, employed women only in the medical branch, no women could have been taken over into the new all-German military, anyway. It is, thus, hard to say whether, in the long term, women in the NVA would have had the same career options as their male colleagues; what we can say is that the military was not a vehicle for speeding up the social advancement of women in the GDR (*0.2* Fingerle, Waffen in Arbeiterhand?, 323–326).

Everyday Life, Culture, and Sports

Training and Maneuvers

Similar to any other army, the largest share of everyday duty was taken up by battle and weapons drill. The results were evaluated at regular intervals by the respective higher authorities; this was a central element in young officers' fitness reports and, therefore, had immediate consequences for their career perspectives. That, however, gave the more experienced privates, the "EKs", a substantial potential for pressure. The subalterns knew that their promotion depended, to a certain degree, on their subordinates' willingness to cooperate, and the subordinates knew that as well, opening the door for downright blackmail. Again and again, the lax discipline was criticized among the NVA's top brass and even in its political leadership. But it was largely due to the fact that many junior officers plainly could not afford to enforce a strict discipline against the interests of their more experienced conscripts.

This went above all for technical drill and weapons systems drill which, as we have seen, made up a large part of routine duty. The call for continuous battle readiness implied that the highly complex weapons systems would be permanently cared for; their technical readiness was also subject to regular inspections. As a consequence, only a very few of them would be used for training purposes, while the others would be serviced daily and, thus, maintained in top condition. Many of those Bundeswehr officers who, in the autumn of 1990, were the first to see NVA barracks were shocked that the garages for heavy equipment were often in better conditions, and better heated, than the accommodation for the soldiers who were expected to operate the tanks or heavy guns.

Combat training would take place in the training areas available in all garrisons, and they would also permit handgun and rifle firing. In some instances, additional training infrastructure was created for specific needs. Small town centers were built at the Streganz training ground used by the Border Troops from around Berlin, as well as at the Lehnin training area created for the 40th Parachute Regiment (*Luftsturmregiment* 40), to train for combat in inner city areas, as these units were preparing to take part in an eventual attack on West Berlin and had to practice accordingly. Engineer training areas along the river Elbe or near Storkow (between Berlin and the Polish border) were specially equipped for training for river crossings.

The high points of year-round training were the annual large exercises. The latter could range from division-sized exercises to maneuvers covering the entire north of the GDR, with contingents from several or even all Warsaw Pact member states taking part; inversely, NVA units might attend such large-scale exercises in other Warsaw Pact countries. The invasion of Warsaw Pact armies into Czechoslovakia in 1968 had initially been camouflaged as exercise "Danube." These international maneuvers would always include preplanned, very rehearsed mobile displays as well as a final parade. Despite all the set piece and propaganda elements, the exercises always served to test new structures and procedures, while also practicing transnational cooperation within the alliance.

"Permanent readiness" required that eighty-five percent of personnel had to be present inside barracks at any given time. Some career and volunteer soldiers had permission to spend the night outside and stay with their families; they had to ensure, however, that could return to the "object" immediately.

Accommodation
Similar to what had happened in the West at the end of the war, the victorious powers had seized the existing barracks and military infrastructure (unless it had been completely destroyed during the night bombing or the ground fighting). Newly raised German units were left with two options: one was moving into less adequate or more heavily damaged sites, the other meant building new, more modern accommodation. However, there were limits to how much restoration or building could be achieved at a time when civilian housing was badly needed to make up for what had been lost during the night bombing, and what was required to accommodate the many refugees coming into the country from East Central Europe. There was competition between building barracks for the NVA and creating better living conditions for civilians. In the early years of the NVA, some conscripts actually had to live in tents.

New barracks throughout the GDR were mostly created in the thinly populated North-East, around Neubrandenburg, where the KVP had originally set up its Territorial Command North, which later developed into Military District V. The soldiers stationed there would, at times, derogatorily refer to the area as the "Free Tank Republic Eggesin" *(Freie Panzerrepublik Eggesin)* – sarcastically stating that cost reductions, operational planning, and the desire to insulate military from civilian life had combined to create the most unattractive garrisons in the middle of nowhere.

Most conscripts passed their national service in the vicinity of small or medium-sized towns. Larger cities would accommodate major staffs and command authorities where career or volunteer soldiers prevailed.

Sanitary installations and kitchens remained major problems in the accommodation units newly built during the 1960s, right to the very end of the GDR. The country's building industry was geared toward meeting quantitative targets; qualitative restoration or conservation only came second. The existing infrastructure gradually wore out, and the neglect had become conspicuous particularly in the sanitary units by 1990. Even during the mid-1970s, one shower per 25 soldiers was the norm – despite all the heavy physical duty as well as sports training. Similarly, there was an obvious shortage of adequate, functioning toilets.

Disregarding any claims of a "classless society," the NVA also followed Soviet examples in that officers, NCOs, and privates ate in strictly separate messes and canteens. Throughout the entire military history of the GDR, conscripts' complaints about qualitatively and quantitatively deficient food abounded. Here, similar to elsewhere, both the political officers and the Stasi transported such complaints to higher levels of authority. These problems were well-known at the top of the NVA without, however, any serious attempts being made to do anything about them. Contrarily, the soldiers' medical care was generally of a higher standard than in civilian life.

Cultural Events
The community facilities most widely available were the "Clubs" provided by the Party and the political officers. Their purpose was to not only cater to the soldiers' needs during their free time but also educate them in the right political direction. There were usually three "Clubs," one each for privates, NCOs, and officers. Ostensibly, they offered opportunities for those who had not been granted furlough but, according to their own self-understanding and according to those who provided them, the main aim was the political and social "education" of the military.

Singing was among the preferred activities, but creative writing and the arts (usually painting) were also encouraged. However, in view of the highly charged ideological atmosphere, the soldiers were rather unwilling to avail themselves of what the "Clubs" were offering. The NVA leadership was well aware of this, and kept criticizing the shortcomings.

A rather well-known institution was the "Erich Weinert" army orchestra, which had been founded as early as 1950 by the KVP, and then continued by the NVA. Its concerts included a mixture of German and Russian popular songs, interspersed with ideological propaganda so as to make another contribution to "socialist culture."

The Churches and the Military
In reality, looking after the soldiers in barracks increasingly became the task of the political officers. At times, they themselves would complain that they were assigned an a-political charity role. Yet, there was no one else. Religious or charitable activities by the churches were utterly unthinkable; the only country within the Warsaw Pact to have a military chaplaincy was Poland – which made the GDR's eastern neighbor appear even more suspicious in the eyes of many NVA officers.

see page 201

Even so, some of the young men who served in the Construction Units, but also in the regular NVA, belonged to one of the churches. The Protestant pastors in garrison towns saw the need to look after these young members of their respective hometown congregations while they were on furlough in their garrisons. The Catholic Church, an absolute minority within the GDR, offered young men weekend seminars in preparation for their military service, and occasionally also similar reunions once their time in the military was over. Both the NVA and the Stasi watched these activities of both denominations with critical eyes. Participation in these events was conditional on a recommendation from the home pastor or priest to impede infiltration by Stasi informers, but the church officials were very conscious that overly critical utterances about the state or the NVA were inadvisable.

Alcohol and Suicides

A permanent problem throughout the NVA's existence was the abuse of alcohol by soldiers. This may apply to many other armed forces as well, but there were some notable specificities. Consuming alcohol within barracks was limited to after-duty hours in the KVP and the early NVA, but not generally forbidden. However, investigations into the recurring failures of discipline, violent brawls, and accidents caused by carelessness showed that the vast majority of these had been committed under the influence of alcohol. The problem was one of all ranks; the fact that officers openly consumed substantial quantities within military installations made it all the more difficult to enforce the comprehensive ban on alcohol among the ranks. The abuse of alcohol soon moved to high-proof beverages as spirits were easier to smuggle in.

Defense Minister Hoffmann (himself well-known for his penchant for drinking) issued Order 30/66 in 1966; in 1974, he repeated it as Order 30/74, generally forbidding the consumption of alcohol within military premises. The only exceptions were to be clubs, messes, and pubs outside barracks. However, this hardly helped to reduce alcohol abuse by the troops, but it did spread the problem into the garrison towns. Once soldiers were granted furlough, they drank without limits, resulting in complaints from the town citizens about the comportment of inebriated soldiers in public. To the very end of the GDR, the NVA leadership never managed to develop a practicable strategy against excessive alcohol consumption, the chief reason being that it flatly refused to see the root causes: restriction to barracks around the clock, the deficient living conditions, the long periods away from home, and the lack of proper care.

The Soviet Army was known to have high rates of attempted or accomplished suicides. The living conditions in the NVA, as described above, would suggest the that GDR military would also have a higher rate of suicides than the civilian population. Reliable conclusions are methodologically difficult to draw, as the SED regime refused to register suicides separately over substantial periods of time and the sources do not always provide the framework of reference for the figures given.

Fig. 13:
The ideal of "meaningful" activities in the Club: soldiers who collectively spend their time either productively or on intellectually challenging games.
ZMSBw Potsdam

Fig. 14:
Several orders were issued to reduce alcohol abuse by soldiers. "Order 30/74" issued by the Minister of National Defense was colloquially often referred to as "Order 15/37," as no more than half of all NVA personnel ever complied.
MHM Dresden/BAAU4043

Fig. 15:
The "Red Prussians": Every Wednesday (here on February 11, 1987), the NVA Guard Regiment paraded in Berlin, Unter den Linden, illustrating for all to see that the NVA saw itself as the inheritor of the "field grey" tradition.
BArch, Bild 183-1987-0211-300/ Bernd Settnik

Surprisingly enough, the existing sources suggest that there were roughly as many suicide attempts and suicides in the NVA as in the GDR population at large (about 20 cases per 100,000 inhabitants per year).

Garrison Life of Longer-serving Personnel

The GDR civilians generally assumed that professional NVA soldiers (officers and senior NCOs) enjoyed a number of privileges, with greater chances of obtaining housing and better shopping facilities as the most important. Upon closer inspection, it is, indeed, true that a number of housing areas were built for the military. As telephones in private homes were a rare exception, the housing areas even had loudspeakers installed so that in case of an alarm, the officers and NCOs living there could be called back into barracks even more efficiently. However, the housing units designated for NVA personnel never sufficed to meet actual requirements. What made matters worse was that tenants of such apartments could stay in them when they had been transferred elsewhere, or even after retirement from the service, leading to a gradual decrease in the number of housing units available to personnel on active duty. On the other hand, the civilian housing agencies, part of the local authorities, often flatly rejected applications from NVA families, pointing out that the army had its own housing program. And if – after much hassling – an apartment had finally been found, and the family had eventually moved in, the next posting was already on the horizon, and the wheel would come full circle. Consequently, long periods away from their families were the norm, for career soldiers as well, and the insufficient housing situation was one of the chief reasons for petitions by soldiers or their wives to the Party hierarchy.

Army Sport Club *Vorwärts*

Sport was an essential part of military training. Over and above the official sports training, the NVA also organized sports clubs – as did many other major GDR employers, including the Stasi with its "Dynamo" clubs. The Army Sport Organization *Vorwärts* ("Foreward") consisted of local clubs and groups in most garrisons. Their corporate design was brown sports clothes with red and gold stripes. They not only encouraged grassroot sports but were also part of the GDR effort to achieve top performances in international sports events. Among the winners of Olympic gold medals who originated from the *Vorwärts* sport clubs were Uwe Beyer, hammer thrower from Potsdam, canoeist Birgit Fischer, also from Potsdam, and boxer Henry Maske from Frankfurt/Oder.

Soviet Idols and German Traditions

The HVA, KVP, and NVA all employed substantial numbers of former Wehrmacht and, at times, also Waffen-SS soldiers during their early recruitment periods (see Chapter 2: Chronological Overview) (*0.13* Niemetz, Das feldgraue Erbe, is still unsurpassed in this respect, but see also *1.29* Loch, Deutsche Generale, and *0.20* Bröckermann, Landesverteidigung, 503, 870). Yet, the former Wehrmacht officers were the objects of constant suspicion; they were employed predominantly as specialists (e.g., medical doctors) in staff or teaching posts. Their influence on the political attitudes of the nascent East German military, therefore, remained negligible. The NVA adapted many Wehrmacht regulations and norms in its early phase. The ordinances for barracks and guard duty were largely written by former Wehrmacht officers. Under the cover of "socialist awareness," the old militarist spirit of the Reichswehr and Wehrmacht quite often resurfaced unhindered behind the new barracks walls.

The HVA and KVP soldiers had worn uniforms whose design had been a copy of the Soviet model. The founding of the NVA, however, occurred at a time when both the Soviet Union and the GDR went on the political offensive against the Bonn government. Both were united in an attempt to hold Adenauer's policy of strong ties with the West responsible for the division of Germany. The line "Germany, united Fatherland" in the GDR national anthem adopted in 1949 indicated a claim that the GDR was not only a faithful Soviet ally, but also the true Germany representative of all the best traditions of the entire German past. The Bundeswehr was vilified during the mid-1950s as being in the pay of the Americans *(Söldnerarmee)* as shown by its new helmets, and dividing the country *(Spalterarmee)*. In marked contrast to that, the NVA's public appearance, its uniforms, parade formations, goosestep, and military band music quoted older German traditions – a decision partially due to Soviet guidance.

Apart from such external appearances, the NVA's military tradition was quite different. "Revolutionary" themes were predominant here, and they included the early 16th-century peasant revolts (in particular Thomas Müntzer), Prussian reformers, such as Gerhard von Scharnhorst and August Neidhardt von Gneisenau, the revolutionaries of 1918/9, the Republican fighters of the International Brigades in the Spanish Civil War *(Interbrigadisten)*, Communist resistance against the National Socialist regime and World War II, as well as members of the National Committee "Free Germany," which had been comprised of German prisoners of war in Soviet captivity.

Including any "progressive" elements into NVA traditions made it easy to overlook the question whether anyone had already fought for the cause of the "working classes" – none of the "heroes" of the pre-19th century period would have met that criterium, anyway. During the years after Franz-Josef Strauß had resigned as Federal Minister of Defense, the Bundeswehr sought allegedly "a-political" idols who had lived according to "timeless soldierly virtues," most of them from the First and Second World Wars. These were obviously excluded from the NVA pantheon, but during the 1970s and 1980s, the NVA had fewer inhibitions including individuals from the monarchical periods of German history in its military tradition.

The Prussian military reforms of the early 19th century and their chief protagonists were an illustration of that. Initially, the core group of reformers, such as General Gerhard von Scharnhorst and Field Marshal August Neidhardt von Gneisenau, had been deemed worthy of inclusion into NVA tradition. The East German Army's highest decoration was the "Scharnhorst Order" in honor of the "progressive military theoretician." A "Blücher Order" had been prepared for times of war, but was never awarded. The historiography of the GDR always represented the Napoleonic Wars of 1812–1815, often referred to as the "Wars of Liberation" in Germany, and the Prussian reforms as a single entity. Yet, the decoration was named after the aged Prussian warhorse Field Marshal Gebhard Leberecht von Blücher, who could not really be included in the circle of Prussian reformers, however far one might stretch the term. In time of war, a stronger reference to "apolitical" soldierly virtues obviously seemed more important than ideological purity.

The NVA traditions were ordained from above. The Bundeswehr regulations regarding military traditions, dating from 1968 and 1982, respectively (since superseded by regulations dated 2018), allotted the chief responsibility for traditions to local commanders and limited themselves to defining the limits within which such tradition could be formed; this kind of thinking was utterly alien to the NVA leadership. The NVA tradition since the mid-1960s largely took the form of awarding "names of honor" to military units and institutions such as schools and academies. Unlike in the West German military, naming barracks after people was the great exception and occurred in only a few cases. The military academy in Dresden became the "*Militärakademie* Friedrich Engels" (after Karl Marx's closest collaborator). Most of the names selected, however, referred to the working-class (i.e., usually Communist) resistance against the National Socialist regime during the 1933–1945 years. The Ministry of State Security's guard regiment (which was, therefore, not part of the NVA) was named after the founder of the NKVD, Feliks Dzierzynski – an example of those names which served to underpin the close ties with the Soviet Union with historical references.

The regular Changing of the Guard outside the Neue Wache memorial in Berlin's boulevard Unter den Linden, the huge parades every May 1 (Memorial Day of the Working Classes), and the anniversaries of the founding of the GDR every October 7 underlined the determination of the GDR leaders to represent themselves as the "red Prussians" (even if a number of them spoke very audibly with a Saxonian accent!). Reintroducing the "Grand Tattoo" *(Großer Zapfenstreich)* in 1962 only added to that list. However, the potential conflicts between this identification with German, and specifically Prussian, history, and the adaptation of Soviet instructions were never fully resolved throughout the GDR's existence.

The Enemy: The Bundeswehr, Desertion, and Opposition

The SED Party leadership was well-informed about details of Western defense planning, and also about the Bundeswehr's and the other NATO armies' equipment, training, and stationing. The NATO member states had predominantly open societies, and most information could be collated with a bit of effort from open sources. What was more, both the Stasi HVA and NVA's own Military Intelligence had penetrated the West German and West Berlin security services to a degree that enabled them to produce a substantial amount of covert intelligence (*3.12* Wegmann, Die Militäraufklärung der NVA; *3.6* Herbstritt/Müller-Enbergs, Das Gesicht).

While a vast amount of individual bits of information were generated in this way, collating them into a coherent picture was subject to an ideological filter and, thus, proved more difficult. The unquestionable premise throughout the GDR leadership, and especially at its top, was that a Western attack could happen at any time. Any suggestion that the Bundeswehr and other NATO forces were structurally incapable of starting a war would have been in contradiction to the axiomatic, top-down belief in capitalism's permanent aggressive intentions, and could, thus, not be transported bottom-up through the hierarchy.

Paranoia would regularly reach its peak during NATO exercises, particularly the annual series of autumn maneuvers throughout West Germany. It hardly mattered whether these involved corps-sized forces, with up to 100,000 men, or were only designed as war games at staff level: any announcement in Western media of such exercises made the HVA and Military Intelligence double their efforts. The NVA and Border Troops might well be placed on a higher alert level as well.

The NVA's official picture of the Bundeswehr was marked by these assumptions; the strict prohibition on "contacts with the West" was also to ensure that NVA staff did not gain access to such sources of information about the West German military which could not be controlled by the Party authorities.

Among the axiomatic beliefs about the Bundeswehr was the assumption that its purpose was to promote "capitalism." Allegedly, it served US and not German interests; the term *Spalterarmee* (divisive army) was commonly used during the 1950s and 1960s. To support the claim, GDR propaganda would point at the US-style helmets and uniforms. What was more, the GDR claimed to be the "anti-fascist state" on German soil; conversely, the Federal Republic had to be the "fascist" continuation of the Nazi regime. That some of the elites of the "Third Reich" were reemployed in West Germany, especially in the justice system, the diplomatic service, and the military, helped underpin this accusation. The Federal Republic's claim to be the sole representative of all Germany was taken as an "objective" proof of this. In this fashion, GDR propagandists construed a continuity from Bismarck through Hitler right down to Chancellor Adenauer, which, in turn, suggested a high degree of aggressive readiness to start a war among the West German political and military leadership.

In all this, the GDR propaganda had to gloss over the fact that the regular Bundeswehr conscript private usually also came from the "working classes." Even so, once he was drafted into the Bundeswehr, he was part of those elements which were to be fought at all costs, and not only in war. Even in peacetime, the West German military was to be the object of intense hatred. "Education to hate" was one of the staple formulas of indoctrination within the GDR's armed forces for many years, even if many of its officers attempted to deny or, at least, relativize this after 1990.

The effects of this "education to hate" remained limited, in any case, as did those of most other forms of political indoctrination. The Stasi repeatedly reported that the conscripts were not really convinced of the class enemy's aggressiveness. In the early years, it was national sentiments among the young men which stood in the way of an all-encompassing hatred of their West German contemporaries; over the years, GDR citizens were increasingly aware of what life in the West was like, so that the belief in a Bundeswehr on a permanent war footing and paid by the Americans wore rather thin (*0.15* Rogg, Armee des Volkes?, Chapters II.6 and V.7).

see table page 210

What was perceived as especially serious during the early years of the NVA was the number of desertions, which remained high in spite of all the countermeasures, and that although all personnel serving before 1962 had joined as volunteers. Here, too, the Politburo blamed Western infiltration and agitation, above all the West German *Bundesministerium für Gesamtdeutsche Fragen* (Federal Ministry of All-German Affairs), which was accused of systematically organizing desertions and subsequent illegal escapes into the West. The GDR military justice system dealt out harsh sentences for those deserters on whom it could lay hands. Anyone who had crossed into the West was also supposed to have betrayed military secrets to the Western intelligence services (and, indeed, such deserters were routinely questioned by the West German *Bundesnachrichtendienst* and the American CIA); if they returned to the GDR, they would usually also be charged with treason.

Even back in the KVP years, desertion had been denounced as "betraying the democratic order"; this did nothing to stop the number of desertions from rising to a total of 1,940 during 1953; that figure included 82 officers (*0.9* Wenzke, Staatsfeinde in Uniform?, 76). The figures gradually declined between 1956 and 1961,

Fig. 16:
"Militarism without mask."
GDR placard, 1957. The "anti-fascist" state alleges that the Federal Republic is the continuation of the Nazi state.
Source: Deutschland im Kalten Krieg, 3
Akademie der Künste, Berlin, Kunstsammlung, Inventar-Nr.: KS-Plakate 30062a

varying between 100 and 250, but rose again sharply during the first eight months of 1961 when another 144 NVA personnel, including seven officers, went West.

By then, the NVA leaders had begun to acknowledge that not every desertion was due to political subversion by the class enemy. Living and working conditions in the NVA, abuse or, at least, incorrect treatment of soldiers, or fear of punishment for other offences, were by then quoted more often as reasons for defections.

The *Deutsche Gesellschaft für Sozialbeziehungen* (German Society for Social Relations) was founded in 1963 to integrate escaped NVA military personnel into life in the West. It was jointly funded by the West German Ministries of Defense and All-German Affairs. Its chief aim was to convince the young and inexperienced men not to return to the GDR despite initial bouts of depression and homesickness, or falling for attempts by Stasi agents to persuade them to come home (*3.2* Buchbender/Rothe, Hilfe).

Annual NVA desertion figures gradually decreased after the building of the Berlin Wall. They suddenly rose again in the early 1980s, but after that, they remained below fifty per year. It must be noted that the soldiers who had left their units almost always intended to flee to the West, but only about a third (usually Border Troops soldiers) succeeded in doing so. Desertion had ceased to be a mass phenomenon, but the NVA, nevertheless, saw them as a "serious political and military problem" (*0.9* Wenzke, Staatsfeinde in Uniform?, 293).

Opposition Attitudes

Social control within the NVA was strict. The military hierarchy, the political and Party organizations, and the Stasi continuously watched over the armed forces and kept an eye on the political reliability of its personnel. *see page 210 f.*

The KVP had, by and large, been able to demonstrate political reliability during the uprising of 1953. Even so, there had been individual cases of "capitulation," i.e., flinching in the face of the protesters. Quite a few KVP soldiers quietly agreed with the demands that were being voiced in the streets. At that time, no separate military justice system existed, therefore, the Stasi had to investigate and eventually indict the soldiers concerned in the civilian courts.

see page 202

The NVA promulgated a new Regulation for Discipline and Complaints in November 1957. On the one hand, it improved the soldiers' legal position and was designed to end the worst abuses; on the other hand, it provided massive sanctions in cases of culpable infringements of military discipline. At about the same time, the *Strafrechtsergänzungsgesetz* (Supplementary Penal Law) came into force, which created specifically military criminal offences. This included absence without leave and desertion, but unspecified other "felonies against military discipline" were now subject to criminal prosecution. Additionally, in the autumn of 1957, the prosecutors within the *Volkspolizei* were converted into military prosecutors; however, for the time being, they still had to take their cases to the regular (civilian) courts at district or regional level. A separate Military Criminal Code was introduced only after the introduction of general conscription in 1962; at the same time, a system of military courts was established, with three Higher Military Courts in Berlin, Leipzig, and Neubrandenburg, and ten Military Courts below. Soldiers who had been sentenced to up to two years in prison originally served time in the custody of the Ministry of the Interior. In the late 1960s, the infamous "Military Jail" in Schwedt on the river Oder was built, initially also as an agency of the Ministry of the Interior, but after 1982, within the purview of the military (*3.8* Polzin, Mythos Schwedt, 10).

A new wave of unwanted critical utterances rose within the NVA in the context of the "Prague Spring" and the Warsaw Pact invasion of Czechoslovakia in late 1968. The critical comments which spread throughout the GDR population also reached the armed forces. Many officers had sincerely believed socialism to be a forward-looking movement encouraging reforms of the existing structure; they were now bitterly disillusioned. There never was a coherent opposition movement in the GDR, but there was a noticeable rise in Party disciplinary procedures and the number of military trials during 1968 to 1970. Many of those concerned expressions of sympathy with the Czechoslovak reform communists; such would usually be treated as "seditious agitation"; prison sentences ranged from one to three years.

Nor did the policies of *détente* in the 1970s and the increase in inter-German contacts in the 1980s fail to affect the internal climate of the NVA. Again and again, officers would face Party sanctions or even criminal procedures for asking critical questions about the GDR military and armaments policy. Officers who had addressed loyal and constructive political criticism to their superiors or even to the minister himself were expelled from the Party, demoted, and dismissed from the military. Right into 1989, positive comments about the new policies of the Soviet

Fig. 17:
Military Prison and Disciplinary Unit, Schwedt. View of the headquarters building and the guardhouse; the prison is in the background.
Stadtmuseum Schwedt/Oder

Communist Party or the reform measures initiated by Mikhail Gorbachev (such as reusing the 1950s slogan "Learning from the Soviet Union means learning to win") were persecuted within the Party and subjected to disciplinary procedures within the military. At a time when some of the best NVA officers were studying in various Soviet military academies, and naturally brought back such new thinking from their time spent abroad, this was patently absurd.

Conscription also meant that every time new recruits were drafted into the NVA, they imported civilian values and a critical mass into barracks. The officers whose task it was to train and indoctrinate them were expected to be both efficient technocrats and unwavering representatives of Party policies. Yet, as the professional and academic qualification of NVA officers improved over time and the better qualified officers spent more time abroad in the East or the West, they began to think about new ways of developing socialism. The NVA institutions routinely branded such independent minds as "enemies of the state," thus preventing an improvement and rejuvenation of the system as a whole. In this way, the NVA also contributed to the eventual downfall of the GDR.

The Organization of the Armed Forces

The Ministry of National Defense

see page 203

The MfNV came into existence in 1956 when the KVP ceased to be under the command of the Ministry of the Interior. Following the Soviet example, but also well within Prussian-German military tradition, the minister was always a general or admiral, even if the very first minister, Willi Stoph, had obtained his rank as *Generaloberst* only due to his Party career. All his successors had, in fact, held military command functions before becoming minister.

The Minister for National Defense who had by far the longest term in office was *Armeegeneral* Heinz Hoffmann; he remained at the top of the ministry and the NVA, after serving earlier as Director of the HVA and then as Chief of the KVP, for 25 years, from 1960 until his death at the age of 75 in 1985. Hoffmann was succeeded by *Armeegeneral* Heinz Keßler, ten years his junior. Keßler had been Chief of the air forces (LSK/LV), then Chief of the Main Staff, and finally, Chief of the PHV. Keßler was only dismissed under the pressure of the 1989 events and replaced by one of the moderate reformers, former Chief of the People's Navy, Admiral Theodor Hoffmann.

The pacifist Protestant pastor Rainer Eppelmann took over in Strausberg as part of the first democratically legitimized GDR government under Minister President Lothar de Maizière, which assumed office in the late spring of 1990, but he (Eppelmann) insisted that the ministry be referred to as the "Ministry for Disarmament and Defense."

In its early stages, the MfNV still consisted of only a few administration units and departments, whose chiefs would also serve as deputy ministers for their respective fields of responsibility. The Chief of the PHV was the most important among them. He reported to the minister only nominally as he communicated directly with the SED Central Committee in his core duties. The history of the PHV is characterized by Admiral Waldemar Verner, who served as its head from 1959 through 1978. Among other things, the PHV was responsible for the Party structures within the forces and for the political officers; it also saw to the censorship of publications discussing military matters or questions of defense policy, as well as propaganda and "cultural education" within the military.

As far as military planning, as such, was a national responsibility, this was the job of the Main Staff *(Hauptstab)*, which, thus, took over all the functions usually associated with a national general staff. The first Chief of the Main Staff had been

Generalleutnant Vincenz Müller of Wehrmacht fame. Defense Ministers Heinz Hoffmann and Heinz Keßler had both commanded the Main Staff before being promoted (1958–1960 and 1967–1979, respectively), and during the 1980s, it was led by *Generaloberst* Fritz Streletz. Streletz was relieved of his command at the end of 1989; he was succeeded, in turn, by *Generalleutnant* Manfred Grätz, who had until then served as Chief of Rear Services (i.e., logistics). The Operations Branch *(Abteilung Operativ)*, responsible for all NVA operational planning, and Military Intelligence were the most important elements of the Main Staff.

Apart from the Main Staff and the PHV, the MfNV discharged all the normal functions usually associated with defense ministries: raising and equipping forces, personnel recruitment, military security in rear areas, but not necessarily operational command.

Until 1971, the MfNV had a Deputy Minister for Training. This post was abolished when a separate Land Forces Command was established in Potsdam-Geltow, effective as of December 1, 1972. This gave the land forces a chief who also served as a deputy minister, putting them on a par with the LSK/LV and the People's Navy. The deputy ministers and service chiefs were responsible for training and equipping their respective services in peacetime, while operational command rested with the two military districts in Neubrandenburg (MB-V) and Leipzig (MB-III). They, in turn, officially came directly under the minister; in reality, however, they reported to the Warsaw Pact authorities.

In case of war, the Land Forces Command was supposed to have command functions in securing the rear areas and recruitment, but, above all, it was to serve as a "Special Grouping" charged with planning a nationally controlled operation against West Berlin.

Ever since the Border Troops had come under the purview of the MfNV, there had been a Chief of Border Troops as well, and a Directorate for Civil Defense was also added at the end of 1976.

Some agencies were under the direct control of the MfNV; this applied mainly to its most important academic institutions, which even had the right to award doctorates: the MAFE (Dresden), the Academy for Military Politics *(Militärpolitische Hochschule "Wilhelm Pieck,"* Berlin-Grünau), the Military History Institute *(Militärgeschichtliches Institut der DDR*, Potsdam), and the Section for Military Medicine of Greifswald University (after 1981: Academy for Military Medicine, Bad Saarow).

Decision-making in all matters of military and defense policies, however, was reserved largely for the SED Central Committee. Similar to all the other ministries, the MfNV served primarily to realize the decisions taken by the Party. In that function, however, it was the key player.

Ground Forces, Air Forces and Air Defense, the People's Navy

Land Forces

Land forces certainly formed the core of the NVA. Using a functional term such as *Landstreitkräfte* (Land Forces – LaSK) instead of *Heer* (army), the NVA demonstratively distanced itself from Prussian-German military traditions. As opposed to that, what had been the *Seestreitkräfte* (naval forces) until 1960 was then renamed the *Volksmarine* – the name suggesting continuity with the Communist revolution of 1918 which had originated with seamen from the imperial navy. The *Bundeswehr* had seen no problem in a continued use of the term *Luftwaffe* for its air forces – a term coined by the Nazis – but here, the NVA again opted for a more functional term: *Luftstreitkräfte/Luftverteidigung* (LSK/LV). The asymmetric structure of the MfNV (that had been a continuation of the respective structures at the head of the HVA and the KVP), which until 1971 included separate commands for the air and naval forces but not for the LaSK, was a clear indication that the land forces were the "real" NVA, while the other services were somehow outside additions (*4.2* Wenzke, Die Nationale Volksarmee (1998); *4.1* Kopenhagen/Mehl/Schäfer, Die NVA).

Four territorial commands had been envisaged during the KVP phase, but once the NVA had been created, this was halved to two military district commands, one of which (MB V) was to cover the northern half of the GDR, while the other (MB-III) would be in charge of the south. In peacetime, the two military districts had territorial command responsibilities for all military units in their area, including those of the LSK/LV and the *Volksmarine*. Upon mobilization, they were to command the 3rd and 5th Armies (corps level in Western parlance), respectively. The divisions assigned to them for this were already under their full command in peacetime. Each district was to control two MSDs and one PD (MB-III: 4th MSD, Erfurt; 11th MSD, Halle; 7th PD, Dresden – MB-V: 1st MSD, Potsdam; 8th MSD, Schwerin; 9th PD, Eggesin). Interestingly enough, both tank divisions were located as far away from the inner-German border as possible – and very close to the Polish border.

Since the early 1970s, the two military districts had also controlled "Training Centers" in time of peace, three for MB-III and only two for MB-V. As part of mobilization, these were to be expanded into fully-blown MSDs, giving the NVA a total of eleven wartime divisions, of which only two, however, would have been tank divisions (PDs).

Since the 1960s, MB-V had also disposed of a separate artillery brigade, renamed the "5th Missile Brigade" in 1967. It was matched by a 3rd Missile Brigade as part of MB-III only in 1975/6. Both brigades were scheduled to provide the LaSK with nuclear fire. Both military districts (armies in wartime) also received a regiment each of helicopter gunships in the mid-1980s.

The Organization of the Armed Forces — 93

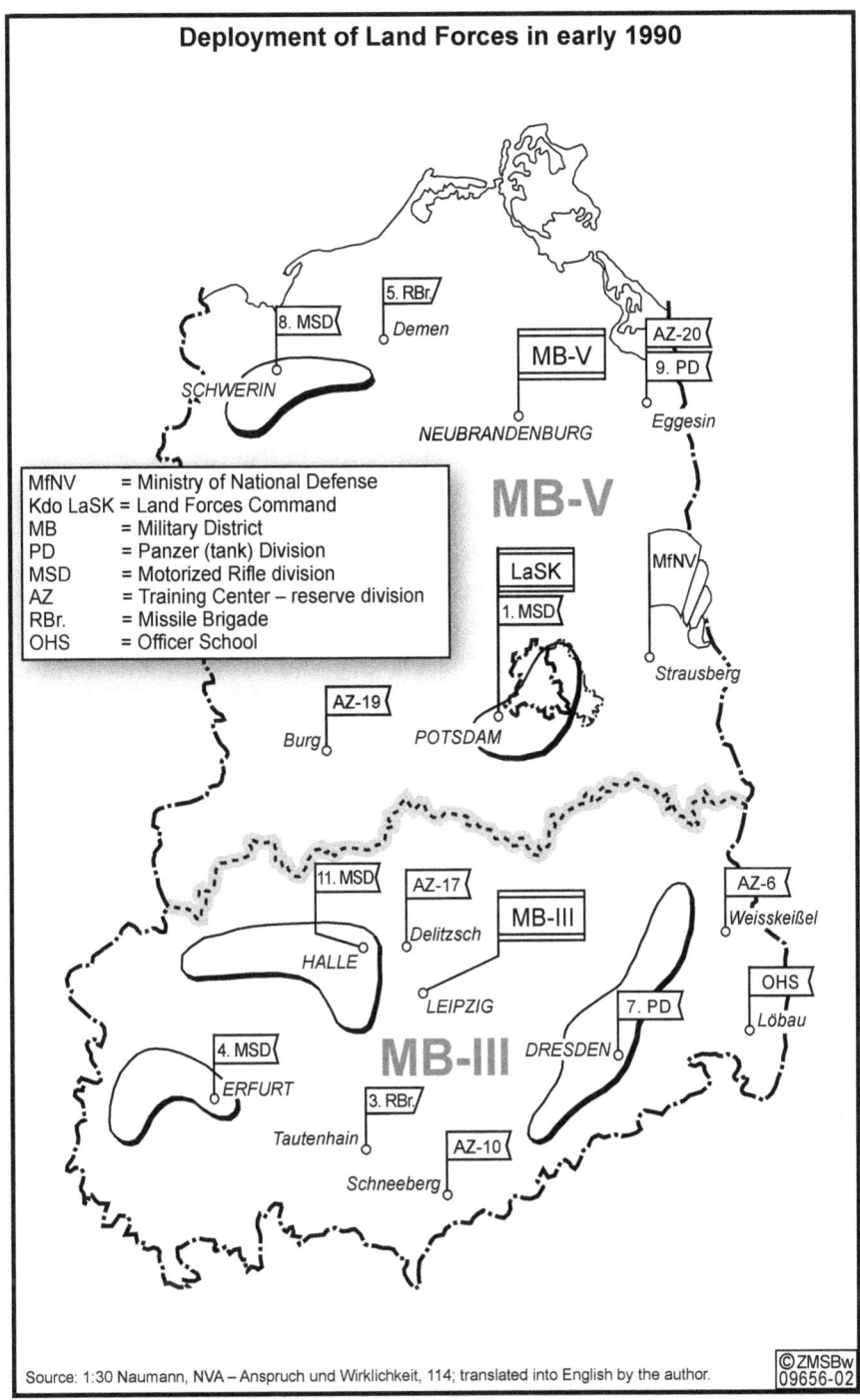

Deployment of Land Forces in early 1990

Separate consideration must be given to the 40th Airborne Regiment *(Luftsturmregiment)* in Lehnin. It had originally been a motorized rifle regiment, which had then been converted into a paratroop battalion. The unit number "40" denoted it as a unit directly under the command of the Land Forces Command – the same as the 40th Artillery Brigade stationed in Berlin-Johannisthal.

The core element of combined arms combat was expected to be the division with its regiments, again in keeping with Soviet doctrine. The four MSDs had a strength of about 10,500 men in peacetime; during mobilization, this figure was to go up to about 15,000 men. Compared to that, the tank divisions were noticeably smaller, with a peacetime strength of just under 9,000 and a wartime complement of well over 12,000 men.

As a rule, an MSD would consist of three motorized rifle regiments plus one tank regiment. They would be complemented by one artillery regiment, an air defense (missile) regiment, and several battalions coming directly under the division to ensure logistics and combat support. The tank division, therefore, would have three tank regiments and one motorized rifle regiment, an artillery and an air defense regiment, and other subordinate units. The divisions structure conformed largely to that of the standardized structure of all Warsaw Pact divisions, even if both types were numerically slightly inferior to their Soviet counterparts.

The East German army, similar to its brothers-in-arms, planned on crushing enemy troops in swift, decisive attacks, requiring highly mobile armored and armored infantry units. The tank and motorized rifle units would bear the brunt of the fighting. The KVP/NVA had initially been equipped with T-34/85 tanks of World War II vintage, but even in the first years of the NVA, the tank divisions were issued the more recent T-54 types. Various versions of T-55 tanks were introduced into the units during the 1960s. The next qualitative improvement came in the late 1970s when the T-72 medium tank became the chief combat vehicle; it was issued to both tank divisions and the tank regiments. On the whole, the GDR acquired more than 500 T-72s, giving their armored units a weapons system roughly equivalent to the West German Leopard 1.

Motorized rifle troops epitomized the concept of mobile or maneuver warfare. Their mobility on the battlefield made any comparison with classical infantry problematic. They were initially equipped with the lightly armored, wheeled vehicles, SPW-152s, which more or less met the demand for mobility on the battlefield. The armored fighting vehicle SPW-40 (NATO usually referred to it by the Russian acronym BRDM) was introduced during the 1960s; it became the standard vehicle of all recce units. At the same time, the motorized rifle units were issued with the eight-wheel armored fighting vehicle SPW-60 (known in the Soviet Union as the BTR-60). With more than 2,000 exemplars, this was probably the most common armored vehicle ever in NVA use. It was gradually replaced by the improved BTR-70 version during the 1980s. However, the tracked BMP-1 began to be introduced as the standard motorized infantry armored fighting vehicle the 1970s. Its greatly improved cross-country capabilities allowed it to stay close to the main battle tanks in almost any terrain. What was more, it was designed for mounted combat; the crew did not have to dismount to fight but could fire from inside the vehicle. The BMP-1 carried a 73 mm cannon; the BMP-2 version was also introduced starting in 1983l; it carried a 30 mm machine cannon, instead, which could also be used for antiair purposes.

Similar to all other Warsaw Pact forces, the NVA had substantial artillery elements. This included the antitank guns which had originally formed part of the combat troop battalions but which were gradually replaced by antitank missiles during the 1960s. Throughout the same period, divisional artillery began to be based on self-propelled guns, greatly improving the agility and protection compared to the towed pieces in use until then; the self-propelled guns particularly offered greater chances of survival on a nuclear battlefield.

This was also when the *"Raketentruppen und Artillerie"* (Rocket troops and artillery), as they became known then, began to comprise tactical/operational missiles designed to deliver nuclear warheads. The 5th Missile Brigade could deploy R-11 (NATO: Scud-A) and R-17 (Scud-B) missiles, while divisional artillery now included tactical missile systems of the Luna/R-30 or Luna-M/R-65 type. As of 1983, these were slowly supplanted by the more advanced 9 K 79 *Totschka* Systems (NATO: SS-21 Scarab), which, however, were not issued to all divisions before the demise of the GDR and the NVA. In 1985, the GDR received four delivery systems for intermediate range 9K714 Oka nuclear missiles (NATO: SS-23 Spider), destined again for the 5th Missile Brigade.

The introduction of combat helicopters into the LaSK brought a marked change in the 1980s; this also followed the Soviet example. Two regiments of attack helicopters were transferred from the LSK/LV to the LaSK in 1984, with one each being assigned to the two military districts. The Mi-24 gunships with their guided missiles were designed primarily for antitank warfare. However, they could also be used against unarmored surface targets, making them more versatile than the antitank helicopters which the *Bundeswehr* was introducing at about the same time.

The LaSK's engineer units, which could bring some spectacular equipment into the field, were equally large. Operating nearer the frontline, they would execute the tasks common to military engineers, such as blocking, mining, or minesweeping. On the level of the two military districts, however, they were also prepared to secure the rear lines of communication passing through GDR territory, effectively ensuring the military contribution to the comprehensive preparation of the entire GDR territory for war. The military transportation system entrusted with this task included railway engineer units with bridging equipment. As part of Warsaw Pact

see table page 211

Fig. 18:
Soldiers of the "Heinz Hoffmann" tank division on a T-72 tank during the parade in honor of the GDR anniversary, October 7, 1988.
BArch, Bild 183-1988-1007-008/ Rainer Mittelstädt

Fig. 19:
Soldier operating a launcher of the Air Defense Missile Regiment "Jaroslaw Dombrowski," July 4, 1979.
BArch, Bild 183-U0704-0010/ Reinhard Kaufhold

Fig. 20:
Gun crew on board coastal protection vessel "Friedrich Engels," February 23, 1962.
BArch, Bild 183-90843-0010/Horst Sturm

maneuvers, they even demonstrated building a makeshift railway bridge across the Oder River into Poland. The bridging equipment provided for this was replaced with more modern systems several times – an indication of the importance the German and Soviet military leadership attached to this task.

The land forces' units were highly mobile; they had been fully equipped, largely with modern, Soviet-built weapons systems, since the late 1960s. They could release an enormous amount of conventional and nuclear firepower and had been trained systematically to fight under the conditions of nuclear and/or chemical warfare. The major maneuvers during this phase indicate that they were principally designed to fight in open terrain. Only much later would select units, such as the 1st MSD and the 40th Airborne Regiment, both scheduled to fight in West Berlin, begin to train for combat in built-up areas.

Officers for the land forces received their training in the Land Forces Academy (*Offiziershochschule der Landstreitkräfte*) in Löbau near Dresden; it was given the honorary name of "Ernst Thälmann" in 1964. The training centers designed to serve as cadres for raising additional divisions as part of a mobilization would operate as NCO schools in peacetime.

The Land Forces were, with a peacetime strength of about 106,000 and a wartime establishment of roughly 258,000 personnel, including 32,000 officers, by far the largest and most important service within the NVA whose operational and even military-political thinking stayed, by and large, within the limits of land warfare.

The elements of both military districts in wartime would have made up a substantial share of the 1st Soviet Front. Compared to other non-Soviet Warsaw Pact troops, they were considered extremely well-trained and -equipped; they gave proofs of their capabilities in recurrent multinational exercises.

Air Forces, Air Defense

The agencies in the KVP designed to prepare an air force had originally received unit numbers from 300 through to 600; later, they had been camouflaged as "aero clubs." In essence, the KVP included three squadrons and, following the Soviet example, they would subsequently be referred to as "regiments." They were stationed in Cottbus, Drewitz, and Bautzen – all on the eastern border of the GDR.

There had been separate directorates for the LSK and LV until 1957, they were then fused into a single command – LSK/LV. This command controlled two air divisions, stationed in Cottbus and Drewitz, with three squadrons each, plus an air defense division headquartered in Strausberg-Eggersdorf. Once the KVP had been transformed into the NVA, it was swiftly equipped with jet fighters, firstly, of the MiG-15 and MiG-17 types; the air defense was based exclusively on antiaircraft guns, similar to that in World War II.

Fighter planes and ground-based air defense were integrated at division level in 1961. Two air defense divisions were created; The 1st *Luftverteidigungsdivision* (LVD) in Cottbus controlled four fighter squadrons and two air defense missile regiments, while the 3rd LVD in Trollenhagen commanded two squadrons and three regiments. At the same time, the GDR LSK/LV began to be included in the Warsaw Pact integrated air defense (*Diensthabendes System der Luftverteidigung*, DHS – *0.18 Finke, Hüter des Luftraumes?*).

see page 203 f.

The DHS was designed to provide an integrated defense against surprise air attack on one or several member states of the Warsaw Pact. Commanded by a Soviet officer, its chief functions were a systematic exchange of up-to-date airspace information and the coordinated deployment of air defense capabilities (both interception planes and air defense missiles). The elements provided by the member nations remained under national control; even the coordination of neighboring countries' assets required bilateral agreements. In this system, the GDR's electronic warfare elements became the country's main contribution to the DHS as their radar swept the frontline airspace.

Unlike all other Warsaw Pact member states, airspace control in the GDR remained a Soviet prerogative until 1990 – a continuation of the rights of the four occupying powers which similarly applied to the Federal Republic as well. What made things more complicated in GDR airspace was that the air corridors agreed between the Soviets and the three Western Powers as well as the flying zone around the former capital, Berlin, made it obvious for everyone that GDR sovereignty over its own airspace had its limits.

The integration of surface-to-air air defense, interceptor planes, and ground-based radar into two air defense divisions (LVDs), thus, needs to be seen in the context of the first inclusion of parts of the LSK/LV in the DHS. As of 1963, Soviet forces and the GDR's LSK/LV operated the DHS for East Germany "jointly," meaning that the German elements were under Soviet command even in peacetime. The LSK/LV Central Command Post was located in an underground concrete shelter near Fürstenwalde/Spree. It continuously transmitted up-to-date information about the GDR airspace to the Soviet allies, but had to note rather often that the "friends" informed the German side half-heartedly at best, and that Soviet planes kept violating the norms and procedures established for the GDR airspace.

There were also recurrent violations of GDR air space by Western planes, both civilian and military. The most spectacular probably occurred when two West German *Luftwaffe* F-84 jet fighters landed at the French air base in Berlin-Tegel in September 1961 – without the LSK/LV or the Soviets having been able to stop them. The diplomatic protests could not obscure the fact that, at that time, the means available were not sufficient to effectively protect GDR airspace.

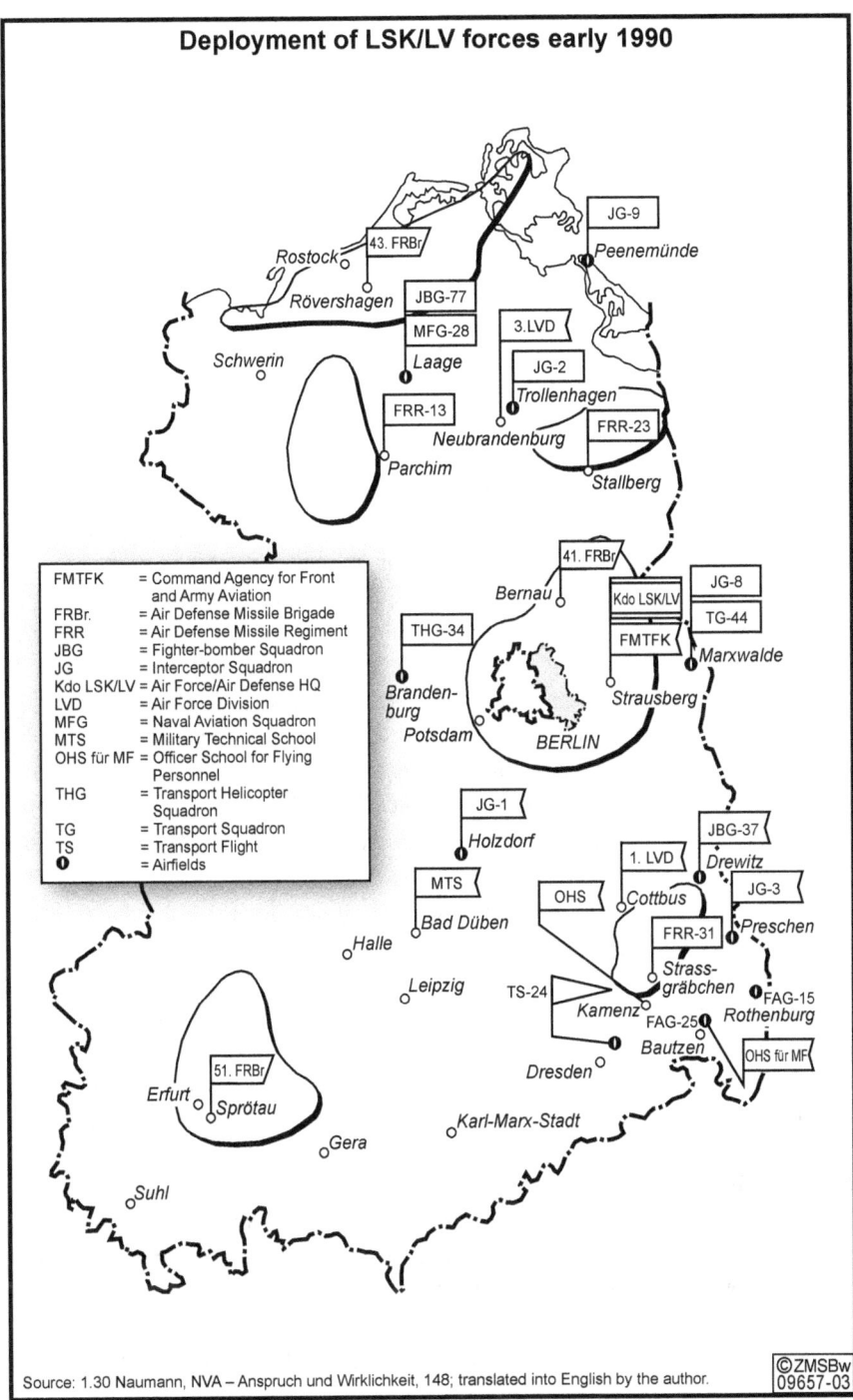

Air defense capabilities were greatly improved during the 1960s when antiaircraft guns were almost completely replaced by guided missiles, also Soviet-designed and produced. In the early 1960s, S-75 Dwina Wolchow missiles were deployed (NATO designation SA-2 Guideline); later, they were reinforced by the more modern S-125 Newa system (NATO designation SA-3 Goa). These missiles could reach great heights but only at a limited range, therefore, they were only suitable to protect individual target sites. A comprehensive air defense would require missiles with a much greater range. The first such system was S-200W "Wega" (SA-5 Gammon), which, however, became available only during the early 1980s. All six fighter squadrons were equipped with MiG-21 interceptors during the early 1960s.

Throughout the Six-Day War of June 1967, Israel managed to vanquish its numerically superior adversaries, *inter alia*, because the Israeli air force succeeded in destroying the Arab air forces on the ground, performing a surprise attack. The consequence for the LSK/LV was that the interceptor squadrons' airfields were equipped with hardened shelters, allowing the jets to be parked dispersed and under cover, protecting them from similar surprise strikes.

The MiG-23 fighters gradually improved LSK/LV's air-to-air capabilities in the early 1970s. When the Combined High Command of the Warsaw Pact called for more Close Air Support to be provided to ground troops, fighter-bombers of the Su-22 type were acquired and assigned to two squadrons. A "Command Agency for Front and Army Aviation" was set up to command these two squadrons as well as the two attack helicopter regiments which had originally been part of LSK/LV, effectively a third air division in all but name. The LSK/LV started receiving what was then the most modern Soviet fighter plane, the MiG-29 interceptor, just before the demise of the GDR, in early 1989.

The LSK/LV officers were generally trained at the Officer School "Franz Mehring" in Kamenz, but pilot officers received their education at the "Otto Lilienthal" officer school in Bautzen.

Due to their integration into the DHS and because they were exclusively equipped with Soviet technology, the LSK/LV were more tightly linked with the Soviet military than any other service. They were also considered to be well-trained and -equipped by Warsaw Pact standards.

People's Navy

While the KVP had had a seagoing element *(Volkspolizei See)*, it had initially been equipped with no more than a few boats for securing coastal waters and minesweeping. Only when the NVA proper was created did the Soviet Union provide the first true fighting units from out of its own inventory: some antisubmarine vessels and fast patrol boats. On this basis, the NVA would be able, in the long run, to make a contribution to the struggle for naval supremacy in the Baltic, and opening up the Baltic Approaches for use by the Soviet Baltic Fleet.

In 1960, what had until then been the "Naval Forces" *(Seestreitkräfte)* was renamed the People's Navy *(Volksmarine)*, an obvious reference to the tradition of the 1918 revolution and the uprising of the Kiel-based sailors who had started it. Soon after, the *Volksmarine* concentrated its offensive seagoing capabilities into a 6th Flotilla stationed in Bug/Dranske, on the northern tip of the island of Rügen. The 6th Flotilla included the early fast patrol boats, reinforced in 1965 by slightly larger units of the "Projekt 206" type, but principally by the missile boats of the "Oka" type ("Projekt 205"), which were, in turn, formed into a Missile Fast Patrol Boat Brigade. The missile boats' crews felt they were the actual spearpoint of the People's Navy, and were treated as an elite.

The "Coastal Border Brigade" based in Rostock became part of the NVA in 1961; until then, it had been referred to as the 6th Border Brigade. Thus, the People's Navy assumed some responsibility for stopping attempts to flee the country across the Baltic into Schleswig-Holstein, Denmark, or to Western ships outside GDR territorial waters. For this, it used boats originally designed for purposes other than border patrol craft, for example, minesweepers.

The People's Navy also created a substantial amphibious capability in the 1960s, which it increased again during the next decade by introducing new, larger units. The amphibious elements of the 1st Landing Brigade would usually exercise seaborne assaults in combination with one battalion from the Rostock-based MSR-28 (28th Motorized Rifle Regiment), which was renamed Coastal Defense Regiment 18 *(Küstenverteidigungsregiment* 18) in 1988. The GDR capabilities alone would only suffice for a tactical landing, but all training was geared toward cooperating with Polish and Soviet units in the Baltic region to perform a combined operation-level landing with an eye to opening the Baltic Approaches.

The People's Navy also comprised a helicopter squadron (eventually designated "MHG-18"), equipped with a special naval version of the Mi-4 helicopter, which was, however, withdrawn in the 1970s and replaced by Mi-8 helicopters. In the late 1970s, these were joined by antisubmarine warfare helicopters of the Mi-14 variant.

Alongside the creation of air-to-ground fighter-bomber squadrons in the LSK/LV, which were to provide close air support to the ground forces, the 28th Naval Aviation Squadron *(Marinefliegergeschwader 28)* was set up during the late 1980s, based at Rostock-Laage airbase, which it shared with the JBG-77 regiment from the LSK/LV; both squadrons were equipped with Su-22s.

The People's Navy was the smallest service; it disposed of no units worth mentioning that would have been capable of operating on the high seas; it was designed exclusively for deployment in the Baltic area. In that limited space, however, it would regularly meet Western naval elements; any forms of contact were strictly forbidden. As part of the United Baltic Fleet of the Warsaw Pact, operating together with the allies and in conjunction with the ground attack along the shores, it would have played an important role in wartime, by far exceeding mere coastal protection duties.

A Special Case: The Border Troops

Every state guards and protects its borders. What was special about the GDR was that it protected its borders less against unwanted intruders than against attempts by its own citizens to leave the country. What is more, protecting borders is usually a police matter; the GDR's Border Troops, however, always had a military dimension as well. The peculiar ambiguity of border police vs. military roles is what sets the GDR Border Troops apart – and justifies their inclusion in a GDR military history (*0.17* Sälter, Grenzpolizisten; *4.3* Diedrich, Die Grenzpolizei; *2.12* Maurer, Dienst an der Mauer).

The Border Troops started as a police force, similar to the NVA. In 1947/8, the DVI (the Soviet-controlled forerunner of the GDR Ministry of the Interior) unified the border forces organized until then by the *Länder* which had been recreated after 1945. The DVI had soon subordinated all border police units and also begun to concentrate them in barracks. It played an important role controlling the "Ring around Berlin" during the blockade of West Berlin in 1948/9; they were supposed to interdict the illegal trafficking of goods between the three Western sectors of the German capital and the Soviet Zone of Occupation surrounding it. Several short-lived changes in affectation followed, but eventually the DGP was allotted to the Ministry of the Interior in 1950; by that time, it was about 20,000 strong. As of January 1, 1951, the DGP commands of the *Länder* were dissolved for good (the *Länder* as a level of political decision-making effectively disappeared in 1952 and were quietly dissolved in 1958).

Yet, the DGP was reassigned again in 1952, this time to the Ministry of State Security. This also meant a changed emphasis in the force's activities. Rather than protecting the GDR economy against smugglers, the new tasks were largely military and political. The Soviet military administration demanded that the border with the Federal Republic be cordoned off; a control zone was created along it which could only be accessed with a special permit. "Unreliable" inhabitants of the border zone were forcefully evacuated in the infamous *Unternehmen Ungeziefer* (Operation Vermin). In a similar fashion, the border between West Berlin and its surroundings was fortified; only the demarcation line between the three Western and the Soviet sectors remained open.

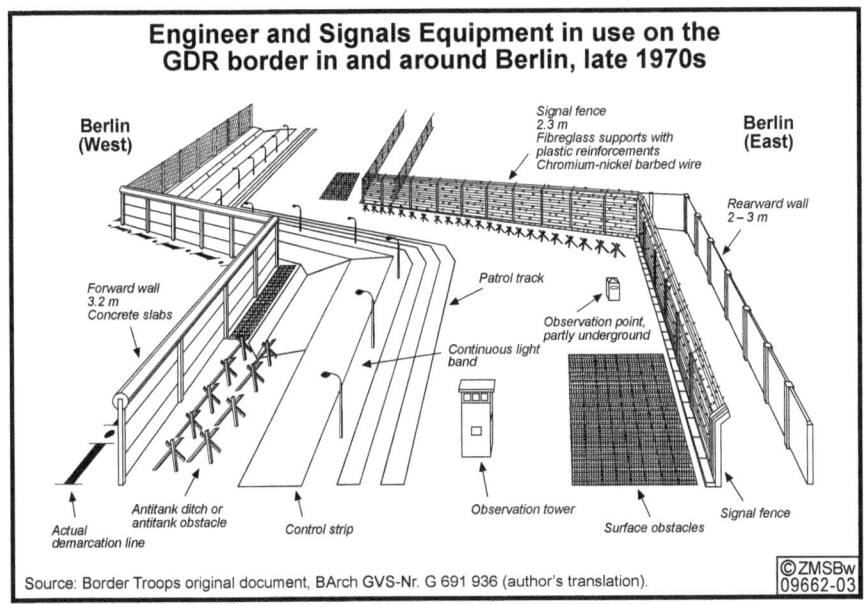

Source: Border Troops original document, BArch GVS-Nr. G 691 936 (author's translation).

After the June 1953 uprising, the Ministry of State Security – and with it the DGP – was made part of the Ministry of the Interior again. At the same time, the DGP was increasingly tasked with paramilitary functions. In case of conflict, it was to form a first line of defense against a Western attack and received military training as well. In 1957, it was reorganized into brigades and equipped with tanks and artillery; regular exercises together with the NVA to train its wartime roles became the norm.

The first generation of border policemen had served to support the Soviet units primarily responsible for guarding the frontiers; during the mid-1950s, the Soviets gradually withdrew from border duties and left the job to GDR officials, not least to demonstrate the increasing sovereignty of its client state. The single exception was controlling the Western Allies at the border checkpoints: this continued to be carried out exclusively by Soviet guards to the end of the GDR as the Western Allies, the victorious powers of World War II, would not tolerate any inspections by German officials.

The NVR officially determined for the first time in 1960 that firearms should be employed to prevent "border violations"; until then, their use had only been permitted in case of armed aggression or in self-defense. The well over 30,000 men of the DGP were commanded by Colonel Erich Peter at that time; he remained at the helm of the Border Troops until his retirement as a *Generaloberst* in 1971.

When the border between the Eastern and Western Sectors of Berlin was eventually sealed off on August 13, 1961 (the "Berlin Wall"), some 5,000 DGP troops were

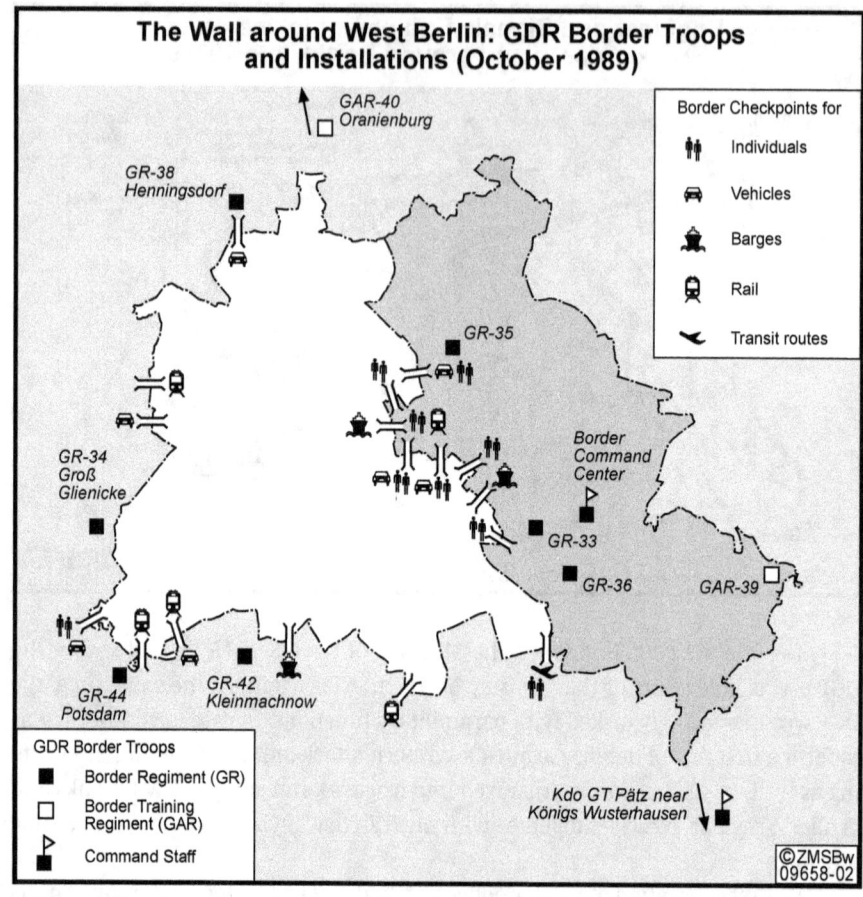

deployed, playing a key role in the operation (*2.9 Die Berliner Mauer*). Weeks later, in September of the same year, the NVR decided to place the Border Police under the MfNV. The new name of "Border Troops" was only the official confirmation of a process of militarization begun much earlier.

This military perspective would characterize the day-to-day duties of the Border Troops to the very end, even if, starting in 1974, they were no longer part of the NVA. Now called the "Border Troops of the GDR," they still remained under the orders of the Ministry for National Defense. The obvious purpose of the new structure and the new name was to keep their manpower out of the conventional force limitation or even reduction talks which were beginning to take place as part of the *détente* process. The same units were to perform border police duties on a day-to-day basis, but were trained, equipped, and structured along military lines in view of their planned role in wartime. Clashes of purpose and interest were unavoidable.

The Border Troops were but one element of the "border regime." In its entirety, it encompassed those informers who would alert the Stasi to their neighbors' apparent preparations to flee the country; inhabitants of the areas closest to the actual border had been recruited as "Volunteer Assistants of the Border Troops" and promised to keep their vicinity under observation; members of the *Volkspolizei* served this purpose as much as the officials of the *Transportpolizei*.

Behind the scenes, the Stasi – operating on behalf of the Party – pulled the strings. The Border Troops had a higher share of "unofficial collaborators" than any other military or paramilitary service. An average of one out of every fourteen conscripts, one out of eight NCOs, and every fifth officer in the *Grenzkommando Mitte* (the Border Troops around West Berlin) also worked for the Ministry for State Security. Even those figures do not yet include the Pass Inspection Units *(Passkontrolleinheiten)* at the various border checkpoints. While wearing Border Troops uniforms during their daily duty, they were, in reality, full-time members of the Stasi. Conscripts could opt to do their national service within the Border Troops, but no one was forced against their will to serve on the border. On the contrary, a rigorous selection process from the very first registration and medical check-up as well as during training and daily routine aimed at keeping potential deserters away from the inner-German and West Berlin border.

The GDR citizens and the world public at large heard next to nothing about failed attempts to flee, especially if such attempts were foiled at an early stage. The GDR, always concerned about its international reputation, tried to intercept potential refugees as far away as possible from the prying eyes of the West. Even if the Border Troops, in this sense, did not have the greatest share in preventing "illegal" border crossings, they publicly represented the GDR's willingness to use lethal force, if necessary, to maintain the existing social and political system.

The Border Troops' other task was to serve as combat units in case of conflict or outright war with the Bundeswehr or NATO as a whole. That is why they also had to maintain a continuous state of readiness. Their units were continuously prepared to concentrate, at short notice, all personnel and equipment into combat-ready units in close proximity to the border.

The problem of training Border Troops soldiers was the inherent contradiction between these two major roles. Police officers are trained to shoot to render a person unable to use violence. The Border Troops only learned to shoot as soldiers; the AK-47 Kalashnikov they used could not be used for any other purpose. The individual soldier's equipment and training was a clear indication that the Border Troops were no border police. However, they were not a regular military unit, either. Normal military forces drill a sense of comradeship into their members; everyone has to be able to rely on each other. Each individual in the Border Troops was trained to mistrust everyone else, particularly the soldier with whom he went on patrol: Would the other man shoot him and then escape across the fence? Peacetime duties required continuous distrust and "watchfulness."

The System of National Defense and the GDR's Other Armed Formations

Sport and Technology Association

Alongside the military units in a narrow sense, several other paramilitary organizations served to safeguard the SED regime against the "counterrevolution" from inside and outside. Among these, such organizations should be counted which were not designed to combat in any sense, but which were to further the militarization of society, or provide or maintain training and qualifications with a potential military application.

The GST was founded following a "suggestion" by Stalin himself. In 1952, he made the GDR leadership provide paramilitary training to male GDR youth (*4.7 Sachse, Aktive Jugend; 4.4 Heider, Die Gesellschaft für Sport und Technik*). The Ministry of the Interior sought the cooperation of the FDJ, the GDR youth organization, under its then Secretary General, Erich Honecker. The same year, the first programs started which involved not only driving, flying, and radio communication, but also formal drill and live firing. After June 17, 1953, the build-up slowed down somewhat, and the focus moved to sports rather than military training. But when, in 1955, the SED reacted to the integration of the Federal Republic into the Western defense system by intensifying the militarization of society, the Politburo demanded that the GST include more paramilitary content in its programs. Thus, it would also serve to advertise recruitment for the KVP, later the NVA, and to encourage potential volunteers to sign up. Once the Ministry for National Defense had been established, it also assumed control of the GST. That, however, decisively tilted the balance of military vs. sports programs. Declining, or rather selective, interest among GDR youth for this volunteer organization resulted in an increased emphasis on sports activities, so that the GST began to run afoul of the East German Sports Association *(Deutscher Turn- und Sportbund)*.

Indeed, many youngsters were far more interested in hang gliding, sailing, wireless communication, or firing weapons, and particularly in acquiring the much sought-after driving license for motorbikes, than in any systematic paramilitary education. In principle, GST membership was open to young men and women, and even to any citizen up to the age of 26, subject to conscription (i.e., male), but in practice, the programs were designed to attract young men below the age of conscription more than anyone else.

The GDR military leadership complained repeatedly about not only the allegedly deficient military and technical training, but also a lack of political education within the GST. Nor did this change when, in 1968, a general on active duty, *Generalmajor* Günther Teller, was appointed to lead the organization. He made an effort to achieve closer cooperation between the GST and the NVA, and pressured the armed forces to provide more instructors. Yet, during the 1970s, the result was not what he had hoped for – instead, interest among the target group declined again.

When the GDR ceased to exist, the GST could muster about 680,000 members – quite a notable degree of mobilization, but then this figure needs to be relativized, as only about a third of all members managed to obtain the "Badge for paramilitary and technical knowledge," which alone indicated a successfully concluded training course. The GST was plagued by a problematic cost and effect relationship throughout its existence.

Air Raid Precautions and Civil Defense
World War II had already shown the need to prepare for protection of the hinterland, and particularly of major conurbations, against the effects of modern war. Faced with a potential nuclear war, such precautions needed to be multiplied. The option of discarding them completely as pointless was never seriously considered anywhere within the Soviet orbit. The "Third Reich" had separated military air defense and civilian air raid precautions. The latter had been part of the police (as had been the fire brigades), placing responsibility on the Ministry of the Interior which had to mitigate the aftereffects of enemy air attacks.

In order to disguise the true purpose, the GDR had initially used the term "active fire prevention" *(aktiver Brandschutz)*, later the World War II term *Luftschutz* ("air raid protection"), which eventually gave way to the term "Civil Defense" *(Zivilverteidigung)*. This went hand in hand with an enlarged spectrum of responsibilities and the gradual inclusion of other organizations. Eventually, the idea was not only to protect civilians against the immediate effects of enemy weaponry, but rather to maintain infrastructure in general, whether it served civilian or military purposes. In this sense, Civil Defense transcended a mere air raid protection service, as it included a wide range of precautionary measures to secure the rear areas and logistic bases of Warsaw Pact troops fighting in central Europe (*0.12* Heitmann, Schützen und Helfen?).

Not only did this organization originate within the purview of the Ministry of the Interior, it also remained under its umbrella much longer than, say, the NVA or the Border Troops. Following the Soviet example again, the former "Adminis-

Fig. 21:
Members of a Border Troops Boat Company patrol the river border between East and West Berlin, March 1964.
BArch, Bild 183-C0305-0001-002/ o. Ang.

Fig. 22:
GST troop practicing small caliber rifle fire in Selchow, April 5, 1955.
BArch, Bild 183-29791-0001/ Horst Sturm

Fig. 23:
Civil Defense exercise near Dresden, May 1978.
MHM Dresden/VA005583

tration Air Raid Protection" was renamed "Civil Defense Staff" in 1967, while remaining part of the Ministry of the Interior. At the same time, it was tasked with not only general civil protection measures, but also "operative tasks in case of a state of defense." "Preparing the population for war" was, however, also to have a substantial ideological dimension. The Civil Defense Staff was to both protect and indoctrinate as well as maintain freedom of military operations. Consequently, the organization was finally transferred to the MfNV in 1976; "Civil Defense" had very obviously become part of the "system of socialist national defense."

Some sources from the mid-1970s claim that by then, Civil Defense had grown to include some 700,000 members – a figure which is met with a degree of skepticism in other publications; by the late 1980s, the Ministry believed the organization to have roughly 600,000 members. While the GDR Red Cross Society alone had about 700,000 members, it is not possible to just add those figures up, as a substantial number of individuals were, in fact, members of both bodies, which also had a high share of female members. Numerically, Civil Defense was the single largest element of the "system of socialist national defense."

The attempt to militarize GDR society further by means of the Civil Defense organizations met with limited success. The Stasi reports about the reality of life in the Civil Defense units or among the volunteer firefighters highlight, on a regular basis, that even active and enthusiastic members of such organizations did their best to avoid the ideological elements of their voluntary service.

Riot Police, Transport Police, Volkspolizei

The "true" police forces remained the responsibility of the Ministry of the Interior, yet, they also need to be counted among the "armed formations," as they were also to be deployed in case of war. The Riot Police *(Bereitschaftspolizei)* was formed as a direct consequence of the uprising on June 17, 1953 (*4.9* Steike, Die Bereitschaftspolizei); the originally envisaged garrison pattern for the Riot Police reflected the major centers of that revolt exactly. Yet, the new police unit, initially designated as "Troops of the Interior" *(Innere Truppen)*, was slow in taking shape; in the never-ending competition for scarce resources, it had to contend with many rivals, such as the KVP/NVA or the DGP/Border Troops. The one alleviation was the reintegration of the Ministry for State Security into the Ministry of the Interior, as this permitted the integration of the Stasi's guard battalions into the Riot Police. These units played an important role in sealing off the inner-city border and the subsequent construction of the Berlin Wall in August 1961.

By the mid-1960s, however, the Riot Police's equipment and training was very obviously geared more toward containing and annihilating enemy troops in rear areas; the units began to be equipped with antitank weapons and even light artillery. The GDR conscripts could opt to do their national service in the Riot Police instead of the NVA. The NVR determined that, in future, the military was to be deployed inside the GDR only in an emergency; internal security was to be primarily the responsibility of the Riot Police, and that division of labor was also practiced during major Warsaw Pact exercises, such as the 1970 *Waffenbrüderschaft* maneuver.

Still, the Riot Police's relevance began to erode. It had been just under 20,000 strong in 1961; by autumn 1989, this had dwindled to 10,000 men. There is no clear indication whether it was this reduction in numerical strength or if the Party leadership had lost faith in the Riot Police's political reliability – in any case, it was never deployed to put down the demonstrations in the autumn of 1989 which eventually led to the demise of the GDR.

Very little research has gone into the history of the Transport Police *(Transportpolizei)*, perhaps because at a strength of about 6,400 men, it was one of the smaller elements of the "system of socialist national defense." In case of war, its job would have been to safeguard the strategically important rail links (*4.6* Mittmann, Die Transportpolizei). In peacetime, the Transport Police made a contribution to maintaining the "border regime" by identifying suspect travelers on trains toward border regions or guarding transit trains between West Germany and West Berlin. For that reason, the Transport Police was not represented on the regional or district level contingency staffs *(Bezirkseinsatzleitung, Kreiseinsatzleitung)* but was to be subordinate to the NVA transport offices.

Compared to the Transport Police, there has been far more research into the history of the regular police force, the "People's Police," *Volkspolizei*, or just "VoPo." Since 1949, the official name had been the *Deutsche Volkspolizei* or DVP. Its creation after 1945 was clearly marked from the very beginning by the determination of the Communist Party, later the SED, to achieve control of the police force and never relinquish it afterwards. All top positions went to "reliable" Party members. Yet, for the VoPo, as for the military, the early years were characterized by a lack of training and equipment, high fluctuation and low discipline – deficiencies which could only be overcome gradually. Every GDR citizen knew about the *Abschnittsbevollmächtigter*, the VoPo representative in a block of flats. The "ABV" was the lowest element of an overarching organization which combined security and criminal police roles with political-ideological supervision and administrative duties, such as citizen's registration. In war, the VoPo was supposed to enforce mobilization, protect strategic infrastructure, and assist in air raid protection measures. The VoPo had been comprised of some 60,000 men since the late 1950s, but a quarter of those were actually employed in guarding the industrial and business infrastructure.

Working-Class Combat Groups
The Working-Class Combat Groups *(Kampfgruppen der Arbeiterklasse)* were another direct result of the June 1953 uprising, even if they saw themselves in the much longer tradition of "armed workers' militias." This dimension of their history has been researched quite well (*4.8* Siebeneichner, Proletarischer Mythos), but an analysis of these units from the perspective of military history is still a *desideratum* and would make a valuable subject for further study (*4.10* Wagner, Die Kampfgruppen). In the eyes of the GDR state leadership, not only had the security organs of the state failed in their jobs, but also the SED Party organization on both regional and district levels had not lived up to their duties in time of crisis. In order to prevent any repetition, regional and district crisis staffs (*Bezirkseinsatzleitung* and *Kreiseinsatzleitung*, respectively) were instituted, which, under the command of the respective Party First Secretaries, were to coordinate the fight against "counterrevolutionary" upheavals. Another reaction was that the self-protection forces which some enterprises had already raised were now created elsewhere as well, in fact, all across the country, and were given the generic term of *Kampfgruppen der Arbeiterklasse*. They were also uniformly placed under the command of the SED Party apparatus. They had a double role: On the one hand, they were to prevent strikes and protests at their workplaces; on the other hand, they were to protect industrial assets against outside attacks.

Raising these units suffered initially from the dual purpose: The relative importance of the paramilitary and the propagandistic roles had not yet been decided. Once the entire GDR was increasingly militarized after 1955, the paramilitary tasks began to be paramount. Yet, the aim of mobilizing some 300,000 fighters could only be reached by relaxing the initial baseline that only Party members or candidates were to be recruited. Occasionally, the Politburo had to emphasize that the occasional recruitment of nonmembers should not put into question the character of the combat groups as suborganizations of the SED.

Responsibility for training the combat groups was assigned to the police; they were often armed and equipped with German weapons of World War II vintage which had been discarded by other units after those had received their Soviet-made equipment and weaponry. The first time the combat groups were deployed in earnest was in November 1956 when Berlin Humboldt University students demonstrated in protest; ostentatiously, the combat groups paraded on Unter den Linden. Even this first public appearance was a clear indication that the true purpose of the combat groups had changed from defending their workplaces to maintaining law and order in a very general sense.

The ambitious target of 300,000 fighters remained illusory, but by early 1961, the combat groups could muster some 200,000 men. However, participation in the training classes remained unsatisfactory – a problem which was never completely solved right to the very end of the GDR. Even so, the combat groups gradually improved their training and, thus, their combat readiness; if, initially, many problems had been due to the badly trained commanders, that was eventually overcome. The proof came when the combat groups played a central role during the sealing-off of the inner-city border in Berlin on August 13, 1961 (the building of the "Berlin Wall"). The combat groups' role was repeatedly highlighted in the GDR media on the day itself and during the following weeks.

Two battalions took part in the Warsaw Pact exercise *Waffenbrüderschaft* in 1970; again, this was utilized to give them a high profile in GDR propaganda, not least, to finally recruit the hoped-for numbers of well-trained fighters. Its numerical strength remained at 200,000, which was, by then, the target set by the Party; equipment, training, and readiness had also become what had been hoped for.

Throughout their existence, the combat groups were subordinate to the Party and the Ministry of the Interior, but the company-sized *Kampfgruppenhundertschaften*, which made up about forty-five percent of the overall numbers, were to be placed under the NVA's territorial command authorities in case of armed conflict. This was only changed in 1988; after that, all combat groups were to remain under the Ministry of the Interior in war and peace. This indicated another change in emphasis, back to internal security even in case of war. In spite of this, when the sheer existence of the GDR was threatened from within in the autumn of 1989, the combat groups never played an essential role. The SED leaders were probably no longer convinced that the combat groups were sufficiently reliable ideologically and harbored doubts whether their members might not go over to the demonstrators. What was more, the focus on military roles had resulted in very reduced training for police functions; on that account as well, the combat groups' usefulness might be questionable.

On December 6, 1989, the combat groups were ordered to hand in their weapons, and before the year was out, the GDR government had decided to dissolve them altogether by the next summer.

Reservists

After fulfilling their obligation as conscripts and serving for eighteen months, young men had to be ready to be called up again as reservists (*0.15* Rogg, Armee des Volkes?, Chapter VIII). In case of war, the NVA and almost all other armed formations would require substantial reinforcements, calling for a well-trained and motivated reserve which could be mobilized at short notice. The many claims on the limited personnel resources often led to individuals being slanted for several different posts, especially if they had relatively rare and sought-after qualifications, such as medical doctors. By the end of the 1980s, about 2.6 million men who had undergone military training lived in the GDR; some 280,000 of them were scheduled to join the NVA to bring it up to full strength.

Together with the introduction of nationwide conscription, the GDR decreed an "Order for Reservists." Its aim was to keep the reservists' military training alive and up-to-date, but they were also to be used as multipliers to advertise the armed forces in East German society. To further this, "collectives of reservists" *(Reservistenkollektive)* were formed on a volunteer basis in some firms and housing areas. Here, too, the results did not keep up with expectations. The numbers reported up the hierarchy and the real figures of how many attended scheduled events were rarely congruent. The single most important reason for this was that the regional military commands *(Wehrkreiskommandos)* entrusted with organizing these collectives accorded them only a very low priority. The GDR as a whole called for many forms of "voluntary" engagement, with the armed forces being only one of the many claims on the citizens' time and energy. That made it even more difficult to recruit competent and energetic organizers. Additionally, young men recently released from the military were apt to tell rather negative tales about their time with the colors, which might well undermine the desired "fighting morale." Nor was any involvement with the NVA reserves rewarded by material or financial advantages.

Apart from the voluntary reserve activities, there were obligatory service periods, some of them as practice alerts without any advance warning. Every year, about 80,000 reservists were called up for this kind of short-term duty, but by far the greater part of them never showed up, citing a variety of reasons ranging from sickness to being irreplaceable at work. Even so, damage to the national economy was substantial, especially with drafts at short notice which did not allow employers to adapt. Obviously, many reservists were older than the regular conscripts, and had had some experience in civilian jobs; they might well comment critically on the army's renewed call to arms and, thus, introduce a negative element into the barracks rooms which the young NVA NCOs were ill-equipped to counteract.

Stasi and the "Feliks Dzierzynski" Guard Regiment

The Ministry of State Security, the Stasi, and its paramilitary arms, the Guard Regiment "Feliks Dzierzynski," needs to be listed among the armed formations; these two have already been the object of substantial research (3.5 Gieseke, The History of the Stasi; 4.5 Koch/Lapp, Die Garde). The Stasi Guard Regiment was created in 1952 out of an earlier guard battalion; in 1967, it received the "name of honor" of the NKVD leader, Felix Edmundovich Dzerzhinsky.

Ostensibly, the regiment's purpose was to provide a continuous protective element around all essential functionaries in the state and Party, as well as performing some parade duties (a role it shared with the "Friedrich Engels" NVA Guard Regiment). The Stasi regiment had already shown its mettle in the events

Fig. 24:
Members of the Working-Class Combat Groups safeguard the GDR border West of the Brandenburg Gate, August 13, 1961.
BArch, Bild 183-85458-0002/ Junge

Fig. 25:
After awarding the regiment the "name of honor" of "Feliks Dzierzynski," Minister of State Security Generaloberst Erich Mielke inspects the regiment, December 15, 1967.
BArch, Bild 183-F1215-0029- 001/o. Ang.

Fig. 26:
Warsaw Pact exercise Waffenbrüderschaft 80, held in the GDR from September 4 through 12, 1980: Armeegeneral Heinz Hoffmann, GDR Minister of National Defense (left), and Marshal of the Soviet Union Viktor Georgiyevich Kulikov, Warsaw Pact Commander-in-Chief (second from left), visit the maneuver.
ullstein bild – ADN-Bildarchiv

of June 1953 and was maintained as a reserve unit for large-scale Stasi operations. However, it was trained chiefly to protect the GDR political system in case of internal unrest – a role which gained in importance after the 1956 uprisings in Hungary. The regiment was to guard the planned internment camps for political adversaries; it was also to perform "chekist" roles in occupied West Berlin and West Germany.

The unit kept being designated as a "regiment," even when it grew to include about 11,000 men, the rough equivalent of an NVA division. Among other equipment, the regiment had armored personnel carriers, but since it was not to be employed in a military role, it never had heavy weapons, such as artillery.

The regiment was deployed to serve as a squad of hatchet men during the mass demonstrations of the summer and autumn of 1989, not in its uniform with the red tabs, but in civilian clothes or in the blue shirts of the FDJ organization. Even its brutal use of force, however, failed to prevent the eventual collapse of the SED rule.

Preparations for Mobilization in State, Society, and the Economy
During a visit to the NVA in 1978, Erich Honecker declared: "There is no part in the life of our society which is not permeated by the demands of socialist national defense" (quoted in *0.15* Rogg, Armee des Volkes?, 277). The plethora of "armed formations" which were to protect the GDR against real or imagined enemies was matched by the comprehensive preparation of all parts of the state, society, and the economy for a potential war (*2.2* Diedrich, Herrschaftssicherung). According to the 1960 Soviet strategic doctrine, which the GDR had accepted uncritically, this preparation seemed necessary as the premises were that a war could be waged and eventually won, but that to do so, massive, armored units would have to conduct a series of continuous heavy attacks. Thus, the territory of the GDR would be both the theater of operations and the chief logistic staging area. It would need to be prepared for that role. The armed forces, industry, and civil society were all subordinated to the interests of the Warsaw Pact, i.e., those of the Soviet Union. In March 1961, the Warsaw Pact decided that all mobilization procedures in the member states were to be standardized throughout the alliance. For the NVA, this meant additional demands on its supply stocks and the logistic services which it would have to perform to keep the Soviet troops in Germany supplied. The civil sector would also have to contribute: The GDR undertook to provide 20,000 hospital beds to treat Soviet or allied wounded. While the GDR generally extended in a north-south direction, with its major ports in the north and more industrialized areas in the south, it now had to modernize its east-west links, such as expanding roads into motorways or electrifying its major railway lines. Strategic choke points were to be "doubled," i.e., alternative passages had to be prepared. This meant predominantly the provision of replacement road or rail bridges across the rivers Oder and

Elbe. On this basis, the SED informed all state and civic institutions which jobs they were expected to perform in wartime. The socialist GDR economy, weak as it was anyway, was, thus, overburdened even more.

The 1978 Defense Law contained sweeping regulations for how all walks of life could be subjected to military necessities. The 1982 Conscription Law not only opened military careers to women as well, but its overall aim was to make a larger share of the GDR population available for defense purposes. And indeed, it was during the 1980s that the NVA and many other of the "armed formations" achieved the peak of their performance and combat-readiness. Yet, simultaneously, it became increasingly obvious that the GDR state and economy were overextended by maintaining this level of security preparations. During the GDR's final decade, about 750,000 people were, in one way or the other, working for the security of the state – in other words, one in every twenty adult GDR citizens. No national economy, and certainly not one as inefficient as that of the GDR, could bear that burden for an extended period of time.

Integration into the Warsaw Pact

Any substantive political decisions of the GDR leadership, particularly when it came to foreign and security policies, were based on Soviet requirements. During the immediate postwar period, the Soviets exercised control through not only the Soviet Military Administration (SMAD) but also appointing Moscow-trained cadres or, at least, such Communists that were unquestioning followers of the Moscow line, to all relevant posts within the newly created structures of the East German state. Once the GDR had been founded as the East German antithesis to the Federal Republic, the SMAD was replaced by a Soviet Control Commission, with the change in terminology often being purely semantic. In any case, the Soviet "advisers" kept calling the tune in the nascent military, even after the Soviet Union had formally declared the GDR to be sovereign on March 25, 1954.

That the GDR was a sovereign state was to be underlined further by it becoming a founding member of the "Treaty of Friendship, Cooperation and Mutual Assistance" signed in Warsaw in May 1955 – whereas the Federal Republic had only been invited to join NATO six years after its inception. The Warsaw Treaty created another organization which seemed to serve the purpose of transmitting Soviet hegemonial aspirations.

The Warsaw Pact (this being the common Western terminology) has since been researched rather exhaustively, even if large collections of the Soviet and East German military documents are still unavailable in Russian archives (*2.8* Mastny/ Byrne, A Cardboard Castle?; *4.14* Gilbert, Cold War Europe; *0.16* Diedrich/Heinemann/Ostermann, Der Warschauer Pakt; *0.10* Umbach, Das rote Bündnis; for the effect of the Warsaw Pact on the GDR see also *0.25* Bange, Sicherheit und Staat). The documents of the GDR Foreign Ministry had been taken over by the West German foreign office archive and the latter had been withheld from researchers for 30 years (making them the only GDR files subject to the 30-year rule!); as 30 years have now passed since the end of the GDR, this restriction no longer applies. However, research into national policies vis-à-vis the Warsaw Pact has, in fact, progressed substantially in several former member states: Rumania defines itself as the Pact member which had retained the greatest diplomatic leeway; the Czech Republic and Slovakia are obviously interested in understanding the 1968 events better, and Polish archivists have published military planning documents from the time of the country's Warsaw Pact membership – despite Russian protests.

see page 204

The relevance of the Warsaw Pact alliance can easily be overestimated, at least, for its early years. From a purely legal point of view, it did not constitute any new obligations over and beyond what had been agreed bilaterally before. The *de facto* Soviet hegemony was patently obvious. Modern research tends to assume that the founding of the Warsaw Pact was more of a Soviet attempt to create a chip for potential negotiations about dissolving both "military alliances" (a term which, at least for NATO, was a misnomer; *4.13* Heinemann, Vom Zusammenwachsen). In this sense, the purpose of the Warsaw Pact was to disintegrate NATO, and the fact that it never achieved that was, thus, if one is to believe this interpretation, its first major failure.

In the medium term, instituting a multilateral structure turned out to bring its own problems with it. It created direct links between Soviet satellites, whose links until then had been largely directly with the hegemon, opening up new diplomatic opportunities for them.

It was only during the mid-1960s that the alliance began to gain in military importance. In view of increasing Sino-Soviet tensions, Moscow felt the need to emphasize its central role in the socialist camp. Yet, the Cuban Missile Crisis had marked the failure of a strategy based on nuclear weapons alone, so that East and West alike saw the need to invest more in conventional forces. For the Soviet Union, this meant a greater reliance on its partners, which would have to shoulder a part of that extra burden, increasing their weight within the alliance. Changes followed in the command structure in the 1970s which were decided either without Rumania or even against protests from Bucharest; these were designed to reassert Soviet military and political hegemony. The most important of these was the decision to place all armed forces under a joint command, naturally a Soviet general, in wartime.

The socialist regimes in Central and Eastern Europe needed the Warsaw Pact for their survival in two different ways: It guaranteed their security against outside attack, but also indicated the willingness of all countries involved to safeguard the "achievements of socialism" inside any one of them, if necessary, by military means.

The supreme body of the alliance was the Political Consultative Committee. It met once a year, with the Secretaries General of the Communist Parties, the heads of government and the foreign ministers attending. After 1969, it was supplemented by the committee of defense ministers. While the North Atlantic Treaty as such did not provide for a military command structure, the creation of a Combined Command of Pact Armed Forces was, in fact, part of the Warsaw Treaty; it was always under Soviet command and stationed in Moscow. The Combined Command (later "Combined Supreme Command") was anything but an integrated staff: aside from the Supreme Commander himself, his First Deputy and Chief of Staff, the Air Defense Commander, and the Deputy for Armaments were Soviet officers. Similar to the other allies as well, the GDR was only represented on the staff by lower-ranking generals.

The first major command post exercise held by the Warsaw Pact Combined Command in September and October 1962 was called "Buria" (Storm). The underlying scenario was that a peace treaty between the GDR and the Soviet Union had been concluded, and the resulting blockade of all access routes to and from West Berlin led to a military conflict. Not unlike the NATO doctrine of Massive Retaliation, Soviet doctrine also foresaw a swift escalation to the nuclear level, so that large swathes of GDR, Polish and Czechoslovak territory would have been devastated and contaminated. One of the results of the exercise was that cooperation between allies had not yet worked without problems, and the alliance's conventional potentials were insufficient. The political upshot was that Khrushchev finally gave up on the idea of signing a peace treaty with the GDR (*2.17* Uhl, Storming on to Paris).

The invasion of Hungary in 1956 had still been a unilateral Soviet measure; the Kremlin had seen no need to involve the recently created alliance. Things were different in 1968 when crushing the "Prague Spring" was deliberately designed as an alliance operation. In June 1968, the Warsaw Pact's combined armed forces held exercise *Šumava* ("Bohemian Forest") on Czechoslovak territory and with Czechoslovak troops participating; the occupation of the country in August 1968 was codenamed *Dunai* ("Danube"). That the Soviet leadership decided at the last minute to exclude the NVA from participating constituted a major loss of face for the GDR within its own alliance (*2.21* Wenzke, Die NVA und der Prager Frühling).

Conversely, the GDR leadership called for military intervention when, in the early 1980s, internal unrest seemed to threaten the stability and even survival of the Communist regime in Poland. With its two tank divisions stationed close to the Polish border, the NVA would have been in an ideal position to intervene by force. Politically, however, a joint Soviet-German attack against Poland could not have failed to evoke unwholesome memories of September 1939. What was more, anti-West German propaganda relied heavily on the argument that, unlike the GDR, the Federal Republic had never officially acknowledged the Oder-Neisse border constituted after 1945. This line of argument would have been seriously damaged by an NVA invasion across just this border.

Regarding the Soviet Union, the alliance served to transmit its demands for military and infrastructural support. As a consequence of developments in Poland, the Soviet high command began to have doubts regarding its strategic communications linking Soviet troops in Germany with the home country through Poland. As a result, two strategic bypasses were built: These were the ferry line between Sassnitz and Klaipeda, i.e., the German island of Rügen and the port in then-Soviet Latvia, in the North, while in the South, road and rail links between Saxony (the south of the GDR) and Czechoslovakia were improved and modernized.

The "comradeship-in-arms" *(Waffenbrüderschaft)* with the Soviet Union was made part of the GDR constitution in 1968; it was also part of the oath all GDR soldiers had to swear. Since about that time, the alliance had coordinated not only operational military planning but also the mobilization of the state, society, and the armed forces as well as military training. The Soviet Union maintained a central role in educating the military elites until the end of the Warsaw Pact: Being delegated to study in the Frunze Military Academy almost guaranteed promotion to the top ranks of any allied forces.

It was considered a given throughout the Warsaw Pact top brass that "exercises" would serve to camouflage preparations for a real war, such as the Warsaw Pact forces had done in 1968. NATO's routine exercises every autumn, thus, caused real concerns in Warsaw Pact capitals, and the assumption that they might end in a surprise attack led to increased alert levels and reconnaissance efforts. In September 1983, the erroneous perception that NATO's wargame "Able Archer" might be the cover for worldwide offensive preparations led to such nervousness among the Warsaw Pact military and political leadership that some historians today believe there was a real danger of the situation escalating into a "hot war" (see, however, *2.31* Miles, The War Scare).

The first strategic echelon was to comprise two fronts in what was in Soviet terminology the Western Theater; the Soviet concept of "front" was roughly equivalent to a Western "Army Group," but would include elements of all three services. The 1st Front was to attack in the South, under a Soviet general, whereas the Coastal Front would be fighting in the North, under a Polish general; both were to have NVA elements attached. Thus, none of the top operational commands would ever go to an East German general. This did not change even when Poland became a source of political concern, although the NVA made every effort to turn itself into the Soviets' "model student." The NVA air defense assets were fully integrated into the Warsaw

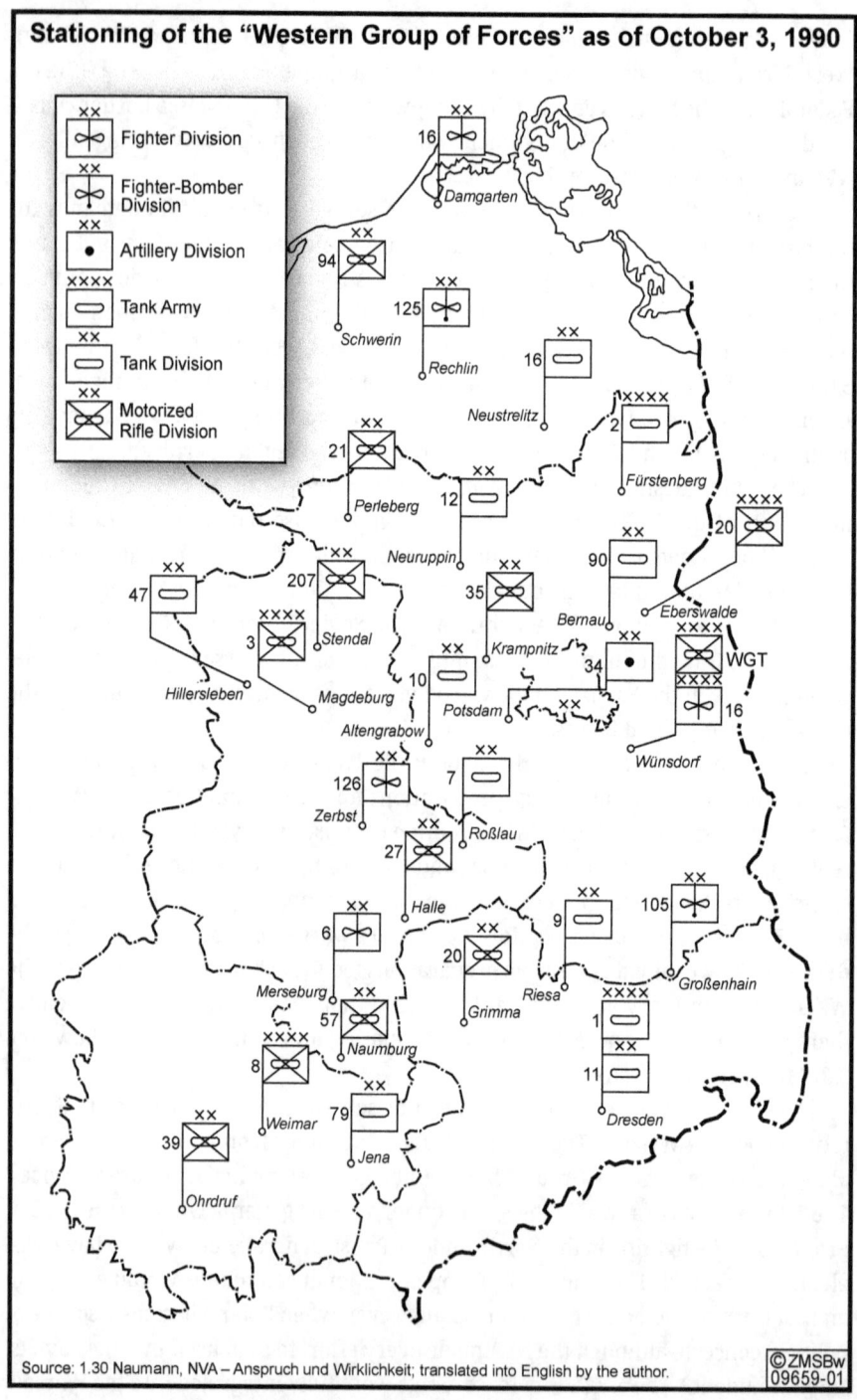

Pact even in peacetime, while the *Volksmarine* was set to become part of the "Combined Baltic Fleet," for which it was equipped and trained.

Compared to the other allies, GDR industry was flourishing and also innovative. It made major contributions to Eastern Bloc arms research and development, most importantly in the fields of computer technology and optronics. However, the GDR never had a dedicated armaments industry. Its most important contribution to the common defense effort were the uranium ore mines in the Ore Mountains; for a long time, they were supposed to be the largest and most accessible sources for uranium within the Soviet sphere of influence. The "Wismut" Soviet Incorporated Company was founded (*Sowjetische Aktiengesellschaft* – SAG) to exploit them; it was renamed *Deutsch-Sowjetische Aktiengesellschaft* "Wismut" in 1954. Heavily guarded and controlled, it provided the basis for the Soviet nuclear weapons program.

In 1954, what had until then been the "Group of Soviet Occupation Forces in Germany" became the "Group of Soviet Forces in Germany," which was again renamed the "Western Group of Forces" in 1988. Over the years, its strength varied between 300,000 and 600,000 Soviet servicemen and -women, so that numerically, the GDR's own military strength never approached that of the Soviet troops in its own country. The NVA and Soviet units would have regular exchange programs which benefitted both sides. Common training programs or maneuvers were the norm, as was mutual technical support. The Soviet policy of almost paranoid secrecy, however, limited the options for cooperation and exchange; the Soviets still mistrusted all Germans decades after the end of World War II, which made frank exchanges difficult. The Soviet officers also found it difficult to explain to their rank and file the obviously higher standard of living in the GDR compared to what they were used to from home, increasing a tendency to insulate themselves against their environment. The initiative for any kind of cooperation would usually come from the NVA units, even if the official events to document "comradeship-in-arms" *(Waffenbrüderschaft)* were a chore for many East German officers and men, especially since the language barrier hindered communication.

However, during the 1980s, the higher and medium-ranking NVA officers became more self-confident when facing their Warsaw Pact opposite numbers. The East German army's combat readiness was now beyond doubt, and the professional quality of its officer corps could stand comparison with the Soviets or any of the other allies.

Membership of the Eastern Alliance was central to the GDR's existence. Ever since 1953, it had been for all to see that the SED was ruling while sitting on the points of Soviet bayonets. When the gerontocratic, ossified SED leadership felt unable to follow the lead of the Soviet reform movements, it alienated itself from

Moscow – and, thus, from its chief power base; the GDR rulers of over forty years gave up what had guaranteed their system of governance.

A Militarized Security Policy

The GDR's "armed organs" were vast and manifold. They provided military protection against outside attack as well as serving to discipline and control the populace inside the country. These aspects interacted in a complex way: The core of protection against outside threat was definitely the NVA, which, in turn, steered and controlled other organizations. Through a variety of mechanisms, the "People's Army," in turn, was controlled by the Party; the Party apparatus in the forces, the political officers, the Party's influence in personnel decisions, the "guidance" offered by the Soviet military, and, not least, the perennial supervision by the Stasi combined to keep the armed forces in line.

The efforts needed to ensure the security of the GDR political system were vast. To estimate the cost, a look merely at the defense budget as part of the overall official state budget will be insufficient. Even before 1989, Western analysts pointed out that the expenses of the vast security apparatus in all Eastern Bloc states were deliberately and artfully camouflaged among various other items of the budget plans. This concerned all institutions of the state, but what was even more pernicious, some of the cost of preparing the territory for war was also to be borne by (state-owned) enterprises. An aspect that can hardly be qualified, but needs to be taken into account, nevertheless, is the cost of the loss of a substantial part of the qualified workforce due to conscription. Some authors claim that no other Eastern Bloc country used a higher proportion of its national income for military expenditure than the GDR; this proportion may have been three times as high as that of the Soviet Union (*2.15* Hertle, The Berlin Wall Story, 116).

Former officers and men of the NVA sometimes argue today that theirs was the "proper" army: dapper in its outward appearance, and unlike the Bundeswehr which would go home every weekend, they would have been able to take to the field at any time. Any NVA unit would have been able to deploy to its assigned dispersal area within an hour. That is, in itself, not wrong, but it does not explain why the GDR eventually succumbed in the systems rivalry with the Federal Republic. But perhaps this line of argument goes a long way toward illustrating one reason for the eventual demise of the GDR.

The premise of arguing along the lines sketched above is, of course, that it takes military efficiency as a chief guarantor of the survival of any political system. This premise characterized the thinking of the GDR leadership, and, for a long time, that of the Soviet Communist Party chiefs as well. Ever since the June 17, 1953, uprising, the GDR chiefs could have reacted to any perceived threat from within or without only by means of using military or an otherwise repressive force.

In the West, none less than President Dwight D. Eisenhower, himself a former five-star US Army general, had realized and argued repeatedly that excessive armaments efforts might erode the social consensus of a liberal society, while simultaneously permitting structures to emerge which could no longer be controlled by democratic institutions. He had warned against a "military-industrial complex" developing in the US in his farewell address of 1961. Eisenhower's own solution had lain in the (cost-effective) nuclearization of defense – but that solution was no longer viable after the "Sputnik Shock" and in view of the prospect of nuclear parity. The attempt to balance "warfare state" and "welfare state" was a characteristic of the Western security debate for a long time (*4.11* Dockrill, Eisenhower's New-Look; *4.12* Gaddis, Strategies of Containment).

This was a debate that could never have been waged in the GDR, nor in any Eastern Bloc state at that. The Soviet Union had had to defend its sheer existence, firstly, in a bloody civil war and then against a murderous attack from abroad; its strategic glacis had also been won thanks to the "glorious feats of the Soviet Army." Added to that, Marxist-Leninist theory took as its premise the theory of an uninterrupted class struggle as the basic pattern of history, thus, excluding any assumption that the other side might be pursuing peaceful intentions. In this sense, "peaceful coexistence" could only be interpreted as transient periods of lessened tensions before the next armed struggle.

This assumption of a perennial counterrevolutionary threat from within and without made the GDR leadership blind to any alternative forms of consolidating its rule, and it stuck to its militarized view of what would safeguard their political system. When the Communist Party of the Soviet Union (CPSU) leadership seriously tried to explore such alternatives in the 1980s, the GDR kept refusing such new thinking. In this sense, the continuous battle readiness of the NVA and the manifold "armed organs" of the GDR may have consolidated SED rule for some time; in the final say, they also contributed to its downfall.

Recruiting

Conscripts, Reservists, and "Construction Soldiers"

The NVA was largely an army of cadres when it was founded in 1956. It consisted of far more officers and NCOs than would have been adequate for its overall numerical strength. Only after the introduction of conscription in 1962 did the personnel structure slowly take the shape of a balanced military force. By the mid-1960s, the conscripted privates made up the numerically largest group within the NVA.

Initially, the young men subject to conscription had been obliged to fill in a questionnaire and deliver it in person to the appropriate military district command. This, however, failed to work properly – as often as not, the young men would not react at all. Instead, in 1968, the police, responsible for civil registration, were made responsible for listing the young men subject to conscription; any information still missing was supposed to be provided by schools or employers. The finalized lists were then sent to the military district commands. These lists, however, contained not only statistical information: Notes on the political and moral "reliability" were actively encouraged. This was particularly relevant for those conscripts who might be willing to sign on for a three-year term as an NCO, and for those who were scheduled to serve in the border troops.

As opposed to the West German *Bundeswehr*, more in the tradition of earlier German and Prussian forces, and, of course, following the Soviet example, the NVA did not have a separate civilian administration. Meeting its personnel and material requirements was the military's own responsibility and was largely carried out by uniformed staff. This organization regularly summoned the young men soon after their eighteenth birthday, either in the spring or in the autumn, to appear for a medical check-up at the military district command. Over and above the purely medical aspects, this was also an occasion when the young men could be put under pressure to sign up for an NCO career. This was the time when the NVA recruited as many three-year volunteers as during all other recruitment drives (schools, GST, workplace) combined.

About ten percent of all young men were excused from national service for medical reasons. They would have to reappear, though, so they could be examined for any improvement in their condition, and if so, might be drafted at a later point. A second medical check-up just before their term started was supposed to make sure that only healthy young men joined the military – a goal that was not, however, reached throughout.

As a matter of principle, the NVA drafted its recruits far from home. The young recruit learned only from his drafting order, about two weeks in advance, where he was to spend the next 18 months of his life. Firms and local communities often organized small parties to bid the young draftees farewell, so they would understand that those left behind would support them in their service for their country. Even so, most of those feted that way would be concerned regarding what awaited them – even more so if they had heard from older colleagues what life in the NVA barracks was like.

Most young men were well aware that the extended absence would impact upon their social contacts back home. East German director Leander Haußmann in his 2005 movie "NVA," has a young conscript break off his relationship with his girlfriend in advance – quite a realistic attitude. The firms where the prospective soldier had been working were obliged to keep him on their books and were also expected to maintain contact with him during his 18 months with the colors, but that remained a largely formalistic obligation designed to support "morale." Private contacts could only be maintained tediously, especially since visits by relatives and friends were the exception. Should such visitors show up, the young soldier was not allowed to take them into the barracks proper, but had to meet them under supervision and in a separate, often rather shabby, visiting room.

The almost completely hermetical life had an effect often observed in social subgroups: the NVA had its own language. This must not be confounded with the officially prescribed specific military language, a requirement in all functioning armies – this was a way of defining an in-group as opposed to the outside, and it also helped to subtly express a critical attitude to military service and its many negative corollaries.

The social hierarchy among the conscripts and among the NCOs who served for three years was usually according to the time which remained to serve in the military. The nearer he came to being discharged, the less the conscript soldier felt bound by the official norms and requirements. That this resulted in a system of everyday indiscipline was known throughout the NVA, right to its very top, but no redress was ever forthcoming.

On the whole, NVA personnel management (if one wants to call it that) was seriously deficient. Complaints ranged from broken promises when recruiting volunteers through rude offensive language to a deliberately "heartless" denial of leave, even in cases of extreme personal hardship, such as the death of close relatives. Petitions addressed by soldiers to the Defense Minister, the Minister President, or even the Party Chairman might help in specific cases but never led to anyone addressing the root causes. The analysis always resulted in a claim that some individual had failed to show sufficient "class-conscious behavior," but the ensuing appeals to improve political indoctrination usually produced little effect.

Any attempt to bring about profound changes would have had to depart from the purely quantitative assessment of performance which was characteristic of the entire GDR and its planned economy. Any kind of systemic change was unthinkable.

All the reports of a lack of discipline or resentment and malcontent must not lead us to overlook the fact that most GDR conscripts did their national service, if not enthusiastically, but without audible protest. Their aim was to survive the eighteen months without any disciplinary problems because they were well aware that grave breaches of discipline might easily bring problems even after their time in the army. If a young man had been dealt with by the military justice system, that fact would get known at home and at work and would forever show up in his personnel ("cadre") file.

Once their time in barracks was over, the young men would return relieved to their homes and workplaces. Little is still known about their professional and social reintegration – nobody seems to have asked about that, and, at the time, no one saw the need to do anything about it. After his discharge, the former soldier had the right to go back to his old job – that was what the law obliged employers to provide for.

Reservists

The former conscript soldier was now also a reservist – and, therefore, liable to be called up again for periods of service in the reserve. Theoretically, this could mean up to three months annually during the first few years after discharge, without much consideration given to any concerns of the civilian employer, and even less to grave family reasons. In reality, however, health reasons were often pleaded to preclude the drafting of specific reservists. The service obligation for NCOs and men continued until they were 50, and for officers until their sixtieth birthday. In case of war, all male GDR citizens would have been eligible until they had reached the age of 60.

Reservists were needed to flesh out the major units which were to be raised in time of war. First among these were the five additional army divisions which were to be formed out of the peacetime training centers and be available to the military districts soon after mobilization. Additionally, substantial elements of the logistic services and combat support units had only skeleton crews and required reservists to bring them up to strength. During the late 1980s, a total of 150,000 reservists were scheduled to be called up as part of mobilization, with about 16,000 officers among them. Plans that these units would be ready to operate within 48 hours were based on the experiences gained in exercises. What was never discussed, though, was what consequences a total mobilization of the NVA and of all the other armed formations would have had for the fragile NVA economy. After all, even in peacetime, the economic survival of the GDR depended on a sizeable number of soldiers (and reservists) being delegated "to production," i.e., to work in power plants, railway stations, etc. What would have happened if these had had to be withdrawn, with the reservists being drafted at the same time, was a question the state and Party leadership never asked itself.

Construction Soldiers
The history of the NVA construction soldiers has been the subject of a number of publications, but most of them authored by men who had experienced this kind of service themselves (5.2 Eisenfeld/Schicketanz, Bausoldaten; 5.3 Zivilcourage und Kompromiss); an independent critical analysis is yet to be written.

When, in 1964, the GDR allowed a national service without weapons, this was unique in the Eastern Bloc. Most of the reason seems to have been that the West German constitution, the *Grundgesetz*, explicitly provided for the right to refuse military service, and that the GDR felt that, to maintain its position in the debates about war and peace, it would also have to offer a similar option. In particular, the Protestant Church in the GDR kept pointing at the liberal West German conditions and put pressure on its own government to match them.

As opposed to the West German system, the construction soldiers were, in fact, members of the armed forces; they were drilled mercilessly, and if they contravened military norms, they were subject to sanctions by the military judicial system. Applications were granted or refused on a largely arbitrary basis as the right to refuse armed service was not codified in law. In any case, to file an application in itself took a lot of courage. Conscripts who took this step knew they would face chicaneries even before joining the force, but their superiors in the construction units also felt that their "spade soldiers" (in lieu of rank insignia, the construction soldiers wore a spade on their epaulettes) were insolent and undisciplined, and, therefore, subjected to even greater repression than elsewhere. Within the NVA, the construction soldiers were kept as separate as possible from the "real" soldiers; the officers and NCOs knew from experience that a frequent exchange between both groups could well lead to "undesirable" ideas being spread among the "real" military. Even after the end of service as an unarmed conscript (which also lasted for eighteen months), refusing armed service did not remain without consequences: most former construction soldiers were not allowed to study in a university.

Until 1973, construction soldiers were often employed building military infrastructure. In the GDR, building barracks and training areas, but also airfields and harbor sites was usually done by the forces themselves, largely by engineer units of the regular military. Construction soldiers seemed to be ideal for these purposes, although there were protests, even at an early stage, that this was an indirect way of supporting armed fighting units.

Since the early 1960s, but even more so during the 1970s and 1980s, NVA soldiers had been detached to work in nonmilitary construction projects. Adapting the "Chinese Principle", the initial concept was that NVA officers should gain valuable experience in the planned economy; soon, however, the sheer economic benefit became the decisive factor justifying such detachments. The oil refinery in Schwedt was built using a large number of NVA personnel, and the same applied to the politically motivated prestigious building projects in "Berlin, Capital of the GDR" – this affected the Border Troops regiments stationed in and around Berlin most of all. The soldiers soon found out that they had to work more hours, while their housing, food, and, not least, pay was vastly inferior to that of the civilian workers – who also tended to leave the least desirable, most dangerous, hazardous, or insalubrious jobs to the NVA soldiers; these would usually come either from the engineer regiments or would be unarmed construction soldiers. This was another reason why applying for the unarmed service took some extra determination: the working conditions down to the health hazards were even worse than those of the regular conscripts.

The Berlin "Palace of the Republic" was one of the most prestigious projects involving the NVA – which availed of the opportunity to prominently display its role to the general public; here, however, under the eyes of the public, no construction soldiers were used. This was very different at another major infrastructure project realized by the NVA: building the port infrastructure in Mukran on the island of Rügen during the 1980s (for its strategic rationale see above). A substantial share of the workforce here consisted of construction soldiers, with particularly harsh working and living conditions, especially during the winter months.

The permission, in the main, to fulfil their obligation by serving unarmed in the NVA enabled the GDR to demonstrate peaceful policies when compared with the West without reneging on the principle of all-encompassing conscription. In the eye of the public, however, the few "spade soldiers" were a rare exception. The norm was that young men would serve with the colors – unloved, often even feared, but usually without protests worth mentioning.

Noncommissioned Officers

German Tradition of a Separate NCO Corps
From the time of the Napoleonic Wars, German armies had formed a separate NCO corps with its own social identity (including its own mess), which, at least partially, performed leadership roles.

Once linear tactics had become outdated and scattered formations became the norm, the role of sergeants and corporals changed profoundly. Their primary role ceased to be that of drillmasters, responsible for exercising the units, and serving in action as reference points for the various formations. Instead, they became responsible for training their soldiers, and led platoons or squads into battle. The Prussian-German military acknowledged this changed role by separately recruiting NCOs, training them in separate NCO schools, and discharging them after nine to twelve years with adequate provision. They would usually receive an appointment as low-level civil servants. That senior NCOs, after serving for twelve years, could be appointed schoolteachers in basic schools was but one out of many facets of a complex social-military reality.

The experience of World War I confirmed the previous position of NCOs. The German armies had lost substantial numbers of officers, particularly in the infantry, so that some officer functions had to be assumed by senior NCOs. The traditional-minded leadership of the Prussian Army would not, however, go so far as to commission these senior NCOs as officers; instead, they would receive the title of "deputy officers" *(Offizierstellvertreter)*. Social mobility allowing NCOs to become officers was a hallmark of the modernizing tendencies in National Socialism; even the Nazis, however, would not go so far as to give up the differentiation between officers and NCOs.

As we have seen, a large segment of the early NVA officer corps had once been Wehrmacht NCOs. That opens up the question to what extent the NVA NCOs saw themselves in the tradition of their Wehrmacht predecessors, or whether the Soviet example was paramount, here as elsewhere.

NCOs in the NVA's Early Phase

The NVA, and before it the HVA and the KVP, differed from all previous German armies in that they did not recruit their officers from the "desirable classes," but instead relied on officers with a proletarian background. That permitted the advancement of able NCOs to officers, which, however, brought with it substantial problems. What it meant, eventually, was that the more able NCOs were commissioned, whereas the less qualified remained behind, characterizing the NVA NCO corps for a long time. The many problems of leadership and discipline, therefore, were not only due to weaknesses among the officers, but also to the NVA's overburdened and underqualified NCOs.

The difficulties were exacerbated by the fact that the NVA, until the introduction of general conscription in 1962, was designed to be a cadre army of potential leaders. That implied a large demand for NCOs, with no pool of conscripts from which to recruit them. The future NCOs would only join for a period of three, sometimes even two, years, causing a periodically large demand for recruits – a demand which could only be met by implicitly disregarding the official standards of qualification. Practically anyone who applied was accepted in order to recruit a more or less adequate number of NCOs.

At that time, training was indubitably along the lines of the Soviet military. The future NCOs were educated in separate NCO training companies, which were, however, part of the regular regiments. Only the technical specialists were schooled at centralized training institutions. The older German tradition still had an effect, in that the question whether these young men would be able to lead in action at all was raised repeatedly, yet, in view of the quantitative problems, this remained largely hypothetical.

Gradually, at first, but then, accelerated by the introduction of conscription, a differentiation between senior NCOs (with a term of engagement of twelve, later ten, years) and the short-term junior NCOs (three years, with four years in the *Volksmarine*) developed. Both groups continued to be undermanned. In the mid-1960s, a quarter of all senior NCO posts were vacant, and the gaps had to be stopped with reservists or else with junior NCOs – worsening the situation among that group.

By that time, NCO training had begun to be centralized in NCO training regiments. The LSK/LV (the air arm) tried educating its NCOs at officer schools, but this was given up after a short time as being impracticable. The Border Troops continued training their NCOs in the units, but that, too, resulted in major deficiencies.

One solution could have been to train the soon-to-be NCOs longer, but that would have meant withholding them from their units for an extended time, thus, increasing the shortage "at the frontline." Alternatively, their period of engagement could have been increased from three to four years; that, however, would have made recruiting even more difficult, not to mention the detrimental effect on the national economy, which was also suffering from a lack of workforce.

Deficiencies were both quantitative and qualitative; the MfNV finally redefined the recruitment, training, and role of NVA NCOs in 1968. The distinction was now formalized between senior NCOs, who were to serve until retirement and be actual superiors of soldiers, on the one hand, and the junior NCOs, on the other hand, who would continue to serve for three years but would assist the senior NCOs rather than give orders themselves. The junior NCOs were now taken to be "excellent specialists," reducing their leadership roles even further. Within the military hierarchy, they moved closer to the conscript recruits.

By the late 1970s, the NVA had postings for some 43,000 NCOs, about half for senior career NCOs and for junior men on a three-year engagement. To fill these posts, some 11,000 junior NCOs and about 1,800 senior career NCOs were to be recruited annually. These were ambitious goals which were never reached, least of all regarding the career NCOs. In 1971, they made up not half, but just about a third of all NCOs. The difficult work and living conditions of soldiers and their families deterred potential candidates. The NVA leadership encouraged advertising this career among the junior NCOs and the conscripts, but they all saw the disadvantages involved far too clearly.

The inflationary use of junior NCO ranks, and their increasing employment as technical specialists, led to suggestions that such technical specialists should be longer-serving privates. That, however, would have made these badly paid jobs even less attractive and almost impossible to find recruits, therefore, this never went anywhere, either.

The NVA introduced the intermediate career of *Fähnriche* in 1973 to make the career of professional NCOs more attractive. Traditionally, and in the *Bundeswehr*, this German term means officer cadets; what was introduced here, however, was closer to what the US and British military knows as "warrant officers." This *Fähnrich* career was to offer highly qualified senior NCOs further promotion up to the rank of *Stabsoberfähnrich*. In that sense, it proved to make the professional NCO career more attractive, but the obvious disadvantage was that, again, those selected (and they were supposed to be the best qualified) were no longer available as NCOs.

Again, only a fraction of the numbers originally planned could actually be recruited, thus, the jobs supposed to be done by *Fähnriche* ended up being done by senior NCOs, with a snowball effect resulting in regular conscripts doing junior NCOs' jobs at the bottom of the hierarchy.

Historian Christian Th. Müller states that for the entire history of the NVA, "the lack of qualified applicants for the senior NCO career led the NVA to hire applicants who met the required standards only with great difficulty. That in turn had the effect that within the armed forces, and within society at large, NCOs held a low social status. That, combined with the unenjoyable conditions of living and working, made the career unattractive for the target group originally envisaged" (*0.6* Müller, Tausend Tage, 42).

Müller's skeptical analysis is aimed largely at the career NCOs, while the *Fähnriche* are attested a predominantly adequate performance. The young NCOs who served for three years were usually employed to assist with the individual training of recruits, according to Müller.

These young men who had agreed to serve for three years deserve a bit more attention, though. After all, in terms of numbers, they were by far the largest group among the NVA's NCOs. Many of them were future university students who had been told that attending university required more than the usual 18-month national service. The fact that these three-year volunteers serving as NCOs usually met the requirements of their job was due, on the whole, to their superior civilian qualifications to start with.

As we have seen, that distinguished them from the career NCOs, whose intellectual capacities were often lacking. The three-year junior NCOs were housed in barracks, much like the conscripts, while the professionals could live with their families – always provided there was sufficient accommodation available. These senior NCOs could leave the barracks at night and over the weekends, while, in this respect, too, the junior NCOs were treated much like the regular conscripts. As a result, there was a wide social gap between the two groups of NCOs. Many young three-year volunteers often found all their superiors, senior NCOs and officers similarly "heartless" or "arrogant."

In view of this lack of social cohesion, it seems doubtful whether one can truly speak of an NVA "NCO corps" in the sense of a coherent social group (*5.1* Lapp, Die Nationale Volksarmee, 1948). At the time, the Bundeswehr had a hierarchically differentiated but socially coherent NCO corps. Sergeant-Majors would take their meals and drink their beers with young corporals or even privates being trained to be NCOs, and the Company Sergeant Major would have a dedicated responsibility for educating the younger NCOs. In this, the Bundeswehr stood in the tradition of the Wehrmacht and even earlier German armies. Contrary to that, the NVA NCO "corps" consisted of three separate groups, with the most junior of them in many ways closer to the conscript soldiers than to the senior NCOs, in both the way they were treated and their self-perception.

Those young men, many of whom had decided to become NCOs for extrinsic reasons only, were often bitterly disappointed. Apart from the conscripts during their third (and last) semester, the NCOs serving their last (sixth) semester were the chief protagonists of the informal hierarchy system, while NCOs in their first and second year of duty found it extremely difficult to exercise any authority over the conscripts waiting for their discharge.

Officers

Cadre Policies

Disregarding the NCO problems, the SED was far more focused on the selection of a reliable officer corps. The chief question it was facing was what should be the relative merits of professional expertise and Party political reliability – the latter usually equated, at least during the NVA's early years, with proletarian extraction. On the other hand, there was also a major problem finding sufficient and appropriate cadets to become officers – or else to modify the selection criteria somewhat.

To achieve its aims, the SED relied on a systematic "cadre policy," which was again, unsurprisingly, based on the Soviet model. In a wider sense, the term "cadre" referred to anyone in the KVP and later the NVA who had a responsibility for leading and educating men; this would include NCOs and even privates who, for lack of alternatives, were employed in junior leadership functions. This must not be confounded with the narrower term of "Party cadres," which covered only the political officers and the Party officials within the armed forces.

The central institution for cadre policies was the Cadre Directorate within the MfNV, with its corresponding subbranches in the various command agencies and staffs. Yet, the role of the political officers should not be underestimated, as they had a say in all and every selection process. All officers who were due to be promoted were also continuously vetted by the Ministry of State Security. Without the Stasi's consent, no one would get anywhere, even if the detailed mechanisms of cooperation in this field still require further research.

The NVA Main Staff *(Hauptstab)* calculated how many officer cadets were required in the various branches, and the Cadre Directorate defined the selection criteria. Advertising, recruiting, and eventually contracting was the job of the Recruitment Directorate *(Verwaltung Auffüllung)*, which controlled the Military District commands.

We have learned a lot about East (and West) German military elite selections from a recently published book which would deserve a translation into English (*1.29* Loch, Deutsche Generale). It details how the Soviet concept of war, based on tenets of Marxist ideology and largely oriented along "scientific," quantitative lines, impacted on the structure of the higher officer corps. The most marked difference from Western career structures was that future generals would be trained from a very early age as either staff workers or military leaders. Only very few would oscillate between command and staff functions. (Brief biographies of all GDR generals can be found in *0.29* Froh/Wenzke, Die Generale und Admirale.)

This complex selection process for top positions was overlaid by the system of *Nomenklatura*, applied to both the military and civilian (Party and government officials) top elites. What it meant was that the Party was the sole decision-maker when it came to nominating candidates to the top positions included in the *Nomenklatura* system. Responsibility for the *Nomenklatura* of all security-related ministries lay with the NVR; its minutes often include, as the final item on the agenda, decisions about "Cadre Questions." The NVR, in turn, had to consult with the SED Central Committee *Nomenklatura* branch. The Politburo had reserved the nomination of the Minister of National Defense and the Chief of the Political Main Directorate for itself, and it had to confirm all promotions to admiral or general. The Central Committee's Security Policy Branch was also responsible for guiding and supervising the work of all lower-echelon cadre (i.e., human resources) branches. The *Nomenklatura* system, again derived from the Soviet model, had the express purpose of ensuring the political reliability of all state agencies, including the security apparatus.

Recruitment

see table page 213

The NVA required a disproportionately large number of officers. Its TOEs provided for one officer for every eight privates; the high figure was also due to the limited role of the NCOs. Altogether, some 18,000 officers served in the NVA during the mid-1950s, the figure rose continuously during the existence of the GDR and had peaked at more than 40,000 by 1989.

Filling this vast number of posts required a substantial effort. The *Volksmarine* generally managed to attract sufficient numbers of cadets, and the same usually applied to the LSK/LV's need for fighter pilots, but in the ground forces (LaSK), about ten percent of all officer posts were normally vacant. The Border Troops were even worse off; their deployment on the fringes of the country as well as the tedious and demanding living and working conditions meant that an even greater percentage of posts remained unoccupied. The NVA attempted to counterbalance this by introducing a career option for officers who would serve for a predetermined period of time, which would also have had the effect of producing more lieutenants and captains without inflating the numbers of field-grade officers, but even this did not allow the East German military to meet its demands.

Party Membership

Since the mid-1960s, almost all NVA officers had been SED Party members; the figure was usually above ninety-five percent. In fact, military officers were by far the single largest group among SED Party members; at times, officers and officer cadets together would constitute about half the SED membership. The few officers who had either joined one of the other "block" parties (called that because they were all politically affiliated to the SED) or had remained aloof from all of them served in the "rear services" (logistics, medical services). A disproportionate number of them served only for a limited period of time as promotion to higher ranks was outside their reach anyway.

Promotion

The earliest research into NVA officer careers was *0.2* Fingerle, Waffen in Arbeiterhand? Regarding the top level generals, this has since been superseded by *1.29* Loch, Deutsche Generale, which allows us to understand elite selection much better.

Military elites can be traditionally selected by performance or seniority, the latter understood as either age, length of overall service, or seniority in the same rank. If the emphasis is on seniority, the career becomes attractive to an increased number of potential cadets, as more or even all officers will be promoted, even if only slowly. However, it puts the better qualified at a disadvantage, thus, rendering elite selection difficult. Right into the 1920s, the German military had relied heavily on selection according to seniority; during World War II, Hitler had insisted on selection according to "performance," understood largely as successful frontline leadership. Rank in the military should also normally be compatible with the level of responsibility and the functions exercised, but this had not always been the case.

Bundeswehr observers who were involved in the process of recruiting former NVA officers into the all-German Bundeswehr noted a number of specific characteristics in the NVA officer corps structure. The extremely high share of officers in the NVA meant that some of them served neither as commanders nor in a real staff function, but even elderly field grade officers at times did jobs which in the Bundeswehr had been entrusted to experienced senior NCOs. Officers might be promoted at a fairly early age, and 40-year-old full colonels were not uncommon. Then, however, a career would often level out – those who had reached Lieutenant Colonel or Colonel at such an early age, but did not qualify for promotion to general, would spend a very long time in their final rank, with little extrinsic motivation.

Thus, only a small group of officers were earmarked from an early stage for promotion to top ranks (*1.29* Loch, Deutsche Generale, 426–434). The group remained so small because the top generals would stay in their posts for an extremely long time; *Generaloberst* Heinz Hoffmann held the post of Minister of National Defense for a total of 25 years, not allowing anyone else to be promoted into this post. Ideally, a top career consisted of a sequence of leadership postings, whether as actual commander or – before that – as deputy. A course in a military academy was required to be promoted to full colonel, and one had to have studied in the Soviet Union, preferably at the Frunze Military Academy in Moscow, to qualify for the highest-ranking posts. In this context, rank was not as relevant as in other armies. An officer with top career prospects and matching qualifications, ranking Lieutenant Colonel, might well be employed as deputy chief of staff in one of the two Military District commands, and might then have several full colonels working under him. On the other hand, most divisional commanders would assume their posts while still ranking colonel and would be promoted to *Generalmajor* during their tenure. At times, they might be transferred to the subsequent stage of their high-flying career even before that, and they would hand over their division to their successor still in a colonel's uniform.

Generals

From a sociological perspective, the 377 generals and admirals who served in the KVP and NVA since the introduction of military ranks in 1952 were not so much a power elite but constituted a substantial part of the GDR's functional elite. They can be divided roughly into three generations.

The founders' generation included a large variety of generals: there were Communists from before 1933 as well as former Wehrmacht officers – with nine former Wehrmacht generals among them. Then there were the Moscow-trained cadres and those emanating from the National Committee "Free Germany." In terms of numbers, the former Wehrmacht officers were a majority, but the Communist Party cadres made sure that all decisive leadership positions remained in their hands; the indispensable experts who were considered politically unreliable were employed in staff and training jobs. This founding generation included men such as Willi Stoph, Vincenz Müller, Heinz Hoffmann, and Waldemar Verner.

The intermediate or build-up generation was characterized by those generals and admirals who had fought in World War II as privates or NCOs, and those who had emerged from the SED youth organizations, particularly the FDJ. For all those, an officer career in the NVA offered a social advancement which would have been unthinkable not so many years before. Characteristic officers in this generation were men such as Horst Stechbarth and Fritz Streletz; both ended their careers as *Generaloberst*.

The third generation included officers fully socialized in the GDR; only a few of them had actually been promoted general or admiral before 1990; names to be mentioned here are Vice Admiral Hendrik Born and *Generalmajor* Hans-Georg Löffler, both of whom had obviously been earmarked for top postings during the 1990s.

The GDR had to balance the official ideology of a "classless society" against the reality and even need of social and political, therefore, also functional, differentiation. As in most armies, the officers' thinking, especially that of the most senior ones, was marked by an ambition to be promoted further, with the prospect of an enhanced social and political role. It was not uncommon for the ensuing rivalry to peak into mutual denunciations to the *Stasi*.

However, they were all agreed in a common loyalty toward a political system which had opened up top careers for them way in excess of what men of their background and origins could have obtained in other political systems. As a consequence, the generals and admirals perceived what they were doing as a "political profession"; while the NVA also had technical specialists, similar to any other army, those were never promoted to the top rungs of the ladder. Not only the chiefs of the Political Main Directorate, but also most other high-ranking officers saw their role as following a "class order." Quite a few among the founding generation had resented the task allotted to them, i.e., having to create new armed forces, as they would have preferred a more politicized role.

The officers' loyalty toward the Party included acceptance of this role as a functional elite. At no time did anyone inside the NVA military leadership ever consider an attempt to take power. Everybody knew that the GDR military was too thoroughly infiltrated by Party and *Stasi* informers for such an attempt to have had any chance of going unnoticed. Personnel selection, cadre policies, training and education – they all served the dual purpose of maintaining the NVA as a combat-ready, highly efficient military force but "in duty bound to the Party."

Ideology vs. Efficiency

That still leaves the initial question unanswered: How were ideological and performance criteria balanced in NVA recruitment and elite selection processes? The system described above primarily reflected a primacy of political and ideological factors, but balanced by the need for military efficiency, with the balance changing over time according to political, social, and military circumstances. During the 1950s, military qualifications gradually gained in relevance, after the systematic preference for cadets from the former lower classes had resulted in a "first socialist intelligentsia." This, and the tendency of members of the traditional elites to leave the GDR (at least until August 1961), opened up opportunities for unheard-of careers – opportunities which, in turn, increased the loyalty of those who profited from them toward the regime that had created them (*0.2* Fingerle, Waffen in Arbeiterhand?, 17–20).

During the 1960s, the "New Economic System of Planning and Management" *(Neues Ökonomisches System der Planung und Leitung)*, as propagated by Walter Ulbricht, required better qualified scientific and technological specialists, which led to a relaxation of the criterium of a "proletarian background." Yet, when Honecker succeeded Ulbricht in 1971, for a while, the ideological selection criteria gained more weight again. By then, children of Party officials were recognized as being of "working-class descent"; in lieu of the traditional elites, a new, self-perpetuating "socialist" elite began to form.

The percentage of true "laborers" in industry and agriculture ("workers and peasants") decreased over time, with a corresponding drop in truly "working-class" youngsters in the GDR during its existence as well as everywhere else. Instead, it sufficed to give proof of an inner attitude loyal toward the state and the Party, which obviously the sons and daughters of Party functionaries could easily provide – this effect helped develop a new, socialist elite. Another consequence was, however, that conformity and an unquestioning parroting of phrases provided by the Party became a decisive precondition for a successful career. In the military, that meant unconditional adherence to all and any orders given by superior officers. The final phase of the GDR has been diagnosed as having suffered from a lack of initiative and perspective – the mechanism described here contributed heavily to that feeling of pointlessness. By the mid-1960s, officers from working-class families made up seventy-five to eighty percent of the total, but the percentage declined continuously after that; by the end of the 1980s, the figure was less than sixty percent. When asked for their own "social status," i.e., their occupation before joining the military, only half of the officers said "worker" in the NVA's final phase; the other half had joined the army straight after school (*4.2* Wenzke, Die Nationale Volksarmee (1998), 454).

Academic qualifications became essential as leadership and command processes in the political, bureaucratic, economic, and military fields became more complex. The NVA met military and ideological requirements alike by combining both specialist expertise and political education in its comprehensive training system as demanded by the SED Party.

Training and Qualification

Ideology demanded that officers and NCOs of all ranks be military leaders and superiors and, at the same time, represent socialist teaching. To achieve this, all training, courses, etc., covered practical military as well as ideological subjects, all of which were equally relevant for passing. On top of that, officers in more technical jobs received specialist, technological teaching.

The integration of political and social studies into the curricula was immediately relativized as these subjects were taught by separate faculties or sections subordinate to the respective political officer, which set them aside from the other fields and revealed the alleged unity of military and political responsibilities as the farce it was.

The various training institutions received detailed instructions about the actual contents of political training, which had to be followed to the letter. That made any adjusting to new developments difficult. Similar to elsewhere in the NVA education system, teaching methods were conventional and aimed at transmitting knowledge and capabilities. Critical thinking, creativity, or even individualism were encouraged rather less. Innovative methods were the exception; front-of-class teaching was the norm.

NCO Schools

As detailed above, NCOs had initially been educated in the units. It was only in the late 1960s and early 1970s that NCO schools were introduced, which, in 1986 (for the Land Forces), were converted into "Training Centers." Each Training Center was simultaneously the core element of a division which was to be formed in case of mobilization. As opposed to that, the Border Troops' NCO School "Egon Schultz," named after an NCO killed in 1974 in a firefight with people trying to flee the GDR (although the authorities knew that he had been killed by a projectile fired from one of his fellow border guards), continued to exist under that name until 1989/90, as did the LSK/LV and *Volksmarine* NCO schools.

Officer Academies

The training of officer cadets was, of course, of central relevance to the NVA. This was the task of the academies set up within each branch:
- LaSK Officer Academy "Ernst Thälmann," Löbau (with some elements in Zittau)
- LSK/LV Officer Academy "Ernst Mehring," Kamenz
- LSK/LV Officer Academy for flying personnel (named "Otto Lilienthal" in 1986), Bautzen
- *Volksmarine* Officer Academy "Karl Liebknecht," Stralsund
- Border Troops Officer Academy "Rosa Luxemburg," Suhl

A Cadet School was created in Naumburg (Saale) in 1956 to prepare working-class boys for a career as an officer, but it was dissolved again in 1960 as it did not meet expectations.

On average, the first generation of NVA officers had only had rather low school qualifications, largely because, for political reasons, officer cadets from the working classes had been preferred in the recruitment process. Since the early 1960s, the NVA had again placed more emphasis on the formal education of their functional elites. By 1962, all cadets had to have had at least ten years of schooling. *(see table page 212)*

In 1963, the various institutions which had preceded them were fused into officer schools of the five branches; this also served the purpose of improving the general educational level of NVA officers. In 1971, these officer schools were transformed into academies. The prescribed course was organized into a four-year academic education at university level. At the end, the alumni should be qualified to command a platoon or a company, and have the basic qualifications for command at the battalion level. To achieve that, the courses were organized according to services: there were courses, for example, for future motorized infantry, tank and artillery officers. The compartmentalization of knowledge, as practiced in all Warsaw Pact armies, thus, started during cadet training. "Social sciences" (i.e., ideological training) made up about twenty percent of the weekly classes; this included "History of the Working Classes" and "Military History" – subjects which were, however, taught separately.

While the courses were labeled as "academic," there was no disguising the fact that they were about military capabilities and qualifications as well as an adequate physical fitness. Course subjects included marching, live firing, tactical training, and a four-week internship in a military unit. The qualifications obtained were usually not recognized in civil life, but since the outcome of the course was to be an officer serving for his entire life, that posed no major problem. Officers training for a career as technical specialists might also obtain a diploma, either as an engineer (the highly prestigious "Dipl.-Ing."), an economist, or an educator – academic grades which had a greater chance of civilian acceptance.

Until the early 1980s, political officers were selected from among the regulars, and then detailed for further studies at the MPH in Berlin-Grünau. In 1983, however, the Officer Academies introduced a separate course for future political officers, so that, from day one, the future Party cadres in the forces were kept apart from their "purely military" comrades. On the other hand, the NVA, thus, recruited a group of younger political officers, whereas previously, political officers had always been elderly men.

Recruiting all officers for a lifelong career would have resulted in a seriously top-heavy officer corps: after all, armies need more platoon leaders than divisional commanders. To meet the additional need for younger officers in the units, the officer academies offered one-year courses for cadets who had engaged themselves for three years. After this course, they would be available in their units for another two years. Most of them were young men who hoped to obtain a place in university for which they would not have qualified otherwise.

As of 1955, future medical officers studied in the Section of Military Medicine in Greifswald University; this course was fully compatible with any medical degree obtained in a civilian university. In this context, the Academy of Military Medicine Bad Saarow should be mentioned. In 1981, it succeeded the Central Military Hospital and took over the further education and training of military medical personnel from Greifswald University.

A different institution was the LaSK Officer Academy "Otto Winzer" in Prora on the island of Rügen, on the Baltic coast. Opened in 1981, it trained officer cadets from "brother nations," i.e., socialist countries, mostly from what was then referred to as the "Third World," such as Angola or Cuba. This was an opportunity for the GDR not only to demonstrate "international solidarity," but also to gain some of the badly needed hard Western currency.

The NVA's Scientific Institutions

The NVA drew a sharp distinction between training and further education. The most important element of the latter was a degree course in the MAFE in Dresden, at the MPH in Berlin-Grünau, or the MGI in Potsdam. All three awarded PhD degrees and were, therefore, fully integrated into the GDR academic system.

None of the three institutions was the object of substantive research after 1990. Little is known about the MPH; some former alumni of the MAFE have published their memoirs. If anything, few publications mentioned the MGI.

Out of these three, the MAFE was certainly the most important. It was founded in 1959 on the basis of what had until then been the "Academy for Officers." To be admitted, an officer had to have commanded a battalion or a regiment successfully, as attested by his respective superiors, and then had to pass a rigorous test. About ten percent of all officers in an age group would be selected for the MAFE course.

Some 200 officers would attend annually, with about ten percent from other socialist nations.

The academy was divided into faculties until 1970, after that, into "sections" roughly according to the branches of the NVA. The course took three years and was designed to prepare officers for command posts at a regimental or divisional level. At the end, the participants would be awarded a diploma as a "Military Scientist." Parallel courses were held for political officers and officers in specialist technical careers; these were nominally equal, but, in reality, the future leaders of the NVA were to be selected from the main course.

While the MAFE offered courses similar to all other academies, what was different was that it also had research obligations. These, however, concerned topics that were of immediate military relevance. Most of the dissertations written there were not published until the end of the GDR in 1989/90. To take but one example: the NVA's preparations for an attack on West Berlin were accompanied by an extensive research project which included two PhD theses written at the MAFE. One of the two PhD students was the Deputy Chief of Staff (Operations) at the LaSK command – i.e., the staff that was to command the "Special Grouping" tasked with taking West Berlin in wartime (7.7 Petroschka, Über die Armeeangriffsoperationen).

There is no known explanation why the Military History Institute was never awarded a "name of honor." On the other hand, it was the sole institution to have "GDR" rather than "NVA" in its title. It had been founded in 1958 as the "Institute for German Military History" and renamed the "German Institute for Military History" in 1967. It also reported to the PHV and served several purposes, the most important of which was legitimizing the GDR. The MGI publications were also to spread socialist ideology within the NVA and the general public. In spite of all this, quite a few of them constituted serious scholarly research and can still be used today. As was customary in more general GDR historiography, authors would select less politically charged topics, such as the Early Modern period, hoping to be able to work without censorship. To take but two examples: The encyclopedic *Wörterbuch zur deutschen Militärgeschichte* is still relevant today, while the volume published on the occasion of the 30th anniversary of the founding of the GDR, published the same year, contains facts correctly organized, while its interpretations are largely propaganda. All titles designed to be published had to be vetted and eventually approved by the PHV in East Berlin. As the MGI was situated on the far side of West Berlin, in Potsdam, coordination required a lot of time and effort.

During the late 1980s, despite all the surveillance by the Party and Stasi, tendencies to come up with alternative concepts for a future GDR grew, initially quite loyal to the regime, in all three institutions alike. These ideas were triggered by the new Soviet military doctrine which became known within the NVA at about that

Fig. 27:
GDR Minister of National Defense, Armeegeneral Heinz Hoffmann, awards the "Scharnhorst Order" to the Institute of Military History (MGI), "honoring its merits in the field of military history research, teaching, publications, and propaganda." On the left: Generalmajor Professor Reinhard Brühl, Director of the MGI (1983).
MHM Dresden/MB083081-003

time, as well as the contacts between the SED and the West German Social Democrat parties. The MGI had also developed international contacts on an academic level, including an informal exchange between East and West German military historians. While surprising at first sight, it had an inner logic that members of all three institutes, after all the forces' ideological hotbeds, should have represented the NVA at the "Round Tables" managing the change over processes within the GDR during 1989 and 1990. The NVA Round Table eventually convened in the MPH.

Training Courses and Academic Degrees in the Soviet Union
The NVA's alignment with the Soviet Union also found its expression in the fact that top cadres regularly received major segments of their education in Soviet institutions. Altogether, some 5,000 NVA officers attended a Soviet military academy of some sort. To be selected for one of those courses not only meant approval of past performances, but also gave rise to the highest hopes for a future career once the course had been successfully absolved.

To get there, the select course participants had to put up with substantial hardships. Pay during the time in the Soviet Union was rather bad, especially since housing was scarce, the family could usually follow only much later, and, until then, the cost of housing back home had to be covered as well. The enforced separation led to a divorce rate of more than twenty percent, which was uncommonly high even for GDR standards. Living conditions in Moscow could be harsh, especially during winter. The strict separation of Soviet officers from their allied colleagues could lead to resentment and misunderstandings. The various non-Soviet groups of students were, however, taught in mixed classes which provided the NVA officers with better contacts with students from brother nations, i.e., other socialist countries.

The degree courses at the M.W. Frunze Military Academy for commanders and staff officers from the motorized rifle troops, the "R.J. Malinowski" Academy for tank officers, or in one of the comparable academies were designed to train the course participants for service as a regimental commander or on a divisional staff. Preceded by a one-year language course, the actual degree course would start, lasting three years, so that, on the whole, NVA officers usually remained in the Soviet Union for four consecutive years.

A total of 283 NVA officers attended the Military Academy of the General Staff of the Armed Forces of the USSR K.E Voroshilov. About three quarters of all NVA generals were among them, thus, in this way, a close affiliation of NVA general officers with the Soviet Union was also ensured.

Right to the end of the GDR, a course at one of the Soviet military academies was a proof of extraordinary qualifications and excellent career prospects. The value of more technical training courses in the Soviet Union, however, seems to have decreased during the 1980s. Some of the GDR training institutions had achieved an excellent status, and their courses were at least equal to the Soviet ones, as could also be seen from the increasing number of non-Soviet student officers attending them. In this respect, the GDR had also developed into the Soviet Union's "model student," except that the former model student was now beginning to best its former teacher.

Fig. 28:
Recruitment Commission, including a medical doctor, an NVA officer, and a representative of the district civil administration. Berlin, March 1971.

bpk/Jochen Moll

Fig. 29:
NVA Recruitment Poster, mid-1960s. Printed on behalf of the NVA Board of Editors of Wissen und Kämpfen (Know and Fight).

BArch, Plak Y 03-0438 (SAPMO)

Fig. 30:
Training of future tank commandants at the Offiziershochschule der Landstreitkräfte "Ernst Thälmann," Löbau, using the "Telepanzer" tank simulator, 1982.
BArch, Bild 183-1982-0422-307/ Ulrich Häßler

Fig. 31:
Poster advertising the harvest support by NVA soldiers, 1963.
MHM Dresden/BAAL1798

Fig. 32:
NVA soldiers on emergency duty reinforce weakened dykes in the Wiche region, district of Osterburg, April 1988.
MHM Dresden/MB088066-008

Armaments and Military Innovation

Methodological Problems

The GDR relied on a centrally planned economic system. Comparisons with Western economic systems are, thus, difficult to make. The value of goods or services in Western economies is equal to the price for which the seller or provider can ask. This system is unworkable without a market with a free agreement between the provider and customer on prices to pay. Establishing performance figures for the planned GDR economy to allow comparisons with Western figures is, therefore, possible only with complex calculations.

Regarding the area of state security policies, the rigorous compartmentalization and almost paranoid secrecy poses yet another methodological challenge. Even before the GDR collapsed in 1989/90, Western experts were very well aware that the figures given in the official defense budget represented only a fraction of what the entire national economy of the GDR had to provide for its country's security policy.

Apart from the actual budget, this included, first and foremost, the cost of the many military and paramilitary "armed formations." Again, a differentiation along the lines of internal and external security, as would be expected for Western countries, is impossible to establish. Would the substantial costs of guarding the border or those of the Working-Class Combat Groups come under external or internal security? And how would one balance the Western currency gains through "selling" prison inmates who had been jailed for attempting to flee to the West against the cost of the border regime? Another field would be the cost of defense technology research and development. The expenses incurred by preparing the GDR territory for war were largely hidden in the budgets of other ministries or had to be borne by the economy. Again, no clear calculation is possible as, for example, the improvement of lines of communication (railways, roads) as a preparation for war also provided a peacetime economic benefit. Part of the paramilitary training was actually done in schools, therefore, a differentiation of costs is almost impossible. On the other hand, the cost of the GST or civil defense (fire brigades!) could not be laid at the door of security policies alone.

What is clearly part of the GDR security expenditure are the expenses incurred by the stationing of Soviet troops in the country. Here, however, the burden to be borne by far exceeded the financial aspect. This would include factors difficult to measure, such as land use, the use of infrastructure, or the immense ecological damage caused by Soviet training and exercises.

But even the figures in the budget were kept secret; when the proposed budget was introduced into parliament (the *Volkskammer*), it would contain only the most general figures for internal and external security, which allowed no guesses regarding for what the money might be used. The real figures were known only to the Politburo, the top level of the Ministry of Finance, and the members of the State Planning Commission. The intention was not only to prevent Western eyes from learning details of the GDR defense effort, but also to disguise the immense economic efforts made to control and supervise it from the GDR's own population.

It was only in the late 1960s that any figures for defense were mentioned in the yearly budget; over time, these figures rose continuously. There were only speculations in the West as to what the proportions were between the publicized and the real sums. As the documents have since been made available, the estimate is that the true expenditures were about twenty percent above the public admissions. All aspects taken together, the amounts made available for defense and internal security can be assumed to have made up about ten percent of the entire GDR national income, a figure which had risen to more than eleven percent by the end of the GDR.

This implies an immense strain on the entire GDR economic system, which exceeded that of the other non-Soviet socialist states. However, while the security expenditures kept going up, their percentage of the regular budget began to diminish in the very last years of the GDR. What happened was that the amounts spent on purchases abroad and keeping prices stable at home rose so drastically that the GDR was inescapably headed for bankruptcy.

One reason for the economic collapse of the GDR state were the immense sums spent on security – but those were not the primary factor. The regime felt it was necessary to spend enormous amounts in order to maintain an adequate standard of living; this was a direct consequence of the events in June 1953 when the forcible armaments efforts had resulted in an uprising which constituted the greatest challenge to SED rule ever. Honecker had propagated the unity of economic and social policies, which constituted the most important factor in the GDR's economic demise, but, in a sense, that had also been part of the regime's concern with (internal) security.

GDR Armaments Industry

After World War I, and then accelerated during the "Third Reich," Germany had begun to move strategic industries into a region roughly defined by the term *Mitteldeutschland* ("Central Germany"). This included what is today eastern Lower Saxony, Sachsen-Anhalt, and Thuringia. Aircraft factories, chemical industries, and others were to produce their goods in a region which was as distant as possible from Germany's borders and, thus, relatively safe from air or ground attack from either East or West. The GDR had no natural resources to speak of, and no heavy industry had existed there prior to 1945. The steel industry along Soviet lines had to be artificially introduced and started from scratch. What it did have was a machine building industry and a chemical industry, but what had been *Mitteldeutschland* before World War II was now perilously close to the inner-German border, and, thus, in a problematic region strategically. For this and other reasons, the GDR contribution to the joint armaments efforts of the Warsaw Pact was segmented and specific. With the exception of light naval vessels built in the shipyards along the Baltic coast, no heavy weapons were produced in the GDR.

The euphemism "special production" designated those armaments firms which, by 1958, had been fused into the *Vereinigung Volkseigener Betriebe Universalmaschinen* (Combined Publicly Owned Enterprises Universal Machinery – VVB UNIMAK), that, in turn, came under the MfNV. The most important products were small arms, ammunition, and shipbuilding. After 1958, repairing heavy and tracked vehicles was added to that list; for that, a tank repair plant had been founded in Neubrandenburg in 1953 and a tank engine plant in Wurzen in 1954. In these fields, the GDR could rely on know-how dating back to the time from before 1945.

The VVB UNIMAK soon turned out to be an inexpedient organization. The firms subsumed into this conglomerate had been detached from the GDR's regular industrial structures, although obviously they had to rely on supplies from the nonmilitary sector. Friction losses were unavoidable, resulting in frequent disturbances in production. The VVB UNIMAK was dissolved in 1961, and the various plants were reintegrated into the appropriate sectors of GDR industry.

A separate point concerns the production of submarines (U-boats) and aircraft in the GDR. A substantial part of the pre-1945 *Kriegsmarine's* U-boat building capacities had been along the Baltic coast, where it had been safe from Allied bombers for a long time; this had particularly included the development of new, technologically superior types of vessel; plans and engineers had been seized by the Soviets. It would have been an obvious choice to establish similar production sites and create a small GDR U-boat arm. However, this process was halted after the events of June 17, 1953, and never restarted. In a similar vein, an aircraft plant had been set up in Dresden – as far away from the inner-German border as possible, building Soviet types of aircraft under license, and even developing a GDR-designed small commercial airplane. All this was also canceled in 1959/61, therefore, from that time on, the LSK/LV had to rely exclusively on Soviet fighter planes and helicopters plus a few smaller transport planes built in Czechoslovakia. Dresden was left with a – quite important – repair plant for military aviation.

Even if came to be only in the late 1960s, at the beginning of the decade, it was obvious that the superpowers would soon arrive at some sort of nuclear parity. This led to the beginnings of a new Western strategy in 1961, which was to become known as "Flexible Response." In 1962, a new Soviet military doctrine was proclaimed. Both provided for an increased role of conventional forces, and the proxy wars in Vietnam and the Middle East illustrated that trend. This meant that the GDR would be required to intensify its armaments efforts.

Subsequently, the GDR's existing capacities were increased quantitatively, particularly regarding the repair of heavy equipment. "Repair" also came to mean "modernization" – the advanced technological know-how of the GDR industry offered ideal conditions for that. Industry's business relations with the NVA and the MfNV were based on the "Delivery Specifications" *(Lieferverordnung)*, which entitled the armaments industry to claim priority when, in turn, ordering from subcontractors. On the other hand, representatives of the military routinely supervised production within the enterprises.

The "New Economic System of Planning and Management" *(Neues Ökonomisches System der Planung und Leitung)*, introduced in 1963, gave individual enterprises more room for decisions and increased productivity across the board, but it dissociated the interests of business from those of the state. All state purchases, including those for the defense sector, thus, became more difficult and more expensive. This was one of the reasons why, after Honecker had succeeded Ulbricht, the system was eventually discontinued.

Having to purchase practically all major equipment in the Soviet Union or one of the other member states of the COMECON placed a heavy burden on the GDR balance of payments. To compensate, the GDR had to furnish high-tech industrial equipment to the other socialist nations. On the other hand, this meant that the GDR had guaranteed buyers for its products, largely removing any incentives to remain competitive on the international market.

The 1970s brought with them a qualitative expansion of the GDR armaments industries, which began to include new fields, such as electronics and optics. East German enterprises, such as VEB Carl Zeiss Jena, soon obtained a leading position within the entire Warsaw Pact; there were similar trends in new chemical products. Notwithstanding all that, the entire armaments sector remained under Soviet control as far as most decisions were concerned, and the Soviet Union remained the chief supplier throughout. Consequently, research and development was not a priority in GDR industry – for a long time, copying Soviet examples seemed more important than the development of new, superior products. The small town of Suhl in Thuringia, for example, had a centuries-old tradition of fabricating first-rate firearms, but during the GDR period, it limited itself to mostly producing Soviet-de-

see table page 213

signed Kalashnikov AK 47 assault rifles (the GDR would refer to them as "submachine guns").

When the two hegemonial powers came to agreements regarding arms limitations and controls for the strategic nuclear sector, this again increased the importance of conventional forces. The resulting claims on GDR industry began to contrast noticeably, however, with the emerging weaknesses of the GDR national economy. The general decline of the worldwide economy after the oil price shock of 1973 did not leave the socialist countries, and the GDR in particular, unaffected. The Warsaw Pact and the COMECON tried to counter this by increased cooperation and a more detailed division of labor among member states. A "Complex Program" agreed upon in 1971 was to optimize armaments cooperation among the council's member states. This placed another burden on the GDR economy, so that exporting goods in all areas of production to "capitalist" countries to obtain hard currency became essential. To achieve that, GDR products were sold abroad at a price which did not even cover the cost of production. The armaments industry also had to open up new markets; this meant increased deliveries to the Arab nations (now oil-rich) and Third World countries. The GDR products soon began to rival Soviet products as they were of modern design and produced to higher standards. At the same time, the enterprises' productivity suffered from their forced fusion into state combines, a process pushed by the military, which resulted in bureaucratization and inefficiency. A plethora of new laws and regulations, including an "Order for Military Economic Planning" (1974) failed to stem that tide.

Similar to the military, the armaments industry was subject to strict secrecy. It was often sited in unattractive regions, with a problematic supply of housing. The personnel required qualitatively as well as quantitively could often be recruited only by offering above-average pay and social services, such as kindergartens, holiday homes, or medical centers. Some firms enjoyed a degree of autarky, including their own electricity and water supplies. All this meant exalted costs and stood in the way of the efficiency and productivity that had been hoped for.

Similar to many other branches of GDR industry, the 1980s turned out to be a phase of stagnation. The worsening economic situation and the decreasing demand for arms and military equipment even resulted in a decline in armaments production during the second half of the decade. In this situation, research and development became more relevant. That the GDR leadership should emphasize this more also indicated that here, as elsewhere, East Berlin was slowly emancipating from the Soviet models. What the GDR industry had to offer was top of the range within the socialist camp, but due to its high cost of production and technological backwardness, it was hardly competitive in the world market. Once the GDR had collapsed, and the guaranteed custom within the COMECON had disappeared, almost all armaments enterprises ceased to exist as well.

Armaments Cooperation and Standardization within the Warsaw Pact

Western analysts always tended to perceive the coordinated armaments and procurement policies of the Warsaw Pact countries as one of the Eastern alliance's major strategic assets. Compared to the NATO members which had to haggle over minimum standardization procedures to provide for a degree of interoperability of military equipment, the uniformized equipment of Warsaw Pact troops seemed to offer substantial advantages.

With hindsight, however, it is necessary to differentiate. For a start, it needs to be stated that Soviet resources were never sufficient to issue all their own units as well as those of their allies with the most modern weapons systems. On the contrary, the most advanced systems usually went to the elite Soviet units while the allies had to put up with older, at times even obsolete, designs. The West was forever concerned about the vast numbers of tanks, armored fighting vehicles, and artillery pieces. To some extent, these exaggerated figures were due, however, to the Warsaw Pact's usage of never decommissioning outdated equipment but preserving it for use by reserve divisions.

The GDR armaments industry soon specialized in modernizing older designs and, thus, allowing them to be used for a longer time. At first sight, this seems to have been a conservative policy which help save scarce resources. Upon closer inspection, this developed into a major drain on resources. Different versions of the same type had to be increasingly deployed – and supported logistically. In view of this variety of types and alternative forms, the efficiency gains achieved by procurement and production in large numbers were almost completely lost.

As the GDR armaments industry was predominantly a repair industry, it was highly dependent on spare parts being supplied by the Soviet Union. However, deliveries increasingly failed to meet the real demand, so that the East Germans were compelled to fabricate those spare parts themselves, usually at a high additional cost. The Soviets had hoped to increase efficiency by imposing a division of labor on their various allies, but what it did was to expand all the problems of a planned economy to the level of an international armaments industry.

A substantive part of the GDR industry's contribution to the joint armaments effort consisted of delivering modern machine tools to the allies as compensation for the military equipment obtained from them. These were often high-tech designs which were not produced anywhere else within the COMECON, and which could not be bought in the world market either, due to the Western restrictions on exporting modern technology to the Communist bloc. In the recipient countries, this top-level industrial equipment was often used primarily in the armaments sector; it was these technology imports which only made it possible for the other partners to provide the GDR with the armaments it required.

Uranium Exports

Once World War II had ended, the Soviet Union saw itself in a position of nuclear inferiority compared to the United States. It soon began to create a Soviet nuclear armaments production, but it only succeeded in detonating a nuclear device of its own in 1949.

One of the limiting factors of Soviet nuclear arms production was a lack of weapons-grade uranium. The uranium ore deposits in the Ore Mountains *(Erzgebirge)*, the GDR's border region with Czechoslovakia, soon began to play a central role.

At the end of the war, the region had been occupied by US Army troops. Even though obtaining uranium was existential for the Americans as well, the US military withdrew during the summer of 1945. It may well be that the relevance of the Ore Mountain uranium deposits had not been fully realized at that time. Even when Soviet troops succeeded the Americans, the strategic importance of the region was slow to be noticed.

Even the name "Ore Mountains" in itself was a clear indication that it had been prospected for precious metals, particularly silver, since the Middle Ages. On the other hand, the great times of silver mining had long been over by the beginning of the 20th century. Instead, the remaining mines extracted tin, cobalt, tungsten, and nickel. However, explorations had already revealed that there were several radioactive sources in the area. Before the war, radioactive substances, such as uranium and plutonium, had been won mostly on the Czechoslovak side of the border, in Jáchymov *(Joachimsthal)*.

After World War II, the Belgian Congo and Canada held the largest known uranium deposits, but they were almost inaccessible, and exploiting them would have required vast expenditures. Thus, the Ore Mountains contained some of the most important deposits worldwide, and they ended up being within the Soviet sphere.

The Soviets soon decided to search for uranium on the German side of the mountains, too. Controlled by the NKVD, a *Sächsische Bergbauverwaltung* (Mining Administration of Saxony) was set up. Its sole purpose was prospecting for and exploiting uranium deposits in the Ore Mountains. For cover reasons, the Soviets spread the rumor that they were also searching for tungsten (*Wismut* in German), with the eventual outcome that the Soviet-German Limited Company which succeeded the "Mining Administration" was called "Wismut." Houses and land were seized, existing or newly created mines were opened up, or new galleries pushed forward in the towns of Johanngeorgenstadt, Oberschlema, Annaberg, and Schneeberg, with no regard for subsistence damages which could be noted very quickly.

The Soviet Limited Company *(Sowjetische Aktiengesellschaft)* "Wismut" was founded in May 1947, comprising all the mining enterprises which the Soviet occupation government had seized so far. They were, thus, exempt from the parallel nationalization of all other Saxonian industrial enterprises decided upon in a referendum. The first Director General of the "Wismut" was a *Generalmajor* of the NKVD, Michail M. Malzew, whose chief previous experience had been in running labor camps.

The expansion of the uranium mining industry was largely financed by drawing upon East German funds, part of the reparations payable anyway. On the other hand, "Wismut" deliveries to the Soviet Union were credited to the East German reparations account – even if the sums credited did not nearly reflect the true value of the uranium provided.

The Soviet Union canceled all further reparation debts in 1954. In this context, what was now the *Sowjetische Aktiengesellschaft* "Wismut" became a "Soviet-German" enterprise *(Deutsch-Sowjetische Aktiengesellschaft* "Wismut"). Nominally under joint control, the true balance of power was unchanged: until 1986, all successors as directors general were from the Soviet Union.

The mining operations suffered from a severe and chronic shortage of labor during the first years of "Wismut." The nascent GDR tried to counter this by forcing unemployed staff from other branches or regions to work for "Wismut." That, in turn, led to an increase in flights to the West, as work in the ore mining industry was arduous and dangerous. What was more, these refugees would also provide Western intelligence with additional information about the Soviet endeavors to obtain weapons-grade uranium.

The SDAG "Wismut" expanded into Thuringia in the 1950s; substantive deposits of uranium were detected and mined in the region around the town of Ronneburg.

Apart from the mines as such, the "Wismut" complex provided the entire infrastructure required for obtaining uranium. This included several kinds of procedures to refill the vacant galleries, as well as the primary processing and eventual transport of uranium. Further processing to obtain weapons-grade uranium or plutonium, on the other hand, was only undertaken within the Soviet Union. Much later, even the fuel rods in the GDR's two nuclear power plants had to be bought from the Soviet Union and were not allowed to be produced in-country.

The huge quantities of residue were stored above ground. These slightly radioactive slag heaps represented a serious environmental threat which was only eliminated many years after 1990. In the early phases, safety precautions were rudimentary or nonexistent, leading to major accidents and conflagrations. Some resulted in the large-scale irradiation and nuclear pollution of drinking water in major regions of the GDR, but no public mention of this was ever permitted.

The Soviet Union and the GDR created a new legal framework for "Wismut" operations in 1962. From then on, the GDR regulations were supposed to apply, which would have led to more safety but were never fully realized. The new arrangement also provided for new modalities of payment. The costs of the operation were to be borne jointly, including such costs as had been carried by the GDR alone so far. The price of uranium, which was to form the basis of the earnings, was to be renegotiated periodically and the subject of separate agreements. The price of goods exported from the GDR, in turn, had a direct impact on how many and which services and goods, including armaments products, the GDR could afford to buy from the Soviet Union. Thus, the price of uranium developed into an important factor in balancing the economic interests of the two states.

Among the costs of "Wismut" to the GDR's national economy were the serious health risks incurred by miners. These did not only include the silicosis common to all kinds of mining but also the additional effects of long-term exposure to massive nuclear radiation. The SDAG "Wismut," therefore, created its own health services, specializing in lung diseases and guaranteeing a far superior level of treatment compared to other GDR hospitals; the "Wismut" health system also allowed the GDR to keep the impact of nuclear mining on the people working there out of the limelight. Still, throughout their existence, "Wismut" enterprises had a noticeably higher rate of employees on sick leave and taking early retirement for serious health reasons.

Apart from its above-average health system, SDAG Wismut had its own leisure and holiday infrastructure. The enterprise continuously invited its employees to identify with their profession and their employer, reviving long-established miners' traditions, such as uniforms and public parades, including distinctive musical bands. The cost for humoring its staff were, however, borne by the GDR alone; throughout the negotiations about the cost of SDAG Wismut, the Soviet Union persistently refused to contribute to these aspects.

In the 1970s, however, the GDR succeeded in getting world market prices for uranium accepted in negotiations with the Soviets. By the mid-1970s, however, the bulk of the East German uranium deposits had been exploited, and mining what was left required a larger economic and ecological expense. When all was said and done, the problem lay elsewhere: the world market price of uranium had actually fallen once much larger and much more easily accessible deposits had been made available elsewhere, including in the Soviet Union itself. The relatively small uranium deposits in the south of the GDR could no longer be exploited economically. In 1987, the GDR government *(Ministerrat)* decided to discontinue uranium production in the Dresden-Gittersee area. In January 1989, the Soviet Union announced that, in the future, it would purchase less uranium. This indicated an erosion of some of the fundamental tenets of the GDR economy: it had been dependent on the Soviet Union buying some of its products at prices way above the world market, while, simultaneously, selling energy to the Germans at prices below par. The major economic problems encountered by the Soviet economy did not allow Moscow to continue this kind of subsidy, and that presaged the impending collapse of the entire GDR national economy.

The Soviet Union had treated the uranium deliveries until 1953 as part of the GDR's reparations. After that, it picked up at least some of the expense of uranium mining, but the GDR still had to bear enormous costs. Figures are quoted in the literature of about 231,000 tons of uranium provided by the Soviet Zone of Occupation/ later the GDR to the Soviet Union between 1946 and 1990; they would have cost the East German economy roughly 25 million marks annually in direct payments, not taking into account the social and ecological follow-on costs. These sums have also to be counted as contributions to the joint security effort of the Warsaw Pact states.

The Military and the Economy

Agriculture

Among other things, the "armed formations" played an economic role, largely by repeated missions in support of the nonmilitary economy. This implied the support given to the agricultural industry during harvest times – a long-standing tradition among the German military from the very first years of its existence right into the 1970s. During those years, the GDR agriculture collectives were suffering heavily from a shortage of manpower, which was a result of the enforced collectivization. What started as an exception to make up for a lack of manpower in emergencies among the agricultural combines soon developed into something the combines came to rely upon as a matter of course and which they factored into their economic plans. At times, up to 12,000 men were working in agriculture rather than undergoing military training.

This delegation to assist in harvesting had an ideological and economic dimension. It was to illustrate the close links between the GDR populace and its military. The SED Party leadership also hoped that the repeated support given by the military would eventually convince the peasant population, which had been rather skeptical of the benefits of socialism so far. Not least, these campaigns might assist the NVA in its recruitment efforts – even if many of the volunteers recruited in this way had worked in agriculture before, and their leaving for a career in the army only exacerbated the problem.

The population in the countryside viewed the support given by the military with mixed feelings. On the one hand, the assistance was obviously welcome. On the other hand, it soon became obvious that the units tasked with sending men and equipment did not always deploy their best officers and men. At times, the disciplinary problems were quite serious. Yet, for many of the soldiers, work in the fields was a welcome change from the dreary barracks routine, and they took to their job with a will. They would often even exceed the targets set by the planning bureaucracies – which obviously could not be in the local farmers' long-term interest, either.

In the beginning, the NVA had lent its support for free, but by the mid-1960s, it began to charge for the work done by its soldiers. That, however, meant that the NVA support became far less attractive for many combines. Additionally, as GDR agriculture became increasingly mechanized, fewer jobs were suitable for untrained NVA soldiers. Simultaneously, the manpower shortages in the GDR economy as a whole tended to be less serious than before, so that NVA work in agriculture seems to have decreased noticeably in the 1970s and 1980s.

Catastrophes

Its air-raid protection service (later "Civil Defense,") provided the GDR with its own emergency management organization. In major catastrophes, however, it would soon reveal its limitations regarding technical equipment and, above all, its command and control capacities. As a consequence, it was up to the *Volksarmee* to provide swift and effective relief in cases of natural disaster. In 1954, the KVP had played a decisive role in combating widespread floods in the north and west of the GDR, and when the Elbe and Havel rivers went into flood again in 1988, this might have resulted in a catastrophe for the regions along both rivers had the NVA not supplied men and heavy equipment. Equally important was the NVA support in snow disasters; what made things worse was that, according to some indicators, the civilian agencies responsible had neglected their preparations as they had counted on military help from the very start.

This became evident in the catastrophic snowfalls in the first days of 1979 (the West German *Bundeswehr* was faced with exactly the same challenges during January 1979 in Northwest Germany). Helicopters, tracked vehicles, and clearing machinery took days and even weeks to remove snowdrifts, evacuate the sick and the pregnant, and keep the road and rail networks open so as to maintain the supply of essential goods to the population. It will not need much explaining that the motivation of the soldiers involved was uniformly high during these deployments, while seeing the army provide emergency relief substantially improved its public standing.

Industry and Construction

The material requirements of the armed forces in the Federal Republic are dealt with by a civilian administration which is even enshrined in the constitution. Contrary to that, but following German military tradition, in the GDR, this was to be done by the military themselves. The recurring shortages in the building industry and the paranoid secrecy surrounding every military project combined to create a situation in which the forces preferred to build their infrastructure using their own means. Airfields, accommodation, or firing ranges were built by men in uniform.

Soon, however, soldiers would also be employed on civilian sites with no connection to military purposes, particularly if prestigious public building projects were in danger of being completed belatedly. The same effect occurred as with the use of military personnel in agriculture: over time, what had started as an emergency measure turned into a matter of routine. Not only were the unarmed "construction soldiers" used for such projects, on the contrary: most such jobs were done by soldiers from regular units. To give but one example: the oil and gas refinery in Schwedt (on the Polish border) was completed, to a large extent, by NVA soldiers. Similarly, prestigious public buildings, such as the "Palace of the Republic" in East Berlin, was only completed on time because NVA soldiers were made available. An entire engineer battalion (i.e., regular troops) was sent to the island of Rügen to build the geostrategically relevant ferry port of Mukran on the Baltic coast.

Military personnel also had a substantial share in maintaining the GDR energy supply, which relied heavily on lignite. As lignite was extracted in open pit mines, it was susceptible to extreme weather. In the catastrophic winter of 1978/9, the GDR electricity supply threatened to collapse as all open-air dumps of lignite had frozen up. Several thousand soldiers were needed to get the supply of lignite to power plants going again. At peak times, the number of NVA soldiers detached to serve in the economy could reach five-digit figures.

This still leaves aside those units which had been raised almost exclusively for the purpose of supporting industrial production, mostly in the chemical industry. Their soldiers would undergo a six-month military training and then spend the rest of their time in some enterprise. In the propaganda, this served to highlight the "unity of the people and its army," but that was only a pretext. The NVA soldiers (both the regulars and the construction soldiers) were anything but cheap for the enterprises and their managers: the sums to be paid to the MfNV for such support were quite hefty. But they were freely available to be employed flexibly, and they could also be put to work in dangerous or harmful environments. At this point, what was being touted as an "honorable duty for the nation" degenerated into a labor service in which the young conscript would at times be placed on a level with convicted felons.

These support duties were centrally organized by the MfNV; on top of them came the innumerable unofficial support services. The twinning of units with enterprises or townships resulted in mutual support being arranged "unofficially," therefore, heavy NVA equipment which was not available in the civilian sector was loaned to the respective partners. In the winter of 1989/90, Minister of National Defense Theodor Hoffmann gave a figure of 48,500 armed forces personnel deployed in the economy; just for comparison, the overall strength of the NVA ran at about 170,000 men.

Problems

As with soldiers deployed in agriculture, their employment in industry was not without its problems. The soldiers would repeatedly complain that they were paid less and treated worse than their civilian colleagues; the latter, on the other hand, had their fears that the soldiers were also being sent to raise the workers' production norms. Regular contacts with the civilian population, and, even worse, at times with workers from West German building firms, threatened military discipline, or so some officers claimed.

In addition, as we have seen, the enterprises treated the soldiers as cheap and readily available labor. Soldiers complained repeatedly that *Volksarmee* personnel would be given hazardous and unhealthy tasks without the safety and protective measures required by law, or that their daily working hours were far in excess of those laid down for civilian workers.

Above all, the huge deployments elsewhere meant that regular military training was being neglected. Moreover, the repeated calls for military readiness around the clock sounded hollow if, at the same time, a substantial share of the units was tied down "in the national economy." When units had been dispatched to help with the harvest during the 1950s, at least there had been a 50 km limit on where they could be sent, so that in case of an alert, they could be back in their barracks within a short period of time. Once the military support for agriculture and industry became a regular routine, this readiness was difficult to maintain. There was no way that soldiers working in the chemical industry or the mines could reach the deployment areas provided for their mobilized units in good time. On top of that, the abrupt termination of military support for strategically relevant production processes might also seriously harm the economy, which might, in turn, affect the mobilization and deployment to wartime positions. If, for example, the GDR electricity supply depended, to some extent, on military personnel, how were the railways or the communication networks supposed to function without them? So far, no war games have come to light in which the top level GDR leadership realistically analyzed the changeover of the entire economic system from peacetime to wartime patterns, under the conditions of war.

The soldiers were well aware of all this, and in their complaints and petitions, they clearly differentiated between the way their military service was glorified in the country's propaganda and the reality in the respective enterprises. It obviously made little sense to recall highly qualified reservists, denying them to their employers, and then not use them against an external enemy but work them as untrained labor in a neighboring plant. And yet that was exactly what happened.

These problems were well-known, right up to the Politburo. The military commanders repeatedly pointed at the need for permanent combat readiness and at the obligations undertaken vis-à-vis the allies. From a Party point of view, all that paled into insignificance compared with the need to maintain an economic system which was, however, doomed to fail eventually even with military support.

Precise statements based on verifiable figures about the sums the GDR spent on external security are practically impossible to elaborate. It would be difficult enough to convert the calculations made within a planned economy into the categories of a market-based system. Equally problematic would be a clear differentiation between the costs of internal and external security. It seems almost impossible to categorize the various expenses not listed in the defense budget or calculate the effects of trade within the Eastern Bloc. What can be said with a degree of certainty is that the overall cost of the GDR's security precautions was so high that it threatened to cripple the East German state rather than stabilizing its political system.

The planned economy required, by definition, coercive measures which could only be enforced by using the tools of political power available to a repressive system. To support this pattern, large-scale security efforts were necessary to guarantee the continued survival of the system. At the same time, the planned economy, rather inefficient to start with, was being overtaxed by the cost of enforcing its survival. The question is moot whether the socialist economic system was ruined by the cost of militarization, or if a similar system without its repressive apparatus might be viable, after all. Without maintaining the means of repression, the entire system could not operate.

Warfare, Operational Planning, and Military Thinking

Sources

Military planning is done in secret in all nations, and the relevant documents are classified. That was so for the GDR as well, but there were a number of additional factors resulting from the paranoid fear of the GDR, and even more the Soviet, leadership that was forever worried about espionage and subversion. The command system in all Warsaw Pact states operated on a strict need-to-know basis; everyone was to hold only the information needed for him to do his specific job. In particular, the knowledge about the "real" operational plans developed for an actual war was limited to a very narrow group – and even those were to know solely which plans had been provided for their specific unit. Only an extremely small number may have had an overview of the entire NVA planning for wartime operations.

Even before the GDR came to an end, it had relatively little knowledge and only a few documents about the Warsaw Pact's operational planning. There are reports that when the GDR Ministers of Defense attended the meetings of the pact's Political Consultative Committee, they would be handed the documents required for the session when entering the conference hall – and had to hand them back upon leaving the hall again. Even fewer files ever came to Germany before 1989/90 regarding nuclear planning and release procedures.

Whatever the GDR held in the way of classified pact documents was delivered back to Moscow in the summer of 1990, as were encryption machines and keys. (It is interesting to note that even when the Soviet Union was being dissolved, Moscow should unquestioningly be considered as the sole legitimate inheritor of Warsaw Pact material.) For that reason, research about GDR operational or nuclear planning cannot be based on a wide selection of original documents, but must rely heavily on eyewitness accounts. An older publication (*7.6* Nielsen, Die DDR und die Kernwaffen) has since been superseded by the publications authored by Siegfried Lautsch, a former NVA colonel involved in operational planning (*7.4* Lautsch, Die Entwicklung; *1.28* Lautsch, Grundzüge).

What has survived in the Federal German Archives in Freiburg, though, are a sizeable quantity of exercise-related files, documents pertaining to the preparation of the GDR territory for war, and those detailing the mobilization plans for the NVA and the GDR's paramilitary organizations.

Yet, the use of exercise material opens up the next methodological question. On the one hand, an old German military adage states that "if you haven't practiced it, it won't work." In any army, training will reflect that army's assumptions about the future war. On the other hand, GDR regulations stated unequivocally that the protection of state secrets required that exercises must never replicate the "real" planning. According to eyewitness reports, all exercise material had to be vetted by officers who knew about the real plans, and if the exercise came too close to the "live" planning, it had to be modified.

After 1991, other Warsaw Pact states gradually opened their Cold War archives, with Poland in the van; the material made available included both exercise and "real" planning. This allows us to understand the complex relationship between the two kinds of sources better. As all Warsaw Pact states followed the Soviet example in these matters, we can assume that the relationship as it existed in Poland was pretty much the same in all other Warsaw Pact countries, including the GDR. The impression one gains from the Polish sources is that exercises and war games at the top command levels *(Kommandostabsübungen)* reflected war planning fairly accurately. With all methodological care, it will still be possible to consult the exercise documents preserved in the Federal Military Archives in Freiburg, together with memoirs and eyewitness accounts to form an impression of what GDR military planning was like (*7.10* Wenzke, Die Streitkräfte).

Surprisingly, it seems that the "real" plans of the various Warsaw Pact armies do not match each other. In the case of the Polish People's Army and the NVA, there are discrepancies regarding which army was to attack where in northwest Germany. This raises the fundamental question whether the tasks allotted to the various allies by the Soviet General Staff reflected what those allies would have been tasked to do should war break out, or if, in order to maintain secrecy, these tasks were only a pretense and, in case of war, everything would have been very different from what the non-Soviet allies had been led to believe. The question will remain open until such a time in the distant future when the Russian Federation opens up its military archives to international researchers.

Integration into the Warsaw Pact

It is not easy to differentiate between the military and the political dimensions of the Warsaw Pact. The pact's multilateral structure overlaid the preexisting network of bilingual treaties of allegiance between the Soviet Union and its satellites. The political dimension was clearly more important right into the 1960s. The outcome of the Cuban Missile Crisis marked the failure of an expansive policy based on nuclear weapons; it also increased the importance of large and expensive conventional weapons so that, in turn, the allies' contribution suddenly appeared more relevant. Even so, historical research has shown that the Pact, from its inception, cannot be thought of as representing a "monolithic" bloc. All the socialist regimes were dependent on Soviet guarantees, especially in view of their lack of any democratic legitimacy, but, even so, they continued to pursue their respective national interests – Nicolae Ceauşescu's Rumania being the most obvious case (*0.16* Diedrich/Heinemann/Ostermann, Der Warschauer Pakt, in particular *7.8* Rijnoveanu, Die Auswirkungen; *0.25* Bange, Sicherheit und Staat).

Even in peacetime, all units of the GDR military were assigned to the Combined Command of Pact Armed Forces and would have come under its full control in war. The Combined Command, based in Moscow, must not be understood, however, as a truly integrated command authority. Rather, it was part of the Soviet General Staff, enriched with a few small liaison and consultative elements from the allied armed forces. "Supreme Command" of the Pact's forces was reserved for the Chairman of the CPSU, who would exercise his authority through the Soviet General Staff. In this fashion, the Soviet General Staff reserved operational control for itself, so that the "Combined Command" cannot be interpreted as an operational-level command staff, either.

A separate High Command for the Western Theater of War was only established in the 1970s; its first test came during exercise Zapad-77. (The Zapad exercise series was normally only for Soviet troops; this seems to indicate that no substantial participation of the allied troops was envisaged by the Western Theater High Command.) During the 1980 *Waffenbrüderschaft* ("comradeship-in-arms") exercise in the GDR, the existence of this Western Theater High Command was already implicitly understood.

It was to command and control several "fronts" (since World War II, the term in Soviet parlance denotes a command level roughly equivalent to a Western "army group"). Two fronts were to operate on the territory of the GDR: the 2nd Front in the north, under Polish command, and the 1st Western Front under Soviet command south of a line from Bremen through the Wendland region to Schwedt. The MB-V was scheduled to convert into the 5th Corps, with three NVA divisions. After 1985, this was referred to as the "5th Army," but with equal strength. It was to fight as the 2nd Front's first strategic echelon. Similarly, Military District III was to become the 3rd Army Command, also with three NVA divisions. Although the GDR was a founding nation of the Warsaw Pact, and while no other member country would be affected as seriously by a war in Central Europe, it was not to command one of the fronts. Nor did this change when, after 1981, Poland had become a rather uncertain ally; presumably, the NVA force contribution was just too small.

Unlike the "Army Group," the rough Western equivalent, a Soviet-style "Front" would own air elements, such as fighter-bombers. The NVA's LSK/LV were assigned in their entirety to the 1st (Western) Front, i.e., came under a Soviet general. Similarly, the policing and defense of GDR airspace was controlled by the Soviets even in peacetime – this was unique among the Warsaw Pact member states. The *Volksmarine* was to be fully integrated into the Pact's United Baltic Sea Fleets, equally under Soviet command. As the East German military was not involved in the command of any "front," it had no access to any information about operational planning at this level.

According to the Soviet definition, the Warsaw Pact defined an "operation" as "a form of commanding combat activities with operational (operational-strategic) forces, and as the entirety of battles, skirmishes, and strikes coordinated in their aims, space, and timing in a theater of a strategic direction according to a unified concept" (*7.6* Nielsen, Die DDR und die Kernwaffen, 32). This definition is rather static and, upon closer inspection, it reveals a weakness which marked the military forces of all socialist nations, and even reflected a general social and political weakness of the socialist systems as such. The way the command staffs at all levels operated was to devise plans and then submit them to the next higher staff for approval. Once approved, the plan of operations was sacrosanct; any deviation required another previous authorization. Thus, the military command system was about as rigid and inflexible as the planned economy system.

Once the GDR had reoriented toward the Soviet Union after its brief flirt with the People's Republic of China, which for the NVA meant an end to the "Chinese experiment", and in view of the improved training and introduction of general conscription, the time had come for the NVA to be integrated into the 1st Strategic Echelon of Warsaw Pact forces in Central Europe. These developments have still not been fully analyzed for the land forces. The NVR passed the draft of the new defense law on August 28, 1961, that provided for an increase of the NVA numerical strength by 5,000, as well as further measures in all walks of state and economic life, which had been "suggested" by the Soviets to "further increase defense readiness," and improve integration of the East German army into the Pact's military organization. This obviously started a lengthy process which included several large-scale allied exercises and war games with major NVA units participating, largely concluded in 1963. When the exercise "October Storm," held in October 1965, was analyzed in the Central Committee, the chief of the Political Main Directorate, Admiral Verner, referred to the NVA as one of the armies of the 1st Strategic Echelon. Similarly, it seems safe to assume that the *Volksmarine* had been prepared for quite some time for a role within the framework of the Eastern alliance. The LSK/LV had been incorporated into the Warsaw Pact's integrated air defense system *(Diensthabendes System der Luftverteidigung)*.

During the following years, the NVA played a somewhat special role within the alliance's framework, even if one does not fully accept the theory that, due to the need for stabilization, smaller allies can exert a much larger influence on the hegemonial power than normally assumed. After all, the basis of both the Western and Eastern alliances included the experience of the partners that many of them had been twice the object of German military aggression during the 20th century. Both alliances had to utilize their German partners' military capabilities, while simultaneously providing security against a potentially renascent German militarism.

Military Doctrines

Soviet military doctrine was based on the Marxist interpretation of history and, therefore, loosely on Clausewitz. Marx and Engels, as well as Lenin, had studied the Prussian philosopher of war. The term "military doctrine" denotes general assumptions about the future war, such as the probable enemy, the nature of warfare, the forces needed, as well as the preparation of the territory for defense. The political elements inherent in this, especially in the general assumptions about the nature of war, resulted in Soviet military doctrine having a decidedly ideological dimension ("class warfare character").

The Soviet doctrine was binding for the entire Warsaw Pact. This was due to not only the Soviet Union providing the bulk of forces but also the political character of the doctrine: The CPSU was unwilling to relinquish its political leadership within the alliance.

The Soviet military had developed a new doctrine in the early 1960s based largely on strategic nuclear weapons. Yet, after the experience of the Cuban Missile Crisis of 1962, it was soon revised and from then on took into account the option of a nonnuclear limited war. Soon after, the Vietnam war escalated rapidly but not into a nuclear conflict, indicating that, indeed, even at the time of massive nuclear armaments, conventional war remained possible.

According to Soviet terminology, a war might occur worldwide or be limited to one or several theaters – such as the North American theater, the Atlantic as a naval theater, the South Asian theater (including the Middle East), or the South East Asian theater (with Indochina as the obvious example).

According to this definition, Europe consisted of three theaters: the North Western, the Western, and the South Western. The North Western Theater meant Scandinavia, the Western Theatre referred to Central and Western Europe, while the South Western Theatre covered Europe south of the Alps, Greece, Turkey, and the Eastern Mediterranean. The Baltic Approaches were assigned both to the North Western and the Western Theatre.

The non-Soviet Warsaw Pact allies naturally focused on the Western Theatre, i.e., Central Europe. No participation of the allies in Soviet global strategy was expected or encouraged, anyway. That explains, to some extent, why GDR strategic and operational thinking remained forever landlocked and limited.

This Soviet military doctrine comprised the common assumptions about the nature of a future war almost to the end of the socialist camp. Only when the Political Consultative Committee met in Strausberg in the spring of 1987 did the Warsaw Pact accept a wider definition, according to which the military doctrine was to include measures for the prevention of war as well (Berlin Document).

The 1980s had, earlier on, brought about a substantive modification of the doctrinal assumptions about what a future war would be like. Until then, the basic idea had been that a war would result from a NATO attack, but that combat would immediately move to Western territory due to the massive offensive operations of the Warsaw Pact.

This was put into question by new Western armaments efforts during the Reagan years, and especially the development of innovative systems, such as anti-tank missiles, low-flying aircraft (MRCA "Tornado"), and cruise missiles, which could overfly enemy (i.e., Soviet) territory at low altitudes. All these combined to make the US FOFA ("Follow-on Forces Attack") doctrine appear realistic. For the Soviet camp, however, that meant that the swift insertion of a second strategic echelon from the Soviet Union through Poland, and across the Vistula, Oder, and Elbe rivers, became uncertain.

Even before the new CPSU Secretary General Mikhail Sergeyevich Gorbachev came to power, the 1983 large-scale Warsaw Pact exercises indicated that the Soviet Union was willing to consider an, at least temporary, operational defense at the beginning of a war. Attack was no longer the sole mode of warfare to be practiced in such exercises, but defense was also considered. It was a change which the GDR could not fail to notice: In a defensive war, its territory would not represent the strategic rearward communications, but would become the actual combat zone.

A Separate Military Doctrine for the GDR?
For the GDR, the priority of Soviet military thinking meant that its own planners just had to adapt the Soviet guidance to the specificities of the GDR political situation and terrain, with the political elements being immutable, so that only the more "technical" aspects needed adaptation. As early as 1962, the Soviet Minister of Defense, Rodion Yakovlevich Malinovsky, had declared that the other socialist states had accepted Soviet military doctrine. It was claimed to be scientific and, thus, formed the framework for the entire "system of socialist national defense." The GDR had cautiously begun to think about a separate GDR military doctrine during the closing years of the Ulbricht era, and, thus, to emancipate itself ever so slightly from Moscow, but the Soviets had clamped down on the attempt almost at once. The "Berlin Document" of 1987 was the first to mention a "Warsaw Pact mil-

itary doctrine," whereas, until then, unquestioned, it had been the "Soviet military doctrine" which had formed the basis of all alliance theories and practical preparations alike. This went, above all, for the East German satellite state: "Until the 1980s, not to have developed an autonomous military doctrine was the real characteristic of GDR doctrinal thinking" (*7.3 Kauffmann, Kontinuität und Wandel*). This also excluded the adaptation of specifically German experiences during World War II or the development of operational thinking based on them. The GDR operational planning, therefore, was idiosyncratically quantitative and schematic in character; every plan required a large amount of calculation; in many ways it reflected the concepts of the GDR planned economy.

The question of a separate GDR military doctrine appeared in quite a different light again in the early 1980s, when the GDR praised the West German movement for demanding nuclear disarmament, while, at the same time, suppressing analogous ideas in its own sphere of power. Additionally, when Intermediate Range Nuclear Forces were eventually stationed in Western European countries (including the Federal Republic), it indicated that the cohesion of the Western Alliance had not eroded as predicted by socialist ideology. Instead, it remained stable, while, simultaneously, in the light of developments in Poland and Rumania, doubts grew about the continuing cohesion of the Warsaw Pact. That, together with the uncertainty caused by the new generation of Western conventional weapons systems, led some NVA officers, together with the small elite involved in security politics, to deliberate again the "specificities of the GDR" – a euphemism camouflaging the idea of a GDR military doctrine adapted to the characteristics of the East German state.

This trend gained traction in the Gorbachev era, when the Soviet planners developed the idea of an initial defensive action – which would have made not the Federal Republic, but the GDR into the battlefield of the initial clashes, threatening the existential basis for the latter's survival. The more reform-oriented thinkers in East German security policy began to understand that any war would result in the annihilation of their country, and not in the victory of socialism. Interestingly enough, intellectuals from the academic institutions of the NVA suddenly found themselves in overall agreement with church-based oppositional peace groups. Another factor that gained relevance was the increasing exchange among the two German states, be it as part of CSCE inspections or in the various international fora.

Finally, the Security Department *(Abteilung Sicherheitsfragen)* of the SED Central Committee submitted the draft of a GDR military doctrine in February 1989 which still referred to the Warsaw Pact as the basis of GDR security, but omitted any reference to the "leading role of the Soviet Union" – until then an essential element in any such document. This followed up the option opened up in the 1987 "Berlin Document" that all member states could formulate their own military doctrines –

in agreement with the Soviet Union. However, the document submitted was never formally discussed, let alone passed, by Party bodies. By the time this might have come to pass, the security and future of the GDR were threatened in a way vastly different from anything for which a military doctrine could provide.

The NVA during the Warsaw Pact Crises

What relevance the other allies attached to the GDR became obvious during the crises affecting the Warsaw Pact. The invasion of Hungary in 1956 was no alliance operation but conducted by the Soviet Union alone. Just a few months after its official inception, the NVA would have been unable to make a meaningful contribution, anyway. The Cuban Missile Crisis of 1962 was perceived as a stand-off between the superpowers (this applied more or less the same way to the Warsaw Pact and to NATO). The smaller partners raised their alert levels but had no political say.

The Prague Spring

Therefore, the first crisis that must be discussed in our context is the participation – or not – of the NVA in the military suppression of the "Prague Spring" in August 1968.

see page 205

The internal developments within Czechoslovakia posed an existential threat for the SED regime. Citizens of the GDR could freely visit the country and did so regularly. It was reasonable to believe that any "counterrevolutionary" ideas circulating there would soon spread to East Germany. As early as in the spring of 1968, the GDR leadership perceived the danger of an ideological softening in the CSSR, and an intervention in Prague from the outside became essential for the GDR regime.

The allied armed forces, including the NVA, conducted a large-scale exercise called "Šumava" ("Bohemian Forest") on Czechoslovak territory in late June 1968. While all troops that had participated left Czechoslovakia after the exercise had ended, the Soviet forces did so only reluctantly.

As Ulbricht had been among those who had demanded a Warsaw Pact intervention most insistently, it seemed a matter of course that the GDR would participate in it, even more so since it would be conducted largely from GDR territory (and that of Poland). The Soviets then sent out invitations for another exercise which was to be called "Dunai" ("Danube"); the NVA's 7th PD and 11th MSD were to take part.

A liaison element of the NVA high command arrived at the headquarters of the Supreme Commander of the Combined Forces, Marshal of the Soviet Union Ivan Ignatyevich Yakubovsky, in Legnica (Silesia, Poland) on July 25, 1968. On August 10, 1968, Ulbricht, in his capacity as Chairman of the NVR, officially approved the participation of NVA units in the preparations for an invasion.

On August 17, 1968, the CPSU Politburo took the final decision in favor of armed intervention in Czechoslovakia. Two days later, on August 19, the order to execute operation "Dunai" reached the GDR MfNV; Walter Ulbricht's general order is dated August 20. Apart from the NVA, organs of internal security, mainly the police and, of course, the Stasi, were to be alerted and ordered to prepare all necessary measures to ensure the operation went smoothly; this was to include restrictions on the transit routes between West Germany and West Berlin – something that would exacerbate international tensions even more. Two regiments of border troops were ordered to seal off the Czechoslovak border and to close all border crossings.

While most of the NVA still remained in its barracks, its alert level was increased substantially, even ammunition was to be issued. The two divisions assigned to the operation (7th PD and 11th MSD) had been placed under Soviet command on July 29 and moved into their deployment areas. The 7th PD was to operate as part of the Soviet 20th Guards Army, while the 11th MSD had been scheduled from the beginning to serve as an operational reserve. The operation started during the early morning hours of August 21, and, later on that day, Minister of National Defense Heinz Hoffmann informed the members of the NVR that the 7th PD had also been detailed to serve as a reserve for the Supreme Commander "at short notice."

What this meant was that neither GDR divisions would leave their country. There were no GDR units among the Warsaw Pact troops that invaded Czechoslovakia on that fateful August 21, 1968. The only GDR military personnel to cross the border were in the liaison team and the signals unit sent to support it, and a few border troops who temporarily crossed the line.

If one is to follow the German sources, technical military reasons alone resulted in the exclusion of German units from Operation "Dunai" (*2.21* Wenzke, Die NVA und der Prager Frühling (2008), 140;). The decision was, however, highly political, and it seems almost inconceivable that mere technicalities should have been at play here. A definitive answer will be hard to arrive at as long as Soviet documents are being withheld by Russian archivists. After all, all this took place close to the 30th anniversary of the Wehrmacht's annexation of the Sudeten, following the Munich Conference of 1938; this may have affected Soviet thinking. We do not know; nor do we know whether the Soviet Supreme Command held doubts as to the political reliability of the NVA units. In any case, the GDR and particularly the NVA provided massive logistical support for the Soviet invasion troops. The increased alert level activated during the night of August 20/21, 1968, was deactivated again in September; in October, all units which had moved into deployment areas eventually returned to barracks.

Even so, the notion seems irrepressible that the GDR actively participated in the suppression of the Prague Spring. This is largely due to the fact that the GDR leadership perceived the exclusion of its troops and units as discrimination and a loss of face. It attempted, therefore, to create the impression (without positively saying so) in the Party-controlled media that the NVA had joined the allied forces in invading its neighbor.

Ever since the uprising of June 17, 1953, the GDR leadership knew all too well that its rule depended on the Soviet guarantee of intervening by force should the Party's control of the state be put into serious question. Moscow's willingness to do so in Prague was, therefore, also a warning to the East Germans.

However, the events and the "Brezhnev Doctrine" resulting from it also posed a dilemma for the GDR. According to this new doctrine, the socialist nations only had "limited sovereignty," justifying an intervention by military force by the others. Yet, GDR foreign policy had always striven to emphasize the country's full sovereignty, denigrating Soviet control as best as possible. It was somewhat difficult to demand that the Federal Republic declare the current borders in Europe (including those of the GDR itself, and the post-1945 western Polish border) inviolate if an intervention by its own allies was simultaneously declared legitimate. Support of the invasion would not only have violated the GDR constitution (which expressly forbade the preparation for a war of aggression) but also all the relevant statutes of the Charter of the United Nations – as the GDR was working hard to be admitted to the United Nations, that would have been a serious mistake.

Poland, Solidarność
In a very similar way, it was again the GDR political elite which put pressure on the Soviets to intervene militarily in Poland once the Workers' Defense Committee (Polish: Komitet Obrony Robotników) had been founded in 1976, and even more so when it fully understood the political repercussions of the election of a "Polish Pope," John Paul II, the former archbishop of Cracow, in 1978, which lent additional weight to the growing opposition. Again, this was particularly sensitive for the GDR. It had not only joined the United Nations in 1973 but also signed the Final Act of the CSCE, which underlined again the inviolability of European borders.

Moreover, since the 1950s, the GDR had presented itself as the peace-loving German state which had legally acknowledged the international border between Poland and Germany as it had emerged after World War II and the Potsdam Conference of 1945. The GDR kept harping about "revanchists" in West Germany who still put the Oder-Neiße Line into question. Although the Federal Republic had never formally resigned itself to the loss of a quarter of German territory, relations between West Germany and Poland had continuously improved after an exchange of letters between the Polish and the German Catholic bishops had initiated the process. By the early 1980s, the GDR found itself in an uncomfortable position between its archrival, the Federal Republic, in the west, and a Polish state in the east which had begun to lean noticeably toward the West. On the other hand, should East German military units take part in an invasion of Poland together with the Soviets, reminiscent of what had happened in September 1939, this would not sit well with the GDR's attempt to be perceived as the peaceful German state.

Opening of the Hungarian Border; GDR Refugees in the West German Embassy in Prague

During the 1989/90 Peaceful Revolution (often in German, and sometimes in English, referred to as *Die Wende*), no military intervention was ever even conceived of against such allies who acted against the interests of the Warsaw Pact as a whole, or of the GDR in particular – not even among the GDR leadership were such plans hatched. In a way, this also indicated the reduced relevance of the NVA.

When the Hungarian government decided in the spring of 1989 to demolish all fences and other devices along its border with Austria, and to allow GDR citizens to cross into the West, this was in clear contravention of several agreements concluded between all socialist states to prevent GDR citizens from "going West." The GDR's only reaction was to denounce the opening of the border as "organized human trafficking" and to make it more difficult for its citizens to travel to Hungary. On October 4, 1989, when hundreds of GDR citizens had found refuge in the West German Embassy in Prague, the GDR also terminated unilaterally an agreement allowing visa-free travel to Czechoslovakia. Any attempt to use force against either ally to make them conform to the agreed procedures again by closing their borders was just inconceivable. The Soviet Union under Mikhail S. Gorbachev had made it abundantly clear that the Brezhnev Doctrine was dead – thus, depriving the GDR regime itself of the basis of its existence.

In its agonal phase, the NVA did not play the stabilizing role which many of its officers had envisaged for "their" army. Nor did it have an opportunity to operate abroad – against its allies. It may be true that the NVA and the GDR's paramilitary formations never took part in aggressive operations against other countries, but that is largely due to the Soviet Union's active refusal of the plans devised by the GDR's political leadership in 1968 and again in 1980/81; by 1989, any such idea would have been rejected outright as utterly absurd. This, too, relativizes the claim that the GDR was a "peace-loving state" *(Friedensstaat DDR)*.

The GDR in the "Third World"

Even if the GDR's security policy was largely limited to a Central European framework, it had a worldwide dimension as well. As early as in the 1950s, the Soviet Union had attempted to instrumentalize the Western dependence on raw materials obtained from what was then referred to as the "Third World" (for this chapter, see, above all, *0.21* Storkmann, Geheime Solidarität?). Moscow had tried to export the East-West Conflict into the global South, particularly by supporting "liberation movements" in the territories held by Western colonial powers. The first example had been the Soviet involvement in the building of the Aswan Dam in Egypt, which had been one of the causes of the 1956 Suez Crisis. During the 1960s, this policy expanded to all of Africa, parts of Asia, and Cuba.

In this game, the Soviets had also assigned a role to the GDR. It was to deliver weapons and equipment, and detailed to offer military training both in the respective countries and at home in the GDR. The GDR government, in turn, could hope to further its own international recognition by massive support for "anti-imperialist" movements.

The first equipment was dispatched to Guinea in 1959, accompanied by training opportunities for the material's potential operators. Yet, the GDR help for the emerging nations remained limited until the Vietnam War escalated; the East German state had enough on its hands equipping and training its own nascent military forces.

see page 206

During the 1960s, however, pressure grew to demonstrate "internationalist solidarity" with Vietnam by means of more concrete measures. The GDR population was encouraged to make "voluntary" donations for humanitarian purposes – which, however, soon mutated into arms and equipment for the North Vietnamese military.

There is no denying the fact that the NVA provided a modicum of humanitarian aid. Medical support ranged from sending medicines and medical equipment for the treatment of injured combatants (plus, at times, privileged members of the respective state and party *nomenklatura*) in GDR hospitals. In 1984/85, an entire squadron of transport aircraft was dispatched to Ethiopia to support the country in its struggle against the effects of drought; the *Volksarmee* also delivered blankets, tents, and other humanitarian equipment.

The most important part of support for independence movements, and then for states that had been liberated from colonialism, was the delivery of arms and equipment. These would initially come from the reserves the NVA had created for mobilization; later, they would also be taken from the small arms production in the GDR. The chief recipient of weapons and equipment remained North Vietnam, but support deliveries also went to Syria, Ethiopia, Mozambique, Egypt, Angola, South Yemen, the People's Republic of Congo, and Nicaragua. Apart from states, independence movements received support; the aid for FRELIMO (Liberation Front of Mozambique) morphed into military aid for Mozambique once the country had gained its independence. Only in special circumstances would the GDR part with major equipment – that would be the role of the Soviet Union. Handing 50

Fig. 33:
The President of the Republic of Zambia, Kenneth David Kaunda, together with Erich Honecker inspects the guard of honor at the beginning of his state visit to the GDR, August 24, 1980.
ullstein bild – ADN-Bildarchiv

MiG-17 jet fighters over to Egypt after the Six-Days' War in 1967 must be seen as an exception to the norm.

The GDR was increasingly short of hard currency during the 1980s and began to insist its deliveries were to be on a "commercial" basis; it expected payment in freely convertible (i.e., Western) currency from countries such as Syria or Libya.

Another, separate element of aid for the "Third World" was the training of military elites – mostly officers but, in some instances, also specialist NCOs who would receive technical training. During the 1970s, the number of trainee officers increased drastically and a separate training facility was required: the Officer Academy "Otto Winzer" in Prora on the island of Rügen, in the extreme North of the GDR. It was convenient to have it close to the *Volksmarine*'s Technical NCO School "Erich Habersath"; furthermore, the *Kraft durch Freude* accommodation facilities built by the Nazis before 1945 could be put to good use. Yet, the remoteness of Prora on an island in the Baltic also played a role in selecting it for this purpose; it was easier to keep the facility secret, and undesirable contacts between the officer cadets studying there and the local GDR population could be controlled and reduced to a minimum. The SED state had both a political and financial interest in supporting overseas "progressive" regimes, but here as elsewhere, the old white men at the top of Party and state had decided that too much intermingling of the young men from, say, Mozambique, Cuba, or Nicaragua with GDR citizens was to be avoided. The opposite option, i.e., sending NVA instructors to countries in Africa and Asia, proved to be far less effective, and was less sought after by the potential hosting nations, on top of carrying greater risks of involvement as well.

As far as can be ascertained so far, about 3,000 foreign military personnel from more than 20 countries received some sort of training in the GDR. Money was also the problem here: While some countries or liberation movements could send their course participants to the GDR for free, Libya and Syria were made to pay in hard currency. Apart from its diplomatic and military dimension, the training business also turned out to be a sizeable boon for the GDR economy.

Regarding the GDR instructors, ideological indoctrination was an integral part of the program offered to "Foreign Military Cadres." That, however, did not always meet the expectations of the countries that had sent them to Europe: They were more interested in the realm of military and technical expertise and qualification. Moreover, the kind of training which would produce good commanders in regular armies did not always prove to be suitable for officer cadets who, upon their return, were to fight underground or as guerrillas.

It was sometimes assumed in the Western media that NVA units had been sent to fight overseas, but that never happened. When soldiers and usually officers were deployed to Third World countries, they went as advisers and instructors. The same is true for members of the other "armed organs of the state," such as the Ministry for State Security (Stasi), who assisted training in "friendly" nations but made sure they would not get involved in operational quagmires.

The cost of these kinds of aid for developing countries never exceeded one percent of the overall GDR defense expenditure (for the problem of exact economic figures, see Chapter 6.1 above). By far the largest share of that went into the provision of arms and equipment, while the cost of training programs always remained very limited.

All decisions about GDR involvement in the Third World were taken by the Party chief himself during the Honecker era. After all, what was at stake when GDR officers took part in international conflicts was the self-perception of the GDR as a "peace-loving state"; the West German *Der Spiegel* (comparable to *Time Magazine*) once appeared with a cover entitled "Honecker's Africa Corps"). But, at the same time, this was about acquiring hard currency, and it affected relations between East Berlin and Moscow.

The more successful GDR training institutions became in attracting Third World cadets, and the more weapons from GDR firms were sought on the world market, the sooner this could be construed as East Germany competing economically, and eventually politically, with the hegemon in Moscow. That was why all decisions in this field were taken under the political guidance of the Party; any particular interest the NVA might have had vis-à-vis the Party and state took second place. The demand for instructors and support personnel began to exceed the limited NVA capacities during the 1980s, but that did not enter into consideration, either.

West Berlin

The mere existence of a separate political entity securely tied to the West in the middle of its own territory was always a thorn in the side of the GDR. All attempts and pressures between 1958 and 1961, including the threat of a renewed blockade of West Berlin, were designed to force the Western Allies to accept a peace treaty giving the GDR the full sovereignty over its territory and air space, including the access routes to West Berlin. The long-term Western presence in the city had resulted from the Potsdam agreements of 1945 but would, thus, have become impossible to maintain.

From a GDR perspective, aside from the political considerations, there were tangible military reasons to perceive the Western presence in West Berlin as a threat. To start with, Berlin lay astride the main East-West lines of communications, i.e., the principal links with home of any Soviet units deployed against NATO. A railway bypass had been built after 1961 *(Berliner Außenring)*, and the motorway around Berlin started by Hitler had eventually been completed, neither of which ran across West Berlin territory, but they were all under the surveillance and possibly within artillery range of the Western Allied garrison, which, altogether, amounted to a weak division.

West Berlin and the access routes were invaluable for all kinds of military intelligence. The many planes of the three Western Allies did not only carry goods and people to and from Berlin; they also served as platforms for optical and electronic intelligence. The transit roads from the West into Berlin (and further into Poland) also offered opportunities for exchanges, such as smuggling spies in or out, and of gathering military intelligence *en route*. The Allies had installed substantial assets for electronic intelligence in West Berlin itself, with the US signals intelligence installations on Teufelsberg as the best-known.

It should not surprise us, therefore, that concrete plans were developed to attack West Berlin in case of a military conflict in Central Europe. What does seem surprising is that the GDR should have been entrusted with this task. The first general deliberations to be found in the GDR and NVA files date from the early 1970s. Whether the Soviets had developed such plans at an earlier stage must remain open, nor can we explain with certainty why they should have transferred the responsibility for this operation to the East Germans at that particular point in time. We can suspect that the NVA had perfected its training and education sufficiently, or that there was a connection with the Four Power Agreement over West Berlin in the sense that the Soviets felt they had to compensate for conceding access rights to the Western Allies over the head of the GDR, or that this came with Honecker's succession of Ulbricht, engineered by Moscow – but all this is guesswork. That the decision must have been taken at about that time can be deduced from several events. The Land Forces (LaSK) Command was created on December 1, 1972, which, as we will see, was to command the Berlin operation. Also in 1972, the former Parachute Battalion 5 was renamed Parachute Battalion 40 *(Fallschirmjägerbataillon 40)*; it was later to be enlarged into *Luftsturmregiment 40* (Airborne Regiment 40); the battalion was also transferred from Military District V, subordinated directly to the

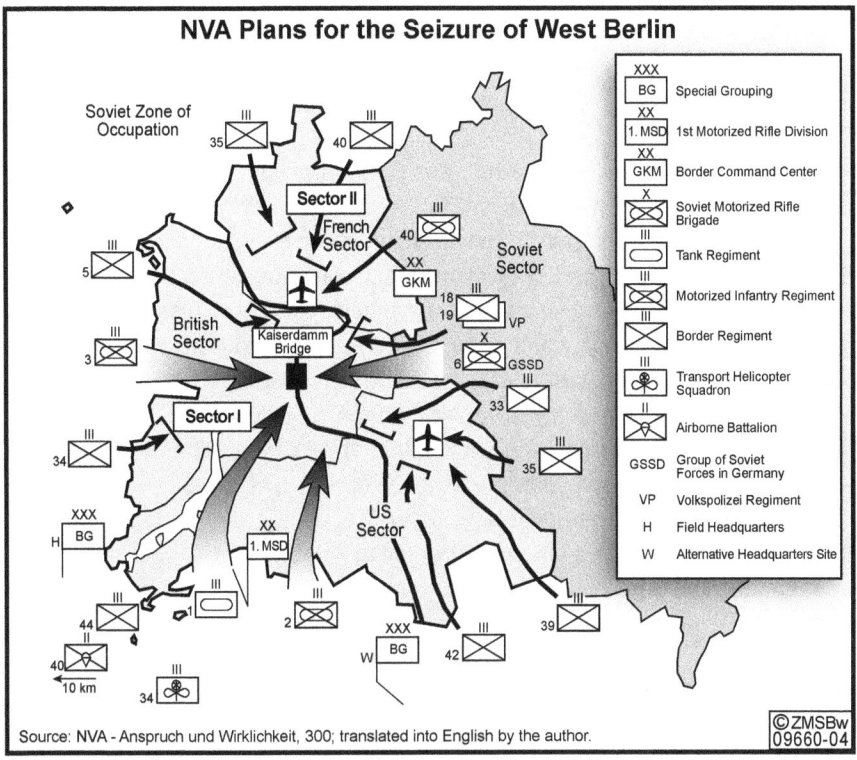

LaSK Command, and eventually relocated to Beelitz, south of Berlin. In 1973, we see the first exercises which obviously envisage a Berlin operation; one of them was to demonstrate a "Border Regiment Performing a Hasty Attack against a City" (Source: *Anordnung Nr. 32/73 des Stabschefs über organisatorische Maßnahmen zur Vorbereitung und Durchführung der Truppenübungen des GAR-40 und des GR 35.* BArch, GT 5728, f. 140–55). In the autumn of 1972, the LaSK Command ordered a war game to be held under the code name *"Turnier 73"* (Tournament 73). A "Special Grouping" *(Besondere Gruppierung)* commanded by the LaSK staff and comprising the 1st MSD (Potsdam) and the Border Command Center *(Grenzkommando Mitte,* i.e., the Border Regiments deployed around West Berlin) was to practice the "organization and command of combat operations to conquer a major city in the border region during the initial phase of the offensive operations conducted by an Army without the use of nuclear weapons."

These war games were intensified and held regularly during the 1980s; their code name was changed to *"Bordkante"* (Curbstone). The documents pertaining to these exercises reveal that the "Special Grouping" increased in size: apart from the 1st MSD and the Border Command Center, it would comprise the Soviet 6th Independent Motorized Rifle Brigade (which was almost the strength of a division, but

see page 206 f.

was not commanded by a general, thus, no Soviet general officer would be serving under an NVA superior), the Airborne Regiment 40, and other NVA units, as well as elements from the other "armed organs" including, of course, the Ministry of State Security (Stasi).

During the Cold War, West Berlin was a prime target for intelligence operations, be it by the Stasi Main Directorate for Intelligence or the NVA's Military Intelligence branch. They were interested in the strength, order of battle, and equipment of all three Western Allies, and in the routes they would need to take to deploy. The obvious intention was to slow down Western deployment and disrupt the concentration of their forces. Again and again, the exercise scenarios provided for a swift attack from the east and west so as to cut the enemy (Western) forces into a northern and southern half at a very early stage. Although Magdeburg was the preferred site for these war games, parallels with Stalingrad 1942/3 were more than obvious, and so were those with the plans for West Berlin.

A Berlin Operation was inconceivable as a separate strike. All those concerned knew that an attack against West Berlin would inevitably lead to war. A Berlin Operation could, thus, only be conceived of as part of a larger conflict which had erupted elsewhere. (What we do not know is whether the Warsaw Pact had also planned for a scenario where there would have been war in Central Europe, but West Berlin would have been bypassed and not attacked.) None of the exercises for a seizure of Berlin ever envisaged a nuclear strike; here, too, all Warsaw Pact planners knew that the use of nuclear warheads against West Berlin would have had devastating consequences for the "Capital of the GDR."

As far as has become known to date, the Western Powers never stored nuclear weapons in their half of the city. Had they done so, they would have found themselves in an unenviable situation in case of attack: Outnumbered as they were, they might have had decide whether to use their warheads or to let them fall into Eastern hands. Altogether, we probably know less about the Western Allies' plans for the defense of the "Free Berlin" they had pledged to protect than about the GDR's plans to attack it. Again, documents relating to this touchy subject (What would have been defended? What would have been surrendered straightaway? Which demolitions had been planned?) have not yet surfaced.

In all of its plans, the GDR military assumed that the Berlin Operation would have been led by a German command staff, the "Special Grouping Command," which would have been largely identical with the peacetime "LaSK" command in Potsdam. Some memoirs of GDR officers, however, show that there remained some doubts among high-ranking East German commanders as to whether this was really to happen if the moment came. There are some indications that the Soviet Union was also preparing a Berlin Operation under its own control, employing Soviet units.

"Policy of Peace" and Offensive Operational Planning

All plans of the Warsaw Pact Combined Forces were based on the premise that Western aggression had caused a war in Central Europe. Yet, as the distinction between external and internal aggression was somewhat blurred in Marxist-Leninist ideology which assumed a uniform "counterrevolution" by one multifaceted enemy instead, what exactly Moscow would define as "Western aggression" remained a subject for speculation. Even with hindsight, the Western scare of an offensive Soviet war does not seem to be totally unfounded.

Right into the 1980s, Soviet strategic and operational planning was characterized by the traumatic experience of the summer of 1941 – of an unexpected attack which had resulted in a devastating war in the Soviet Union itself. The chief Soviet aim was that nothing similar must ever happen again. That was why, if the Cold War turned hot, operations would have to be carried into enemy territory from the very beginning, if possible, by a preventive strike which would preempt the Western aggression. While the GDR public was being told continuously that their country pursued exclusively defensive aims, all military planning emphasized the offensive. All preparations assumed that the fighting would happen in West Germany; the overall strategic aim was to conquer Western Europe as far as the Atlantic.

Once the Cold War had come to an end, a number of studies were published rather quickly, usually based on documents found in the former GDR; some of them have still retained some value until today (*7.1* Basler, Das operative Denken; *7.9* Wettig, Warsaw Pact Planning). Later publications have covered the subject more exhaustively, particularly studies from other former Warsaw Pact countries which had held on to their files after the Pact collapsed (*7.2* Diedrich, Die DDR als Operations- und Durchmarschgebiet; *7.5* Moszumanski, Die Polnische Küstenfront; *7.8* Rijnoveanu, Die Auswirkungen). These publications offer a better understanding of the complexities and limitations of military planning within the Warsaw Pact structures, especially regarding the Soviet hegemony in this field as in all others. The willingness of former senior NVA generals to disclose past secrets continued to be very limited (most have since died without disclosing details), and testimonies in print remained rather general and sweeping. In some instances, later publications are even more taciturn than earlier ones by the same author.

As the Warsaw Pact forces were far superior in numbers, all planners took it for granted that, sooner or later, NATO would be forced to counterbalance its conventional inferiority by resorting to tactical nuclear weapons. Should this happen, an immediate massive nuclear reaction was foreseen; a politically controlled escalation, such as that envisaged by the NATO strategy of "Flexible Response," was inconceivable within the Eastern Alliance.

In NATO, not only the US as the hegemonial power owned nuclear weapons, but also the United Kingdom and France (albeit with different degrees of independence from US strategists). As opposed to that, in the Warsaw Pact, the Soviets alone had nuclear warheads. The NVA had, since the early 1960s, owned nuclear delivery systems which could have carried Soviet warheads to their targets. This included tactical nukes as well as intermediate range missiles, which could also be employed in an operational role. The first generation of nuclear-capable systems to be deployed within the GDR consisted of the "3R9 Luna" or "3R10 Luna-2" tactical ballistic missiles, known in the West as "Frog-3," and the medium-range "Scud-A" ("R-11 Elbrus") missiles. These were soon replaced by a second generation, which included "Frog-7" ("R-65 Luna-M") and "Scud-B" ("R-17") systems. All these were delivery vehicles whose targeting was so imprecise that they only made sense if fitted with nuclear warheads. During the 1980s, however, the "R-400 Oka" (NATO codename "SS-23") systems were introduced, which, at a range of about 500 kms, were sufficiently precise to also be useful if equipped with conventional warheads. There is no clear indication of whether GDR jets were ever expected to deliver atomic bombs in the proper sense; but the NVA missiles could also have been used to deliver chemical weapons.

In any case, the NVA placed a lot of emphasis on training its soldiers for combat in irradiated or contaminated terrain. The use of the protective suits and masks as well as decontamination procedures were practiced regularly.

Soviet military thinking did not envisage the prior definition of a *Schwerpunkt* (point of main effort) but relied on "massive strikes" in several directions. Two strategic directions had been defined for Germany: North German and South German. The North German one aimed at Denmark, the German and Dutch North Sea Coast, as well as the industrialized area of the Ruhr. The Polish Coastal Front was to operate in the North, with the 1st (Western) Front of the Soviet Forces in Germany to its left. What characterized all planning for the Polish Coastal Front was that its axis of attack was to be divided between the North (Denmark) and the West (along the North Sea Coast). The Polish Coastal Front was to include the NVA's 5th Army (effectively MB-V), while the Soviet 1st (Western) Front was to include the NVA's 3rd Army (i.e., MB-III). To its south, the 3rd Soviet (South-Western) Front was to attack, starting from Czechoslovakia. From the GDR perspective, the industrialized centers along the Rhine and Ruhr rivers, as well as that of Lorraine, were prioritized goals, while from the Soviets' global strategic perspective, what counted above all was to open up the Baltic Approaches and, thus, give the Red-Banner Baltic Fleet access to the open seas.

After 1990, some NVA officers claimed that the Soviets made an effort to avoid Polish troops facing British units, while East German elements should not be facing West German ones; however, the sources do not bear this out.

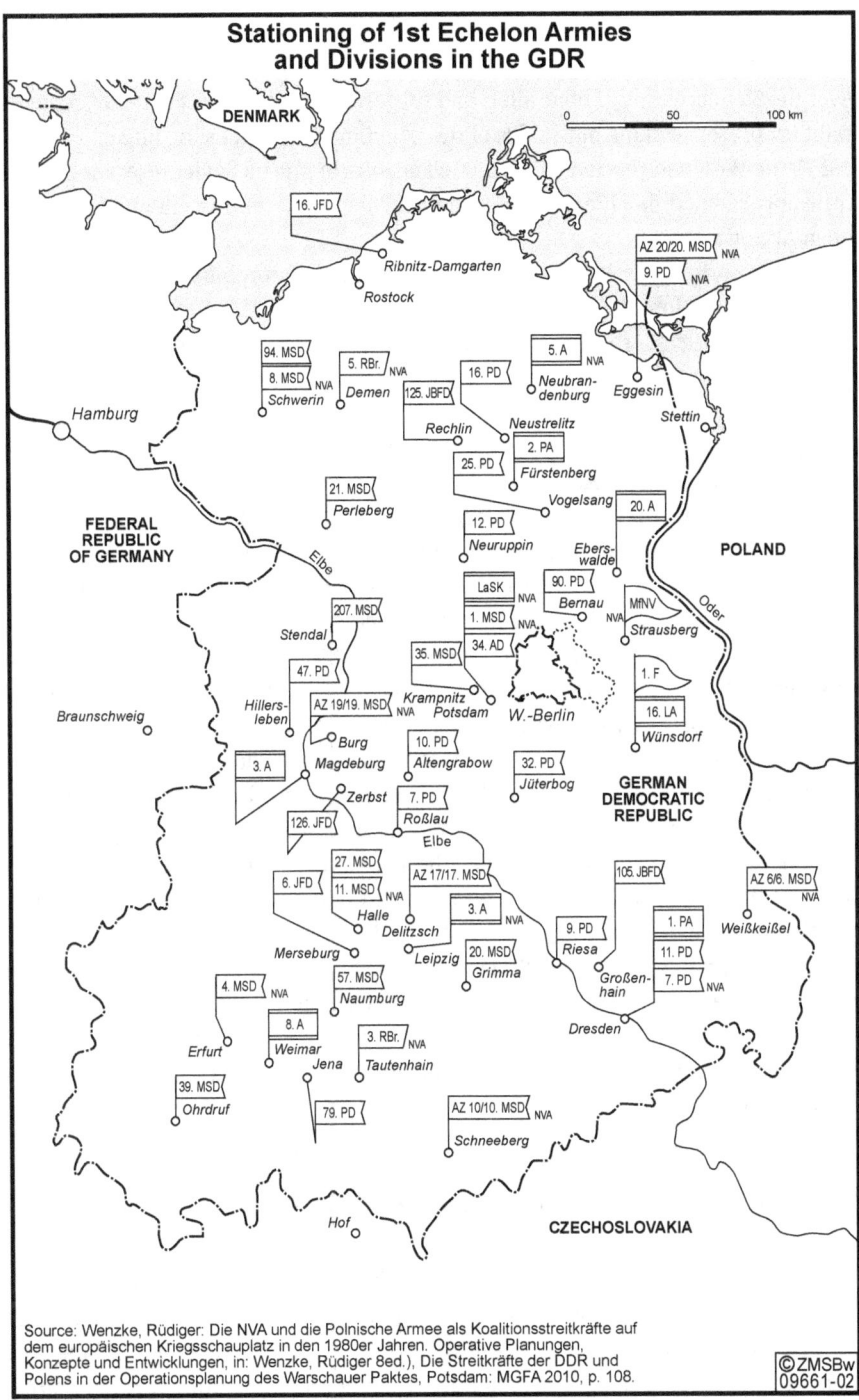

All these plans assumed that this 1st Strategic Echelon would be followed by a second one, which would be introduced from deep inside the Soviet Union. Whenever the Soviets or any of their allies had suggested the creation of zones of reduced military presence along both sides of the Iron Curtain (such as the Rapacki Plan of 1957), the West had reacted with skepticism, as bringing up Soviet reserves by land transport seemed much easier than the transfer of US reinforcements across the open Atlantic.

In the early 1980s, however, several developments combined to put into question the assumption of the unhindered approach of a 2nd Echelon. After the unrest in Poland in 1980/1, the lines of communication through that country could no longer be taken for granted. At the same time, NATO began to adopt the US FOFA ("Follow-On Forces Attack") concept, which aimed at cordoning off the 2nd Echelon along the Polish-German border and degrading it substantively before it even reached the battlefield. Accordingly, NATO introduced several weapons systems which could deliver nonnuclear munitions over intermediate distances.

That NATO should actually deploy these represented, first and foremost, a diplomatic defeat for the GDR, which had expected to weaken the Western alliance's cohesion by supporting the West German peace movement sufficiently and, thus, stop the deployment of intermediate range ballistic missiles (Pershing-2) and Cruise missiles. Both of these as well as the "Tornado" fighter bomber used by several European air forces (which was capable of flying at extremely low altitudes and, thus, avoiding Eastern Bloc radar) made it seem possible that, in case of war, NATO forces might slow down and degrade the 2nd Strategic Echelon. Ten years earlier, the Soviet Union would have countered a situation like that by making increased armaments efforts. By the mid-1980s, the resources of the socialist hegemon no longer sufficed for such a course of action. In addition, there had been change within the Soviet Union itself – a change that the GDR had failed to foresee.

The nomination of Mikhail Sergeyevich Gorbachev as Secretary General of the CPSU indicated that a new generation of efficiency-minded technocrats was succeeding the old, ideology-driven cadres. This made room for not only glasnost and perestroika but also a new strategic thinking which could not fail to affect the GDR's security policies.

The New Soviet Military Doctrine of the 1980s

The beginnings of new Soviet doctrinal thinking go back to before the Gorbachev era, although there is no indication that the non-Soviet allies had any indication of it during the Brezhnev years. This probably indicates that the new thinking was not due so much to ideological relaxation as to inherent necessities. In other words,

Gorbachev did not start the upheavals which would eventually bring about the end of the Soviet Union, but he was the one who channeled processes of change which had predated his coming into office.

In December 1984, the Chief of the Soviet General Staff, Marshal Sergey Fyodorovich Akhromeyev, pointed out that the future Warsaw Pact strategic doctrine would have to be defensive in character. Throughout 1985, the NVA command structure revised its operational planning in this sense, expecting to be fighting in its own country.

This change did not occur without protest. Gorbachev had to convince critics both in his own country and among his allies. All this posed several existential problems for the GDR. The specter of fighting on its own territory inevitably led to the question of whether defending the GDR made any sense at all if it was to be devastated to such a degree that it would cease to exist as an independent political entity. This would be exacerbated even further by the early use of weapons of mass destruction, which was then still considered to be the norm. On the other hand, the term "Alliance doctrine" was used for the first time, and the Berlin Document's reference to separate doctrines of each member state seemed to promise the non-Soviet Warsaw Pact countries more political and military leeway than before. This could and should have meant the development of a new military doctrine for the GDR which would take into account the changing circumstances.

However, the rigid and gerontocratic GDR leadership was unwilling to accept the winds of change that were blowing over the Soviet Union. The SED's chief ideologue Kurt Hager, member of the Party's Politburo, put it succinctly: "If your neighbor repapers his apartment, would you feel like you should also repaper your apartment?" There was no clearer way of illustrating how estranged the East German state had become from the Soviet Union.

The GDR began to reduce troop strengths by about 10,000 men in early 1989; six tank regiments and one LSK/LV squadron were stood down. All propaganda to the contrary notwithstanding, this was not motivated by *détente* policies, but was simply due to the fact that, in view of declining demographics, the GDR population could not maintain its current numbers. In spite of reductions, the political leadership of the GDR insisted that the NVA and the Soviet troops in Germany should defend as far West as possible and oust an invasion from GDR territory at the earliest possible moment. What this demand overlooked was that none of the socialist nations, and certainly not the GDR, were able to provide the resources in personnel and matériel that this would have required.

The situation demanded a degree of adaptation and change that the political and military top brass of the GDR was incapable of accepting. Thus, the GDR put an increasing distance between itself and the Soviet Union. That meant conflicting demands placed upon the armed forces by being part of a Soviet-controlled military

Fig. 34:
On June 21, 1989, journalists – including those from the West – observe the dismantling and scrapping of T-55 A tanks from six NVA tank regiments which had been taken out of service as part of troop reductions and disarmament.
BArch, Bild 183-1989-0621-040/ Matthias Hiekel

alliance and, simultaneously, part of a system designed to maintain the SED regime in power.

The GDR alienated itself from its true power basis by estranging itself from the Soviet Union. The East German state had always been a political entity sustained by Soviet determination and will. When Moscow was no longer willing to sustain it, the GDR had reached the end of the line.

Appendix

Abbreviations

BArch/BA	Bundesarchiv (Federal Archives)	DVdI	Deutsche Verwaltung des Innern (German Administration of the Interior)
BMP	Schützenpanzer (Armored Infantry Fighting Vehicle)		
BND	Bundesnachrichtendienst (Federal Intelligence Service)	DVI	Deutsche Verwaltung des Innern (The Soviet-controlled forerunner of the GDR Ministry of the Interior)
BRDM	Gepanzertes Aufklärungs- und Patrouillenfahrzeug (Armored Reconnaissance and Patrol Vehicle (ARPV))	DVP	Deutsche Volkspolizei (German People's Police)
		EK	Entlassungskandidat (Candidate for discharge)
BStU	Bundesbeauftragte/r für die Unterlagen des Staatssicherheitsdienst der ehemaligen Deutschen Demokratischen Republik (Federal Commissioner for the Documents of the State Security Service of the former GDR)	FDJ	Freie Deutsche Jugend (Free German Youth)
		FOFA	Follow-on Forces Attack (Angriff auf nachrückende Kräfte)
		FRELIMO	Liberation Front of Mozambique (Befreiungsfront von Mosambik)
COMECON	Council for Mutual Economic Assistance (Rat für gegenseitige Wirtschaftshilfe (RGW))	FRG	Federal Republic of Germany (Bundesrepublik Deutschland)
		GDR	German Democratic Republic (Deutsche Demokratische Republik)
CPSU	Communist Party of the Soviet Union (Kommunistische Partei der Sowjetunion (KPdSU))	GST	Gesellschaft für Sport und Technik (Sport and Technology Association)
CSCE	Conference on Security and Co-operation in Europe (Konferenz über Sicherheit und Zusammenarbeit in Europa)	HA I	Hauptabteilung I (Main Department)
		HVA	Hauptverwaltung für Ausbildung (Training Main Directorate)
CSSR	Czechoslovak Socialist Republic (Tschechoslowakische Sozialistische Republik)	KGB	Committee for State Security (Komitee für Staatssicherheit)
		KPD	Kommunistische Partei Deutschland (Communist Party of Germany)
DDR	Deutsche Demokratische Republik (German Democratic Republic)	KSZE	Konferenz über Sicherheit und Zusammenarbeit in Europa (Conference on Security and Co-operation in Europe (CSCE))
DEFA	Deutsche Film-AG (German Film Corporation of the GDR)		
DGP	Deutsche Grenzpolizei (German Border Police)	KVP	Kasernierte Volkspolizei (Barracked People's Police)
DHS	Diensthabendes System der Luftverteidigung (Duty Air Defense System)	LaSK	Kommando Landstreitkräfte (Land Forces Command)

LSK	Luftstreitkräfte (Air Force)	PD	Panzerdivision (Armored Division)
LV	Luftverteidigung (Air Defense)	PDS	Partei des demokratischen Sozialismus (Party of Democratic Socialism)
LVD	Luftverteidigungsdivision (Air Defense Division)		
MAFE	Militärakademie Friedrich Engels (Military Academy "Friedrich Engels")	PHV	Politische Hauptverwaltung (Political Main Directorate)
		SAG	Sowjetische Aktiengesellschaft (Soviet Incorporated Company)
MB-V	Militärbezirk V (Military District V)		
MfNV	Ministerium für Nationale Verteidigung (Ministry of National Defense)	SAPMO	Stiftung Archiv der Parteien und Massenorganisationen der DDR (Special Archive of the Former Political Parties and Mass Organizations of the GDR)
MfS	Ministerium für Staatssicherheit (Ministry for State Security)		
MGFA	Militärgeschichtliches Forschungsamt (Bundeswehr Military History Office)	SDAG	Sowjetisch-Deutsche Aktiengesellschaft (Soviet-German Joint Stock Company)
MGI	Militärgeschichtliches Institut der DDR (GDR Institute of Military History)	SED	Sozialistische Einheitspartei Deutschlands (Socialist Unity Party)
		SMAD	Sowjetische Militäradministration in Deutschland (Soviet Military Administration in Germany)
MHM	Militärhistorisches Museum (Military History Museum)		
MPH	Militärpolitische Hochschule (Academy for Military Politics)	USSR	Union of Soviet Socialist Republics (Union der Sozialistischen Sowjetrepubliken))
MRCA	Multi-Role Combat Aircraft (Mehrzweckkampfflugzeug Tornado)	VEB	Volkseigener Betrieb (Publicly Owned Enterprise)
MSD	Mot.-Schützendivision (Mechanized Infantry Division)	VVB UNIMAK	Vereinigung Volkseigener Betriebe Universalmaschinen (Combined Publicly Owned Enterprises Universal Machinery)
NATO	North Atlantic Treaty Organization (Nordatlantische Vertragsorganisation)		
NCO	Non-commissioned officer (Unteroffizier)	ZAIG	Zentrale Auswertungs- und Informationsgruppe (Central Evaluation and Information Group, MfS)
NKVD	Narodnyy Komissariat Vnutrennikh Del (People's Commissariat for Internal Affairs)		
NVA	Nationale Volksarmee (National People's Army)	ZMSBw	Zentrum für Militärgeschichte und Sozialwissenschaften der Bundeswehr (Bundeswehr Centre of Military History and Social Sciences)
NVR	Nationaler Verteidigungsrat (National Defense Council)		

Rank equivalents

(Army, LSK/LV accordingly)

GDR	US/UK
Generalmajor	Brigadier General (UK: Brigadier)
Generalleutnant	Major General
Generaloberst	Lieutenant General
Armeegeneral	General

Bibliography

The military history of the GDR has not yet found major interest among English-speaking scholars. The literature available in English is, therefore, sparse; most titles in this bibliographical overview are in German. Wherever possible, English-language titles are listed.

General
The best overview in German is the book series published by the *Militärgeschichtliches Forschungsamt/ Zentrum für Militärgeschichte und Sozialwissenschaften der Bundeswehr* in Potsdam, *Militärgeschichte der DDR*. For that reason, it is listed separately here. At the end of this general list, two titles are included which do not, strictly speaking, form part of this series, but which are indispensable and include material which can facilitate any approach to this subject.

0.1 Diedrich, Torsten, and Rüdiger Wenzke: Die getarnte Armee. Geschichte der Kasernierten Volkspolizei der DDR 1952–1956, Berlin: Ch. Links 2001 (= Militärgeschichte der DDR, 1)

0.2 Fingerle, Stephan: Waffen in Arbeiterhand? Die Rekrutierung des Offizierkorps der NVA und ihrer Vorläufer. Die "Arbeiter-und-Bauern-Armee" zwischen Anspruch und Wirklichkeit, Berlin: Ch. Links 2001 (= Militärgeschichte der DDR, 2)

0.3 Ehlert, Hans (ed): Armee ohne Zukunft. Die NVA und die deutsche Einheit. Zeitzeugenberichte und Dokumente, Berlin: Ch. Links 2002 (= Militärgeschichte der DDR, 3)

0.4 Wagner, Armin: Walter Ulbricht und die geheime Sicherheitspolitik der SED. Der Nationale Verteidigungsrat der DDR und seine Vorgeschichte (1953–1971), Berlin: Ch. Links 2002 (= Militärgeschichte der DDR, 4)

0.5 Hagemann, Frank: Parteiherrschaft in der Nationalen Volksarmee. Zur Rolle der SED bei der inneren Entwicklung der DDR-Streitkräfte (1956 bis 1971), Berlin: Ch. Links 2002 (= Militärgeschichte der DDR, 5)

0.6 Müller, Christian Th.: Tausend Tage bei der "Asche". Unteroffiziere in der NVA. Untersuchungen zu Alltag und Binnenstruktur einer "sozialistischen" Armee, Berlin: Ch. Links 2003 (= Militärgeschichte der DDR, 6)

0.7 Ehlert, Hans, and Armin Wagner (eds): Genosse General! Die Militärelite der DDR in biografischen Skizzen, Berlin: Ch. Links 2003 (= Militärgeschichte der DDR, 7)

0.8 Ehlert, Hans, and Matthias Rogg (eds): Militär, Staat und Gesellschaft in der DDR. Forschungsfelder, Ergebnisse, Perspektiven, Berlin: Ch. Links 2004 (= Militärgeschichte der DDR, 8)

0.9 Wenzke, Rüdiger (ed): Staatsfeinde in Uniform? Widerständiges Verhalten und politische Verfolgung in der NVA, Berlin: Ch. Links 2005 (= Militärgeschichte der DDR, 9)

0.10 Umbach, Frank: Das rote Bündnis. Entwicklung und Zerfall des Warschauer Paktes 1955–1991, Berlin: Ch. Links 2005 (= Militärgeschichte der DDR, 10)

0.11 Diedrich, Torsten, and Ilko S. Kowalczuk (eds): Staatsgründung auf Raten? Auswirkungen des Volksaufstandes 1953 und des Mauerbaus 1961 auf Staat, Militär und Gesellschaft der DDR, Berlin: Ch. Links 2005 (= Militärgeschichte der DDR, 11)

0.12 Heitmann, Clemens: Schützen und Helfen? Luftschutz und Zivilverteidigung in der DDR 1955 bis 1989/90, Berlin: Ch. Links 2006 (= Militärgeschichte der DDR, 12)

0.13 Niemetz, Daniel: Das feldgraue Erbe. Die Wehrmachtseinflüsse im Militär der SBZ/DDR (1948/49–1989), Berlin: Ch. Links 2006 (= Militärgeschichte der DDR, 13)

https://doi.org/10.1515/9783111588414-011

0.14 Wagner, Armin, and Matthias Uhl: BND contra Sowjetarmee. Westdeutsche Militärspionage in der DDR, Berlin: Ch. Links 2007 (= Militärgeschichte der DDR, 14)

0.15 Rogg, Matthias: Armee des Volkes? Militär und Gesellschaft in der DDR, Berlin: Ch. Links 2008 (= Militärgeschichte der DDR, 15)

0.16 Diedrich, Torsten, Winfried Heinemann, and Christian Ostermann: Der Warschauer Pakt. Von der Gründung bis zum Zusammenbruch (1955–1991), Berlin: Ch. Links 2009 (= Militärgeschichte der DDR, 16)

0.17 Sälter, Gerhard: Grenzpolizisten. Konformität, Verweigerung und Repression in der Grenzpolizei und den Grenztruppen der DDR 1952–1965, Berlin: Ch. Links 2009 (= Militärgeschichte der DDR, 17)

0.18 Finke, Julian-André: Hüter des Luftraumes? Die Luftstreitkräfte der DDR im Diensthabenden System des Warschauer Paktes, Berlin: Ch. Links 2010 (= Militärgeschichte der DDR, 18)

0.19 Diedrich, Torsten, and Walter Süß (eds): Militär und Staatssicherheit im Sicherheitskonzept der Warschauer-Pakt-Staaten, Berlin: Ch. Links 2010 (= Militärgeschichte der DDR, 19)

0.20 Bröckermann, Heiner: Landesverteidigung und Militarisierung. Militär- und Sicherheitspolitik der DDR in der Ära Honecker 1971–1989, Berlin: Ch. Links 2011 (= Militärgeschichte der DDR, 20)

0.21 Storkmann, Klaus: Geheime Solidarität? Militärbeziehungen und Militärhilfen der DDR in die Dritte Welt, Berlin: Ch. Links 2012 (= Militärgeschichte der DDR, 21)

0.22 Wenzke, Rüdiger: Ulbrichts Soldaten. Die Nationale Volksarmee 1956 bis 1971, Berlin: Ch. Links 2013 (= Militärgeschichte der DDR, 22)

0.23 Wenzke, Rüdiger (ed): "Damit hatten wir die Initiative verloren". Zur Rolle der bewaffneten Kräfte in der DDR 1989/90, Berlin: Ch. Links 2014 (= Militärgeschichte der DDR, 23)

0.24 Maurer, Jochen: Halt – Staatsgrenze! Alltag, Dienst und Innenansichten der Grenztruppen der DDR, Berlin: Ch. Links 2015 (= Militärgeschichte der DDR, 24)

0.25 Bange, Oliver: Sicherheit und Staat. Die Bündnis- und Militärpolitik der DDR im internationalen Kontext 1969 bis 1990, Berlin: Ch. Links 2017 (= Militärgeschichte der DDR, 25)

0.26 Wenzke, Rüdiger: Wo stehen unsere Truppen? NVA und Bundeswehr in der ČSSR-Krise 1968. Mit ausgewählten Dokumenten zur militärischen Lagebeurteilung, Berlin: Ch. Links 2018 (= Militärgeschichte der DDR, 26)

0.27 Beßer, Udo: Vom Soldatsein. Offizier in zwei deutschen Nachkriegsarmeen. With an Introduction by Rüdiger Wenzke, Berlin: Ch. Links 2019 (= Militärgeschichte der DDR, 27)

0.28 Niemetz, Daniel: Staatsmacht am Ende. Der Militär- und Sicherheitsapparat der DDR in Krise und Umbruch 1985 bis 1990, Berlin: Ch. Links 2020 (= Militärgeschichte der DDR, 28)

0.29 Froh, Klaus, und Rüdiger Wenzke: Die Generale und Admirale der NVA. Ein biographisches Handbuch, Berlin 2000 (5th Ed): Ch. Links 2007

0.30 Diedrich, Torsten, Hans Ehlert and Rüdiger Wenzke: Im Dienste der Partei. Handbuch der bewaffneten Organe der DDR, Berlin: Ch. Links 1998

A volume published by the GDR Military History Institute (MGI) is useful for dates and times, but tendentious in its evaluations:

0.31 Armee für Frieden und Sozialismus. Geschichte der Nationalen Volksarmee der DDR, (East) Berlin: Militärverlag der DDR 1985

Chapter 1:

For GDR history in general, see:

1.1 Timmermann, Heiner (ed): Das war die DDR. DDR-Forschung im Fadenkreuz von Herrschaft, Außenbeziehungen, Kultur und Souveränität, Münster: Lit 2004 (= Dokumente und Schriften der Europäischen Akademie Otzenhausen, 128)

1.2 Timmermann, Heiner (ed): Die DDR in Deutschland. Ein Rückblick auf 50 Jahre, Berlin: Duncker und Humblot 2001 (= Dokumente und Schriften der Europäischen Akademie Otzenhausen e.V., 93)

1.3 Mählert, Ulrich: Kleine Geschichte der DDR, Munich: C.H. Beck 2009

1.4 Richter, Hedwig: Die DDR, Paderborn: Schöningh 2009

1.5 Scholtyseck, Joachim: Die Außenpolitik der DDR, Munich: Oldenbourg 2003 (= Enzyklopädie deutscher Geschichte, 69)

1.6 Schroeder, Klaus: Der SED-Staat. Geschichte und Strukturen der DDR (1949–1990), Böhlau (3rd Ed.), Cologne 2013

1.7 Weber, Hermann: DDR. Grundriß der Geschichte 1945–1981, Hannover: Fackelträger 1982

1.8 Weber, Hermann: Die DDR 1945–1990, Munich: Oldenbourg 2000 (= Oldenbourg Grundriß der Geschichte, 20)

1.9 Wehler, Hans-Ulrich: Deutsche Gesellschaftsgeschichte, 5: Bundesrepublik und DDR 1949–1990, Munich: C.H. Beck 2008

1.10 Wolle, Stefan: Die heile Welt der Diktatur. Alltag und Herrschaft in der DDR 1971–1989, Berlin: Ch. Links 1998

1.11 Grieder, Peter: The German Democratic Republic, Basingstoke: Palgrave Macmillan 2012

1.12 Deutscher Bundestag (ed): Materialien der Enquete-Kommission "Auf-arbeitung von Geschichte und Folgen der SED-Diktatur in Deutschland" (12. Wahlperiode des Deutschen Bundestages), 9 vols., Baden-Baden: Nomos 1995

1.13 Deutscher Bundestag (ed): Materialien der Enquete-Kommission "Über-windung der Folgen der SED-Diktatur im Prozeß der Deutschen Einheit" (13. Wahlperiode des Deutschen Bundestages), 8 vols, Frankfurt: Suhrkamp 1999

1.14 Fulbrook, Mary: Anatomy of a Dictatorship. Inside the GDR, 1949–1989, Oxford: Oxford University Press 1995

1.15 Fulbrook, Mary (ed): Power and Society in the GDR, 1961–1979. The "Normalisation of Rule"?, Oxford: Berghahn Books 2009

For an overview of the state of the art, see:

1.16 Hoyer, Katja: Beyond the Wall. East Germany, 1949–1990, Dublin: Allen Lane 2023

1.17 Eppelmann, Rainer, Bernd Faulenbach, and Ulrich Mählert (eds): Bilanz und Perspektiven der DDR-Forschung, Paderborn: Schöningh 2003

1.18 Kocka, Jürgen: "Eine durchherrschte Gesellschaft", in: Kaelble, Hartmut, Jürgen Kocka und Hartmut Zwahr (eds): Sozialgeschichte der DDR, Stuttgart: Klett Cotta 1994, 547–553

NVA history in general:

1.19 Backerra, Manfred (ed): NVA. Ein Rückblick für die Zukunft. Zeitzeugen berichten über ein Stück deutscher Militärgeschichte, Cologne: Markus 1992

1.20 Born, Hendrik: Es kommt alles ganz anders. Erinnerungen eines Zeitzeugen an die Volksmarine der DDR und das Leben danach, Hamburg: Mittler 2018

1.21 Brühl, Reinhard: Die Hoffnung bleibt. Erinnerungen eines Militärhistorikers, Potsdam: Knotenpunkt 2018

1.22 Echternkamp, Jörg (ed): Militär und Gesellschaft in Ost- und Westdeutschland 1970–1990, Berlin: Ch. Links 2021 (= Deutsch-deutsche Militärgeschichte, 3)

1.23 Fischer, Egbert, Hansjürgen Usczeck and Werner Knoll (eds): Was war die NVA? Studien – Analysen – Berichte. Zur Geschichte der Nationalen Volksarmee, ed. by der Arbeitsgruppe Geschichte der NVA und Integration ehemaliger NVA-Angehöriger in Gesellschaft und Bundeswehr beim Landesvorstand Ost des DBwV, Berlin: no publisher 2001

1.24 Fischer, Egbert (ed): Was war die NVA? ... nachgetragen. Studien – Analysen – Berichte. Zur Geschichte der Nationalen Volksarmee, ed. by der Arbeitsgruppe Geschichte der NVA und Integration ehemaliger NVA-Angehöriger in Gesellschaft und Bundeswehr beim Landesvorstand Ost des DBwV, Berlin: no publisher 2007

1.25 Fischer, Egbert (ed): Was war die NVA? Zapfenstreich. Studien – Analysen – Berichte. Zur Geschichte der Nationalen Volksarmee, ed. by der Arbeitsgruppe Geschichte der NVA und Integration ehemaliger NVA-Angehöriger in Gesellschaft und Bundeswehr beim Landesvorstand Ost des DBwV, Berlin: no publisher 2010

1.26 Hoffmann, Theodor: Das letzte Kommando. Ein Minister erinnert sich, Herford: Mittler 1993

1.27 Koop, Volker, and Dietmar Schössler: Erbe NVA. Eindrücke aus ihrer Geschichte und den Tagen der Wende, Waldbröl: Akademie der Bundeswehr für Information und Kommunikation 1992

1.28 Lautsch, Siegfried: Grundzüge des operativen Denkens in der NATO. Ein zeitgeschichtlicher Rückblick auf die 1980er Jahre, Berlin: Miles 2017

1.29 Loch, Thorsten: Deutsche Generale 1945 bis 1990. Profession – Karriere – Herkunft, Berlin: Ch. Links 2021 (= Deutsch-deutsche Militärgeschichte, 2)

1.30 Löffler, Hans-Georg: Soldat der NVA von Anfang bis Ende, Berlin: edition Ost 2006

1.31 Naumann, Klaus (ed): NVA – Anspruch und Wirklichkeit nach ausgewählten Dokumenten, Berlin: Mittler 1993

1.32 Port, Andrew I.: Conflict and Stability in the German Democratic Republic, Cambridge: Cambridge University Press 2007

1.33 Stechbarth, Horst: Soldat im Osten. Erinnerungen und Erlebnisse aus fünf Jahrzehnten, Hüllhorst: Stadt und Buch 2006

1.34 Wenzel, Otto: Kriegsbereit. Der Nationale Verteidigungsrat der DDR 1960 bis 1989, Cologne: Wissenschaft und Politik 1995

Chapter 2:

2.1 Diedrich, Torsten: "Die Kasernierte Volkspolizei (1952–1956)", in: Diedrich, Torsten, Hans Ehlert and Rüdiger Wenzke: Im Dienste der Partei. Handbuch der bewaffneten Organe der DDR, Berlin: Ch. Links 1998, 339–69

2.2 Diedrich, Torsten: "Herrschaftssicherung, Aufrüstung und Militarisierung im SED-Staat", in: Ehlert, Hans, and Matthias Rogg (eds): Militär, Staat und Gesellschaft in der DDR. Forschungsfelder, Ergebnisse, Perspektiven, Berlin: Ch. Links 2004 (= Militärgeschichte der DDR, 8), 257–83

2.3 Diedrich, Torsten: Waffen gegen das Volk. Der 17. Juni 1953 in der DDR, Munich: Oldenbourg 2003

2.4 Millington, Richard: State, Society and Memories of the Uprising of 17 June 1953 in the GDR, Basingstoke: Palgrave Macmillan 2014

2.5 Ostermann, Christian F., and Malcolm Byrne: Uprising in East Germany 1953. The Cold War, the German Question, and the First Major Upheaval behind the Iron Curtain, Budapest: Central European University Press 2001

2.6 Diedrich, Torsten: "Prägende Veränderungen im Militär- und Sicherheitssystem der DDR nach 1953 und 1961 im Vergleich", in: Torsten Diedrich and Ilko S. Kowalczuk (eds), Staatsgründung auf Raten? Auswirkungen des Volksaufstandes 1953 und des Mauerbaus 1961 auf Staat, Militär und Gesellschaft der DDR, Berlin: Ch. Links 2005 (= Militärgeschichte der DDR, 11), 119–37

2.7 Helfert, Rolf: "Gesamtdeutsche Offiziertagung" in Ost-Berlin 1955. Feldmarschall Paulus, Ulbricht und die deutsche Einheit, in: Militärgeschichte 5 (1995), 31–5

2.8 Mastny, Vojtech, and Malcolm Byrne (eds): A Cardboard Castle? An Inside History of the Warsaw Pact, Budapest: Central European UP 2005

2.9 Die Berliner Mauer. Vom Sperrwall zum Denkmal, Bonn: DNK 2009 (= Schriftenreihe des Deutschen Nationalkomitees für Denkmalschutz, 76/1)

2.10 Harrison, Hope M.: Driving the Soviets up the Wall. Soviet-East German Relations, 1953–1961, Princeton, N.J.: Princeton University Press, 2003

2.11 Henke, Klaus-Dietmar (ed): Die Mauer. Errichtung, Überwindung, Erinnerung, Munich: dtv 2011

2.12 Maurer, Jochen: Dienst an der Mauer. Der Alltag der Grenztruppen rund um Berlin, Berlin: Ch. Links 2011

2.13 Schmidt, Leo: "The Architecture and Message of the 'Wall'", 1961–1989, in: German Politics and Society 29 (2011), 2, 57–77

2.14 Taylor, Fred: The Berlin Wall. 13 August 1961 – 9 November 1989, London: Bloomsbury 2006

2.15 Hertle, Hans-Hermann: The Berlin Wall Story. Biography of a Monument, Berlin: Ch. Links 2016

2.16 Storkmann, Klaus P.: Das chinesische Prinzip in der NVA. Vom Umgang der SED mit den Generalen und Offizieren in der frühen NVA. Eine Dokumentation, Berlin: Köster 2001 (= Beiträge zur Friedensforschung und Sicherheitspolitik, 1)

2.17 Uhl, Matthias: "Storming on to Paris. The 1962 Buria Exercise and the Planned Solution of the Berlin Crisis", in: Mastny, Vojtech, Sven Holtsmark, and Andreas Wenger (eds): War Plans and Alliances in the Cold War. Threat perceptions in the East and West, London: Routledge 2006, 46–71

2.18 Bischof, Gunter, Stefan Karner, and Peter Ruggenthaler (eds): The Prague Spring and the Warsaw Pact Invasion of Czechoslovakia in 1968, Lanham, MD: Lexington Books 2010

2.19 Gildea, Robert, James Mark and Annette Warring (eds): Europe's 1968. Voices of Revolt, Oxford: Oxford University Press 2013

2.20 Tismaneanu, Vladimir: Promises of 1968. Crisis, Illusion, and Utopia, Budapest: Central European University Press 2011

2.21 Wenzke, Rüdiger: Die NVA und der Prager Frühling 1968. Die Rolle Ulbrichts und der DDR-Streitkräfte bei der Niederschlagung der tschechoslowakischen Reformbewegung, Berlin: Ch. Links 1995 (= Forschungen zur DDR-Geschichte, 5)

2.22 Bange, Oliver: "The German Problem and Security in Europe. Hindrance or Catalyst on the Path to 1989–1990?", in: Mark Kramer and Vít Smetana (eds): Imposing, Maintaining, and Tearing Open the Iron Curtain. The Cold War and East-Central Europe, 1945–1989, Lanham, MD: Lexington University Press, 2014, 197–210

2.23 Geiger, Tim: "Der NATO-Doppelbeschluss. Vorgeschichte und Implementierung", in: Becker-Schaum, Christoph, et al. (eds): "Entrüstet Euch!". Nuklearkrise, NATO-Doppelbeschluss und Friedensbewegung, Paderborn: Schöningh 2012, 54–70

2.24 Morgan, Michael Cotey: The Final Act. The Helsinki Accords and the Transformation of the Cold War, Princeton, NJ: Princeton University Press, 2018

2.25 Ploetz, Michael, and Hans-Peter Müller: Ferngelenkte Friedensbewegung? DDR und UdSSR im Kampf gegen den NATO-Doppelbeschluß, Münster: Lit 2004 (= Diktatur und Widerstand, 6)

2.26 Selvage, Douglas, and Walter Süß: Staatssicherheit und KSZE-Prozess. MfS zwischen SED und KGB (1972–1989), Göttingen: Vandenhoeck & Ruprecht 2019

2.27 Szporer, Michael: Solidarity. The Great Workers Strike of 1980, Lanham, MD: Lexington Books 2012

2.28 Villaume, Poul, and Oliver Bange (eds): The Long Détente. Changing Concepts of Security and Cooperation in Europe, 1950s–1980s, Budapest: Central European University Press 2017

2.29 Wilke, Manfred, Reinhardt Gutsche, and Michael Kubina: Die SED-Führung und die Unterdrückung der polnischen Oppositionsbewegung 1980/81. Cologne: BIOS 1994 (= Berichte des Bundesinstituts für Ostwissenschaftliche und Internationale Studien, 36)

2.30	Olschowsky, Burkhard: Einvernehmen und Konflikt. Das Verhältnis zwischen der DDR und der Volksrepublik Polen 1980–1989, Osnabrück: fibre 2005 (= Veröffentlichungen der Deutsch-Polnischen Gesellschaft, 7)
2.31	Miles, Simon: "The War Scare that Wasn't. Able Archer 83 and the Myths of the Second Cold War", in: Journal of Cold War Studies 22 (2020), 86–118
2.32	Farwick, Dieter (ed): Ein Staat – eine Armee. Von der NVA zur Bundeswehr, Frankfurt: Report 1992
2.33	Heinemann, Winfried: "East German Army Personnel and Equipment in the Bundeswehr After 1990", in: Caplovic, Miloslav, Mária Stanová and André Rakoto (eds): Exiting War. Post-Conflict Military Operations. 6th International Conference, Military History Working Group, Bratislava: MGFA 2007, 215–23
2.34	Koop, Volker: Abgewickelt? Auf den Spuren der Nationalen Volksarmee, Bonn: Bouvier 1995

Chapter 3:

3.1	Borchert, Jürgen: Die Zusammenarbeit des Ministeriums für Staatssicherheit (MfS) mit dem sowjetischen KGB in den 70er und 80er Jahren. Ein Kapitel aus der Geschichte der SED-Herrschaft, Münster: Lit 2006 (= Diktatur und Widerstand, 13)
3.2	Buchbender, Ortwin, and Rolf Rothe: "Hilfe für geflüchtete Soldaten aus der DDR. Die Deutsche Gesellschaft für Sozialbeziehungen e.V., 1963–1991", in: Deutschland-Archiv 42 (2009), 1023–32
3.3	Giese, Daniel: Die NVA als Parteiarmee, in: Ehlert, Hans, and Matthias Rogg (eds): Militär, Staat und Gesellschaft in der DDR. Forschungsfelder, Ergebnisse, Perspektiven, Berlin: Ch. Links 2004 (= Militärgeschichte der DDR, 8), 285–302
3.4	Gieseke, Jens: Mielke-Konzern. Die Geschichte der Stasi 1945–1990, Stuttgart: dva 2001
3.5	Gieseke, Jens: The History of the Stasi. East Germany's Secret Police 1945–1990, Oxford: Berghahn 2014
3.6	Herbstritt, Georg, and Helmut Müller-Enbergs: Das Gesicht dem Westen zu ... DDR Spionage gegen die Bundesrepublik Deutschland, Bremen. Ed. Temmen 2003 (= Analysen und Dokumente, 23)
3.7	Kaminsky, Anna: Frauen in der DDR, Berlin: Ch. Links 2016
3.8	Polzin, Arno: Mythos Schwedt. DDR-Militärstrafvollzug und NVA-Disziplinareinheit aus dem Blick der Staatssicherheit, Göttingen: Vandenhoeck & Ruprecht 2018 (= Analysen und Dokumente, 49)
3.9	Rehlinger, Ludwig A.: Freikauf. Die Geschäfte der DDR mit politisch Verfolgten 1963–1989, Frankfurt: Ullstein 1991
3.10	Schütz, Gertrud, et al. (ed) Kleines politisches Wörterbuch, (East) Berlin: Dietz ³1978
3.11	Seubert, Heribert: Zum Legitimitätsverfall des militarisierten Sozialismus in der DDR, Münster: Lit 1995 (= Studien zu Konflikt und Kooperation im Osten, 3)

3.12 Wegmann, Bodo: Die Militäraufklärung der NVA. Die zentrale Organisation der militärischen Aufklärung der Streitkräfte der Deutschen Demokratischen Republik, Berlin: Köster 2005 (= Beiträge zur Friedensforschung und Sicherheitspolitik, 22)

3.13 Wenzke, Rüdiger: Ab nach Schwedt! Die Geschichte des DDR-Militärstrafvollzugs, Berlin: Ch. Links 2011

3.14 Wolf, Stephan: "Das Ministerium für Staatssicherheit und die Überwachung der NVA durch die Hauptabteilung I", in: Ehlert, Hans, and Matthias Rogg (eds): Militär, Staat und Gesellschaft in der DDR. Forschungsfelder, Ergebnisse, Perspektiven, Berlin: Ch. Links 2004 (= Militärgeschichte der DDR, 8), 323–36

Chapter 4:

4.1 Kopenhagen, Wilfried, Hans Mehl, and Knut Schäfer: Die NVA. Land-, Luft- und Seestreitkräfte, Stuttgart: Motorbuch-Verlag 2006

4.2 Wenzke, Rüdiger: "Die Nationale Volksarmee (1956–1990)", in: Diedrich, Torsten, Hans Ehlert, and Rüdiger Wenzke (eds): Im Dienste der Partei. Handbuch der bewaffneten Organe der DDR, Berlin: Ch. Links 1998, 423–535

4.3 Diedrich, Torsten: "Die Grenzpolizei der SBZ/DDR (1946–1961)", in: Died-rich, Torsten, Hans Ehlert, and Rüdiger Wenzke (eds): Im Dienste der Partei. Handbuch der bewaffneten Organe der DDR, Berlin: Ch. Links 1998, 201–223

4.4 Heider, Paul: Die Gesellschaft für Sport und Technik. Vom Wehrsport zur "Schule des Soldaten von morgen", Berlin: Fides 2002

4.5 Koch, Hagen, and Peter Joachim Lapp: Die Garde des Erich Mielke. Der militärisch-operative Arm des MfS. Das Berliner Wachregiment "Feliks Dzierzynski", Aachen: Helios 2008

4.6 Mittmann, Wolfgang: "Die Transportpolizei (1945–1990)", in: Diedrich, Torsten, Hans Ehlert, and Rüdiger Wenzke (eds): Im Dienste der Partei. Handbuch der bewaffneten Organe der DDR, Berlin: Ch. Links 1998, 537–550

4.7 Sachse, Christian: Aktive Jugend – wohlerzogen und diszipliniert. Wehrerziehung in der DDR als Sozialisations- und Herrschaftsinstrument (1960–1973), Münster: Lit 2000 (= Studien zur DDR-Gesellschaft, 7)

4.8 Siebeneichner, Tilmann: Proletarischer Mythos und realer Sozialismus. Die Kampfgruppen der Arbeiterklasse in der DDR, Cologne: Böhlau 2014 (= Zeithistorische Studien, 55)

4.9 Steike, Jörn: Die Bereitschaftspolizei der DDR 1950–1990. Geschichte – Struktur – Aufgaben – rechtliche Ausgestaltung, Munich: tuduv 1992

4.10 Wagner, Armin: "Die Kampfgruppen der Arbeiterklasse (1953–1990)", in: Diedrich, Torsten, Hans Ehlert, and Rüdiger Wenzke (eds): Im Dienste der Partei. Handbuch der bewaffneten Organe der DDR, Berlin: Ch. Links 1998, 281–337

4.11 Dockrill, Saki: Eisenhower's New-Look National Security Policy, 1953–61, Basingstoke: Macmillan 1996

4.12 Gaddis, John Lewis: Strategies of Containment. A Critical Appraisal of Post-war American National Security Policy, New York: Oxford University Press 1982

4.13 Heinemann, Winfried: Vom Zusammenwachsen des Bündnisses. Die Funktionsweise der NATO in ausgewählten Krisenfällen 1951–1956, Munich: Oldenbourg 1998 (= Entstehung und Probleme des Atlantischen Bündnisses bis 1956, 1)

4.14 Gilbert, Mark: Cold War Europe. The Politics of a Contested Continent, London: Rowman & Littlefield 2016

Chapter 5:

5.1 Lapp, Peter Joachim: "Die Nationale Volksarmee 1956–1990", in: Deutscher Bundestag (ed): Materialien der Enquete-Kommission "Aufarbeitung von Geschichte und Folgen der SED-Diktatur in Deutschland" (12. Wahlperiode des Deutschen Bundestages), vol. 2, Baden-Baden: Nomos 1995, 1900–1972

5.2 Eisenfeld, Bernd, and Peter Schicketanz: Bausoldaten in der DDR. Die "Zusammenführung feindlich-negativer Kräfte" in der NVA, Berlin: CH. Links 2011

5.3 Zivilcourage und Kompromiss. Bausoldaten in der DDR 1964–1990. Bausoldatenkongress Potsdam, 3.–5. September 2004, Berlin: Robert-Havemann-Gesellschaft 2005 (= Schriftenreihe des Robert-Havemann-Archivs, 9)

Chapter 6:

6.1 Karlsch, Rainer: "Die Rüstungsindustrie der DDR im Überblick", in: Ehlert, Hans, and Matthias Rogg (eds): Militär, Staat und Gesellschaft in der DDR. Forschungsfelder, Ergebnisse, Perspektiven, Berlin: Ch. Links 2004 (= Militärgeschichte der DDR, 8), 173–185

Chapter 7:

7.1 Basler, Horst-Henning: "Das operative Denken der NVA", in: Naumann, Klaus (ed), NVA – Anspruch und Wirklichkeit nach ausgewählten Dokumenten, Berlin: Mittler 1993, S. 179–219

7.2 Diedrich, Torsten: "Die DDR als Operations- und Durchmarschgebiet der Vereinten Streitkräfte auf dem Westlichen Kriegsschauplatz", in: Militärgeschichtliche Zeitschrift 79 (2020), 396–418

7.3 Kauffmann, Thomas A.: Kontinuität und Wandel. Entwicklung der Militärdoktrin und Kriegsplanung des Warschauer Paktes im Verlauf der 80er Jahre unter Berücksichtigung der Landesverteidigung der DDR, Munich (Phil.Diss.), 2002

7.4 Lautsch, Siegfried: "Die Entwicklung der militärischen Konzeptionen der Warschauer Vertragsorganisation in den letzten zwei Jahrzehnten des Ost-West-Konfliktes", in: Krüger, Dieter (ed): Schlachtfeld Fulda Gap. Strategien und Operationspläne der Bündnisse im Kalten Krieg, Fulda: Parzeller 2014 (= Schriftenreihe Point Alpha, 2), 87–113

7.5 Moszumanski, Zbigniew: "Die Polnische Küstenfront auf dem Westlichen Kriegsschauplatz", in: Wenzke, Rüdiger (ed), Die Streitkräfte der DDR und Polens in der Operationsplanung des Warschauer Paktes, Potsdam: MGFA 2010 (= Potsdamer Schriften zur Militärgeschichte, 12), 71–83

7.6 Nielsen, Harald: Die DDR und die Kernwaffen. Die nukleare Rolle der Nationalen Volksarmee im Warschauer Pakt, Baden-Baden: Nomos 1998 (= Internationale Politik und Sicherheit, 30)

7.7 Petroschka, Bruno: Über die Armeeangriffsoperationen zur Einnahme eines Ballungsgebietes aus der Bewegung ohne Einsatz von Kernwaffen, Diss. Militärakademie "Friedrich Engels", Dresden (unpublished) 1985 (available at: Bundesarchiv, Abteilung Militärarchiv, DVH 7/45632)

7.8 Rijnoveanu, Carmen: Die Auswirkungen der Krisen des Ostblocks 1956 und 1968 auf das rumänische Sicherheitskonzept, in: Diedrich, Torsten, and Walter Süß (eds), Militär und Staatssicherheit im Sicherheitskonzept der Warschauer-Pakt-Staaten, Berlin: Ch. Links 2010 (= Militärgeschichte der DDR, 19), 149–65

7.9 Wettig, Gerhard: "Warsaw Pact Planning in Central Europe. The Current Stage of Research", in: Cold War International History Project Bulletin 3 (1993), 51

7.10 Wenzke, Rüdiger (ed): Die Streitkräfte der DDR und Polens in der Operationsplanung des Warschauer Paktes, Potsdam: MGFA 2010 (= Potsdamer Schriften zur Militärgeschichte, 12)

Texts

Armeegeneral Heinz Keßler: Letter addressed to Erich Honecker, February 25, 1988

The GDR Minister of Defense asks the SED Secretary General for instructions on how to proceed in the light of Soviet press reports about disarmament questions.

In the Soviet journal "New Times" 7/88, an article was published entitled "Why do we dismantle more missiles?".

After an analysis, allow me to report the following opinions and attitudes from the perspective of the Ministry of National Defense.

The author of this article mainly takes the positions represented by enemy propaganda, supporting the lie that we are threatening the West, and justifying the continuous increase in NATO armaments expenditures. In fact, he places the US and the USSR, and NATO and the Warsaw Treaty [Organization] on the same level, and accuses both sides of conducting an armaments race.

The impression might be created that military decisions of the Warsaw Treaty are determined by an attempt to achieve military superiority.

One indication is the Western argument, repeated here without any objection, that there are substantial imbalances in conventional arms [...] between NATO and the Warsaw Treaty. [...]

If you agree, I will take up this article at the earliest possible opportunity with our Soviet comrades, and will make clear our concerns regarding such publications.

May I ask you to take note, approve of my suggested course of action, or give further instructions?

Source: BArch, DVW 1/115516.

Deployment of NVA forces in October/November 1989

On December 7, 1989, the GDR MfNV formed a committee to investigate cases of abuse of authority, corruption, and embezzlement within the NVA, the border troops, and the civil defense units. The committee submitted its comprehensive report on March 15, 1990; among other subjects, it dealt with the deployment of the GDR during the peaceful revolution during the autumn of 1989.

Since January 1990, and in close cooperation with representatives of the central Round Table, as well as the Citizen's Committees of Dresden, Leipzig, and Berlin, this committee has investigated the deployment of NVA ad hoc units *[Hundertschaften]*.
Planning to deploy parts of the NVA for a possible police operation in support of the internal order and security organs of the GDR was based on the orders nos 08/89 and

09/89 of the National Defense Council, which were valid at the time, but are entirely unacceptable now.

The organizational basis for the deployment of forces was laid with order no. 105/89 of the Minister for National Defense.

This order had been given as the security instructions for the 40th anniversary of the GDR. It already contained regulations for the structure of "one-hundred-men task forces" alien to army structures, which were to be held in readiness in a number of garrison towns. The order was first applied in Dresden in connection with the passing through of trains from Prague to the FRG [Federal Republic of Germany]. [...]

When advanced combat readiness was called for, orders went out to issue 30 rounds of ammunition for submachine guns, and 12 rounds for pistols. [...]

When the dangers of carrying firearms were realized, upon request of the generals and officers in command in Dresden, it was ordered by the Minister of National Defense on October 6, 1989, at about 10:25 a.m., that firearms and ammunition would remain in barracks. At the same time, batons were beginning to be issued to the units.

By about 9 p.m., on October 6, 1989, five units left their barracks with the aim of sealing off the railway station.

One of these units was deployed together with Volkspolizei to evacuate two police vehicles, and formed part of a chain to clear an area. The soldiers were pelted with stones and other items, and had abuse shouted at them.

Batons were not used against the crowds.

Two soldiers were injured by stones thrown. [...]

Members of the forces today take a more differentiated view of their deployment then, whether actual or planned, and now reject such deployments.

According to the Constitution of the German Democratic Republic (Articles 7 and 23), the NVA and the Border Troops of the GDR have the sole tasks of protecting the socialist achievements against enemies from the outside.

Source: BArch, DVW 1/44503.

Order No. 5/90 of the Minister for Disarmament and Defense, June 5, 1990

In this order, Minister Rainer Eppelmann lays down details for how the NVA is to prepare for, and eventually swear, the new oath as determined by the Volkskammer on April 26, 1990.

By the law passed by the *Volkskammer* of the German Democratic Republic on April 26, 1990, the oath to be sworn by the NVA has been rephrased to meet the new social conditions. All members of the National People's Army who have not yet done so are to take this oath.

For the preparation and administration of the oath, I order as follows:
1. (1) The public administration of the oath in the version of April 26, 1990 (encl. 1), will take place in all command authorities, formations, units, and installations on July 20, 1990.
   All members of the forces who, for valid reasons, cannot take part in this will take the oath before September 15, 1990.
2. Until July 1, 1990, all members of the NVA who are to take this oath will be asked by their respective superiors whether they are willing to swear this oath. [...]
3. To prepare for the swearing of the new oath, an order of the day of the Minister of Disarmament and National Defense is to be prepared.
4. (1) The oath will be administered on the flag of the GDR according to the ceremonial as laid down in encl. 2.
   (2) Prominent members of public life, members of the anti-fascist resistance, if possible, relations of members of the military resistance of July 20, 1944, guests from the FRG [Federal Republic], and media representatives are to be invited. Assistance for the guests and an opportunity to talk to the members of the forces are to be prepared.
5. To prepare for taking the oath, members of the armed forces will be taught about the importance of the new oath and about the resistance movement of July 20, 1944, using appropriate measures of political education.
6. (1) Swearing the oath in the version of April 26, 1990, will render any earlier military oath or promise of service as an officer invalid.
   (2) The new oath will apply by force of law for reservists with prior military service.

Wording of the oath:
I swear,
in accordance with the laws of the German Democratic Republic, that I will always perform my military duties with discipline and honor.
I swear to use all my strength to maintain the peace and to protect the German Democratic Republic.

Source: BArch, DVW 1/44497.

Order Nr. 25/54 of the Minister of the Interior of the GDR, January 28, 1954

This order, signed by Willi Stoph, details which defensive measures are to be taken should inimical groups or organizations endanger the order and security of the GDR state.

1. An Operational Control Staff *[Einsatzleitung]* will be created in the Ministry of the Interior to coordinate the various branches of the *Volkspolizei* and ensure successful operative measures. The Operational Control Staff will be established by order of the Minister of the Interior, upon instructions of the competent agencies.

The members of the Operational Control Staff are
- The Minister of the Interior as Chairman
- The Secretary of State for State Security
- The Chief of the Kasernierte Volkspolizei
- The Chief of the Deutsche Volkspolizei [regular police]
- The Chief of the German Border Police
- The Deputy Ministers of the Interior for Finance and Administration, or their deputies in case of absence.

2. The Operational Command Staff will act upon the orders and guidance of the competent agencies and upon its own decisions, to be taken according to the situation. The Minister of the Interior will forward the decisions of the Operational Command Staff as orders to the chiefs of those branches of the *Volkspolizei* whose remit includes their swift and precise execution. [...]

5. All regions *[Bezirke]* will form command staffs in case of violent disruption of the order of the state or attacks upon the security of the German Democratic Republic. [...] No branches of the *Volkspolizei* will be placed under the orders of representatives of the civil authorities. In a similar situation, and upon instruction by the regional command staffs, the districts will proceed accordingly. [...]

9. Should information become known which might indicate an impending disruption of the order of the state or of public security, all branches of the *Volkspolizei* will increase their reconnaissance activities so as to identify in advance any planned enemy measures.

10. To increase readiness in case of unusual occurrences, the Political Organs of the branches of the *Volkspolizei* and their subordinate agencies will intensify political work, in particular with those elements of the *Volkspolizei* which are actually operating.

The focus of agitation is to be on explaining the situation and on the unconditional willingness of all V[olks]P[olizei] members to disrupt enemy actions aimed against the German Democratic Republic.

Source: BArch, DVH 3/2007, ff. 27-32.

Summary by the GDR Supreme Court of the Legal Situation Regarding Pastoral Care for Young Soldiers, December 3, 1986

According to Article 20, Paragraph 1, of our socialist constitution, every citizen of the GDR has equal rights and obligations, independent of their religious affiliation, and freedom of conscience as well as religious freedom are assured. According to Article 39, Paragraph 1, of our constitution, this includes the right to profess a religious faith and take part in religious activities. This also applies to members of the NVA (Paragraph 21.2 of the Law about General Conscription).

The activities of the Churches and religious groups have to conform to the Constitution and the legal norms of the GDR (Article 39, Paragraph 2, of the Constitution). In view of the principled separation between Church and State, members of the NVA are unable to perform religious activities within military objects during their term of military service. For the same reason, pastoral care for NVA soldiers is inadmissible.

Arising from the need for military protection of the GDR, special rights and obligations apply for the duration of military service which are laid down on the basis of the Law about General Conscription (Paragraph 21.2 of the Law about General Conscription).

In accordance with Ordinance DV 010/0/007 [Ordinance on granting leave], and with due regard for an adequate numerical strength, the tasks defined in Paragraph 22 of the Law about General Conscription do not preclude religious activities of military personnel during their leave or furlough.

In view of this legal situation, members of the armed forces are within their constitutional rights if, during their furlough within the garrison or their leave elsewhere, they turn to spiritual care or else perform religious activities. There are no legal norms or military regulations which would be opposed to that, or which might curtail the soldiers' rights in this respect. However, any organized activities by the churches which are specifically aimed at NVA soldiers which might possibly have negative effects on morale and battle worthiness of the troops are, therefore, in contravention of Article 39, Paragraph 2, of the Constitution.

The complex problem delineated here might require additional political decisions. In this case, cooperation with the Working Group on Church Questions within the Central Committee, the NVA Political Main Directorate, and the Secretariat of State for Church Questions would be recommended.

This summary was harmonized with the Director of the Legal Department of the Ministry of National Defense and the responsible officer within the NVA Political Main Directorate.

Source: BArch, DVW 8/71020.

Pasewalk District Court Sentence Against NCO Cadet G. Charged with "Seditious Agitation," May 5, 1958

The accused served from April 15, 1957, until March 23, 1958, as a member of the NVA, eventually as an NCO cadet. His superiors had already noted during this time that he had no interest in political education classes and did not always execute his duties in a way to be expected from an NVA member. [...] On March 12, 1958, while a political education class was being held in his unit, the accused wrote the following letter:

> The 35th Plenary Session [of the SED]! The 32nd Plenary Session is the, is the same as the 35th, i.e. the exploitation by the Soviet Union continues as before. The NVA gobbles up our parents' and siblings' money, who give this money to the state in the form of social insurance or tax money. Therefore: Struggle for justice, freedom from the yoke of the suppressor! The Editor-in-Chief of this journal, Civilian B.

The accused got the idea to formulate this letter because the political education class was just then discussing the questions of the 35th Plenary Session of the SED. As he himself stated, he wrote this letter so as to be granted a discharge from the NVA. By doing so, the accused created a document with a seditious content. The sedition the accused formulates in this letter is directed against the policies of the Workers and Peasants' State as well as against the Party of the Working Classes, the NVA, and the Soviet Union. The accused is guilty of seditious propaganda as defined in Paragraph 19, Sections 1.2 and 2, Supplementary Penal Law *[Strafrechtsergänzungsgesetz]*.

It is general knowledge that the class enemy abuses the friendly relations between our state, the Soviet Union, and the other socialist nations to agitate against our state. In creating this document, the accused made himself a tool of the class enemy. He openly agitated against the Soviet Union, against the social conditions in our state, and against the NVA. [...] The accused needs to be shown that our state of workers and peasants will not, under any conditions, allow the kind of seditious agitation against the state which the accused undertook. The accused is still relatively young. He will have sufficient opportunity to show by his future behavior that he has learned from today's trial and the subsequent sentence and is willing to draw the necessary consequences.

The Prosecutor pleaded to convict the accused of seditious agitation and to sentence him to four months in prison. In view of all the circumstances, the court decided to follow this plea.

Source: BArch, DVW 13/6996, fol. 24-5.

Law Concerning the Creation of the NVA and the Ministry of National Defense of January 18, 1956

Protecting the workers and peasants' power, the achievements of the working classes, and safeguarding their peaceful work are elementary duties of our democratic, sovereign, and peace-loving state. The reestablishment of aggressive militarism in West Germany and the establishment of the West German mercenaries' army are a constant threat to the German people and to all the peoples of Europe.

The *Volkskammer* has passed the following law to increase the defense readiness and the security of our German Democratic Republic, and on the basis of Articles 5 and 11 of the Constitution:

§ 1
   (1) A "National People's Army" shall be established.
   (2) The "National People's Army" consists of those land, air, and naval forces which are necessary for the defense of the German Democratic Republic. The numerical strength of the forces is limited in accordance with the tasks of protecting the territory of the German Democratic Republic, the defense of its borders, and air defense.

§ 2
   (1) A "Ministry of National Defense" shall be established.
   (2) The "Ministry of National Defense" shall organize and command the "National People's Army" (land, air, and naval forces) on the basis and in execution of the laws, byelaws, and decisions of the *Volkskammer* and the Council of Ministers of the German Democratic Republic.
   (3) The tasks of the "Ministry of National Defense" shall be determined by the Council of Ministers.

Source: Gesetzblatt der Deutschen Demokratischen Republik 1956, I, 81.

Order Nr. 65/61 by the Commander, LSK/LV, dated December 16, 1961

The order by Heinz Keßler, who was, at the same time, Deputy GDR Minister of National Defense, referring to an order no. 3/61, regulates the role of the LSK/LV of the GDR within the framework of the DHS (integrated Warsaw Pact air defense system)

1. The units and capabilities of the 1st and 3rd LVD [air defense divisions] will be deployed to reinforce the air defense DHS of the Group of Soviet Forces in Germany to improve safety in the air space of the German Democratic Republic. [...]

3. The units and capabilities of the air defense DHS will engage upon orders from the Central Command Post. In exceptional cases, the command posts of the Group

of Soviet Forces in Germany can request an engagement directly. Should the request be made in weather below the minimum, the Central Command Post will decide. [...]
5. Interaction between the units and capabilities of the air defense DHS and the Group of Soviet Forces in Germany air defense will be assured according to the conformed plans of cooperation.

Airfields are:
- a) For the fighter units of the 1st and 3rd LVD: Damgarten, Lärz, Templin, Zerbst, Altes-Lager, Merseburg, Großenhain, Altenburg
- b) For the air assets of the Group of Soviet Forces in Germany: Cottbus, Drewitz, Preschen, Bautzen, Neubrandenburg.

Source: BArch, DVL 3/24768: NVA. Chef der LSK/LV. Sekretariat, February 1960 through December 1961.

Report of the Central Committee to the VIII SED Plenary Party Session, June 15, 1978

In his report, Erich Honecker emphasizes the military efforts of the GDR to protect "socialist order" within the framework of the Warsaw Pact.

That it was possible to save mankind from a new World War, and that the imperialist aggressors could be put in their place again, is due to the Soviet Union and the entire community of socialist states. The relevance of the socialist world system as the main revolutionary force of our time and as a bastion of peace has increased again. Its influence over international developments is continuously increasing. [...]

Imperialism has attempted again and again, using military aggression and counterrevolutionary approaches, increasingly plundering other nations, and using ideological diversion, to solidify and even expand its positions – but these attempts have always failed. Under the pressure of the international power system changing in favor of socialism, the imperialists attempt to adapt to the new conditions of the class struggle and achieve their old aims with new methods. Their lack of perspective has been proven. However, we cannot overlook the fact that imperialism still has a large potential and that its incessantly aggressive global strategy conjures up serious dangers.

The German Democratic Republic is a reliable, immovable part of the community of socialist states, linked by a close friendship to the country of Lenin, the glorious Soviet Union. For the German Democratic Republic, being safely tied to this alliance is the elementary precondition for realizing the interests of the working classes and all citizens of the German Democratic Republic. [...]

We cannot talk about the cooperation of the community of socialist states without emphasizing the importance of the Warsaw Treaty for the foreign and security policies, and particularly the military protection of our community.

Together with the Communist Party of the Soviet Union and the other brotherly parties, the Socialist Unity Party of Germany has made great efforts to perfect the military organization and combat effectiveness of our defensive alliance and continuously improve our combat and mobilization readiness. At the same time, we contribute to an effective coordination of the diplomatic activities of the Warsaw Treaty member states. In the future as well, we will continue to conscientiously fulfil our obligations within the Warsaw Treaty.

In protecting the socialist order and the peaceful lives of our citizens, the armed formations of the German Democratic Republic, such as the National People's Army, the organs of the Ministry for State Security, the Ministry of the Interior, and the Working-Class Combat Groups have shown operational readiness. The Central Committee is convinced that those comrades who work in these organs will continue to strengthen public order and security, as well as to uncover, unmask, and defend against the corrosive and subversive activities of the imperialist foe, justifying the trust placed in them.

Source: Die Militär- und Sicherheitspolitik der SED 1945 bis 1988. Dokumente und Materialien, [East] Berlin [1989], 399–402.

Teletype Message by Armeegeneral Heinz Hoffmann to Marshal of the Soviet Union Ivan Ignatyevich Yakubovsky, dated June 10, 1968

In this urgent encoded teletype message addressed to the Supreme Commander of the Warsaw Pact, the GDR Minister of National Defense requests binding commitments regarding the participation of the NVA in the preparations for the invasion of Czechoslovakia.

It is with regret that I have to state, to this day, the Ministry of National Defense of the German Democratic Republic has not received any invitation for its staffs to attend the joint command post exercise which is to be held in the CSSR under your command.

From reports in the press and other sources available to me, I have to come to the conclusion that the participation of the National People's Army in this measure, assumed to be militarily and politically very important for us, is not planned.

I regret this and fail to have any understanding of it. In our opinion, that the National People's Army should not take part in such joint operations of the Supreme Commander of the Combined Forces cannot serve the improvement of the strength and cohesion of the Warsaw Treaty. This usage could very well result in unwanted consequences in the future.

I ask for your consideration and response.

Source: BArch, DVW 1/115612, Bl. 108.

Letter to Walter Ulbricht from Minister of National Defense Armeegeneral Heinz Hoffmann dated November 13, 1969

In his letter to the President of the Council of State, the Minister of National Defense comments on the possible training of members of the Libyan air force and navy and cadets inside the GDR

The German Democratic Republic borders directly on the Federal Republic. If the pilot cadets are not sufficiently trained and prepared, there is a real danger that they might overfly the state border of the German Democratic Republic and land on West German territory, for whatever political reasons. It must be taken into account as well that in such circumstances, corresponding technology [Soviet aircraft technology] might fall into the hands of the enemy.

During the last few months, the Ministry of Foreign Affairs of the German Democratic Republic acquainted me with similar wishes of other Arab states and nation-states, such as the retraining of Iraqi Army MiG-15 pilots to fly MiG-21 aircraft in close air support roles, i.e., the dropping of bombs and air-to-ground fire.

As the chief effort of the aerial forces of the National People's Army are in the field of air defense, for objective reasons, these wishes cannot be met for the time being.

If it is intended to train such large cadres in the long term within the German Democratic Republic, this would require that the German Democratic Republic make additional efforts in the fields of personnel, finance, and matériel [e.g. creating a training facility, purchase of training aircraft].

[...]

In view of the aspects listed above I suggest we do not plan to conduct such training.

Expecting your decision.

Source: BArch, DVW 1/115502.

NVA War game Bordkante-86 ("Curbstone 86")

The exercises held during the 1980s codenamed Bordkante were based on an assumed scenario in which American, British, and French forces, each in about brigade strength, had been cut off from their main forces inside a major GDR city. The 1986 exercise was set in Magdeburg during June and early July. A "Top Secret" document ("Geheime Verschlusssache") of the Commander of the "Special Grouping" laid down the planned operations of GDR forces. Many objects specified in the attack plan did not exist in Magdeburg, such as a "Chamber of Deputies" or a "Governing Mayor"; these existed only in West Berlin.

1. The 1st Front's Special Grouping has been tasked with moving into deployment areas and then to be ready, once signaled to do so, to initiate the attack to disrupt enemy forces in Magdeburg and seize the city in concentric strikes. During the 1st

and 2nd day of operations, a breakthrough through the outer ring of defense is to be achieved, the enemy forces are to be split in two, the main enemy is to be annihilated, and propitious conditions for seizing the city center are to be created. Following that, on the 3rd and 4th days, the enemy in Magdeburg is to be annihilated entirely, and the city center is to be occupied.

2. The enemy forces in Magdeburg have been reinforced; barriers have been erected on important access routes. The enemy defends the city deploying the 28th (US) Brigade, the 2nd (GB) Brigade, and the 72nd (FR) Brigade, in total about 21,000 men, 109 tanks, 154 artillery pieces and mortars, as well as 448 antitank weapons, including police forces. Defense will be from strongpoints in an outer and inner ring of defense. Order of Battle: probably one echelon with reserves. [...]

Based on the task set me, and the expected enemy operations, I have determined:

3. [...] Exploiting our own artillery fire, the strikes by close air support elements, and following advance units, to advance swiftly toward the city center in concentric strikes, to split the enemy formation in two by means of a tactical airborne landing, to disorganize enemy command so as to prevent the enemy from organizing their defense and from withdrawing in an orderly fashion into the inner ring of defense, so as to reach to city center during the 1st day. During the 2nd and 3rd days, the enemy formation to be annihilated piecemeal, the most important objects to be seized, and the entire city to be occupied (Objects 3, 36, 40, 56, 88, 89, 90, 95).

If combat operations permit, the following objects are to be seized without damages: 65 (National Gallery), 69 (Museum), 70 (Cathedral), 79 (State Library). Key to the map of the most important military geographic objects of the city of Magdeburg: 1. Food storage site, 2. Police Headquarters, 3. Liberal Party Headquarters, [...] 54. Academy, 55. University, 56. Signals installation, 57. City Hall, Chamber of Deputies, Governing Mayor, 58. Allied Kommandatura, British Kommandatura.

Source: Übungsanlage "Bordkante-86". BArch, DVH 7/45667, f. 83–94, 27–9.

Tables

Former Wehrmacht Officers in Major KVP Command Positions, May 1953

Position	Number	Total	Percentage
KVP Chief of Staff	1	1	100
Deputy KVP Chief of Staff	1	1	100
Directors of Administrations in the Ministry of the Interior	10	17	59
Branch Directors in the Ministry of the Interior	14	61	23
Commanding Generals, TV	1	4	25
Chiefs of Staff, TV	2	4	50
Deputy Commanding Generals, TV	4	14	29
Commanders, "Readiness Units" (i.e., regiments)	8	16	50
Chiefs of Staff, "Readiness Units"	7	16	44
Deputy Commanders, "Readiness Units"	14	64	22
Directors of KVP Schools	10	20	50
Deputy Directors of KVP Schools	12	20	60
Directors, District Recruitment Authorities	7	15	47

Source: *0.13* Niemetz, Das feldgraue Erbe, 103, based on BArch, DVH 3/3878, fol. 99–110.

Socialist Military Education in the GDR

Age (Years	Organization	Political-ideological content	Military content
0–3	Parents, nursery schools	Distinguish good and bad	Movement, games
3–6	Kindergarten	Our soldiers	Playfully training skills
6–10	School, Young Pioneers	Love of country, readiness to defend country	Playfully training skills
10–16	School, Young Pioneers, FDJ, employer, partnership with military unit	Preparation for Hans Beimler Games	Hans Beimler Games
16–18	High school, in-house professional school, GST	Preparation for military service	Paramilitary training
18–26	Employer, university/academy, SED organization	Preparation for practical job (e.g., technology)	Military training, Civil Defense training in universities
26–35	Employer, SED organization, NVA reserve	Retention of military training and motivation	Military training and specialized training

Source: *0.9* Wenzke, Staatsfeinde in Uniform?, 395.

Desertions from the NVA, December 1, 1989 – August 27, 1990

Branch	Officers	Fähnriche (warrant officers)	Officer Cadets	NCOs, NCO cadets	Fähnrich cadets (in training)	Corporals	Privates	Total
MoD	12	2	-	22	-	2	52	90
Army (LaSK)	23	14	11	321	2	29	519	919
Air Force (LSK/LV)	18	13	4	64	-	7	104	210
Navy (Volksmarine)	4	2	-	35	1	5	82	129
Total	57	31	15	442	3	43	757	1348

Source: 0.9 Wenzke, Staatsfeinde in Uniform?, 292, based on BArch, DVW 1/44513.

Methods of Persecution, Disciplining, and Sentencing in the NVA (selection, in arbitrary order)

- Discussion and personnel talk with superior officers, Party officials, political officers, Stasi, or military prosecutors
- Systematic covert supervision by Stasi informers, mail censorship
- Threats and pressure against personnel concerned, or their family, friends, colleagues
- Intrigues, artificially creating problems on the job, compromising, slandering, or discriminating personnel concerned
- Ostracizing personnel and their families on the job or in NVA housing areas
- Treating personnel as enemies of the state and the Party or publicly branding them as criminals
- Party sanctions or expulsion from the Party, combining Party and military sanctions
- Disciplinary measures without legal basis: dismissal, demotion, degradation from officer to private, annulment of state decorations or honors, seizure of honor dagger, annulment of professional qualifications so as to deny any chances of adequate employment in the civilian sector, denial of transmission allowances for volunteers at the end their term
- Restrictions on furlough or leave
- Immediate and dishonorable discharge from the service as a total rupture in the personal and professional career
- Occupational ban; denial of advanced training or adequately paid jobs in civilian life, limiting a person's standard of living and social status

- Disciplining individuals below the level of actual criminal prosecution by police investigations and searches in homes
- Detention
- Duty in the Schwedt Military Prison
- Remand in custody or prison sentence

Source: 0.9 Wenzke, Staatsfeinde in Uniform?, 10.

NVA Land Forces (LasK) Equipment, 1987 (most relevant systems)

	Wartime authorization	Peacetime authorization	Effective strength	Mobilizable strength
Personnel	257,960	103,996	105,983	152,024
"Oka" launchers	20	20	20	-
"Luna" launchers	40	36	40	-
T-72 tanks	635	635	385	-
T-55 tanks	2163	1084	1969	-
T-54 tanks	-	-	444	-
BMP Armored fighting vehicle	887	880	893	-
SPW Armored fighting vehicle	4112	1912	3196	485
Artillery pieces	1746	887	1746	-

Source: Grundkurs deutsche Militärgeschichte, vol. 3, Munich 2008, 262.

Reasons for Young Men to Enlist for a Life Career in the Military

	Conscripts (percentage)	Employees (percentage)
Political convictions	30.2	23.3
Technical interests in a special field	34.9	33.4
Superior social status of military jobs	11.6	-17.0
Influence of parents/educators	12.5	21.7
Financial reasons	29.6	28.8
Insistent pressure during interview	8.4	14.1
Cannot tell	20.8	9.1
No answer	0.4	0.8

Source: 0.2 Fingerle, Waffen in Arbeiterhand?, 304, based on BArch SAPMO, DY 30, IV B2/2.028/17, f 129.

Social and Educational Backgrounds of NVA Officer Cadets, 1955–1960 (Percentages)

	1955	1956	1957	1958	1959	1960
Social Status						
Workers	63.6	31.5	51.7	83.3	84.0	81.3
Farmers	0.1	0.4	0.3	0.6	0.5	0.2
Employees	13.9	4.7	5.7	5.1	4.9	5.3
Students	22.4	61.3	42.3	10.9	10.6	13.2
Others	-	2.1	-	0.1	-	-
Education						
Abitur (13 years of schooling)	21.8	61.4	38.7	10.1	10.6	12.3
10 years of schooling	11.3	7.7	8.5	7.6	7.3	8.0
8 years or less of schooling	66.9	30.9	52.8	82.3	82.1	79.7
Party Membership						
SED	67.0	59.7	48.7	42.3	44.6	34.7
Others	0.1	-	-	-	-	-
Free German Youth (FDJ)	94.5	99.6	99.7	95.9	97.3	99.1

Source: 0.2 Fingerle, Waffen in Arbeiterhand?, 190.

GDR Armaments Enterprises 1965–1985 (selection, rounded figures)

	Production (million Marks)	Personnel	Percentage of Armaments	Percentage of Exported Goods
Repair Works Neubrandenburg (operating as of 1953)				
1965	54.1	1586	100.0	-
1975	185.0	3208	99.0	-
1985	433.7	4208	93.0	-
Peenewerft Shipyards, Wolgast (operating as of 1948)				
1965	91.4	2820	95.0	
1975	188.5	3230	98.0	
1985	310.3	3856	98.0	
Flugzeugwerk Dresden (operating as of 1961)				
1965	51.9	2381	-	17.0
1975	79.4	2394	-	13.2
1985	200.7	2416	-	14.8
Mechanical Works Königswartha (founded in the 1950s)				
1965	19.9	887	-	-
1975	40.5	1026	-	31.3
1985	120.3	1200	-	4.7
Tool and Appliances Building Wiesa (as of 1960)				
1965	32.3	1032	97.5	-
1975	64.2	1214	83.5	32.5
1985	123.4		-	7.9
Spreewerk Lübben (as of 1961)				
1965	15.7	713	83.3	-
1975	29.5	664	64.3	20.9
1985	67.6	841	85.1	8.8
Wurzen Engine Works (taken over from Soviet Troops in 1954)				
1965	36.7	665	60.0	-
1975	60.6	953	69.9	6.9
1985	83.9	1030	-	9.7

Source: *6.1* Karlsch, Die Rüstungsindustrie, 175-6.

Index

Adenauer, Konrad 4, 20, 25, 83, 86
Akhromeyev, Sergey F. 181
Bahr, Egon 16
Beyer, Uwe 82
Biermann, Wolf 47
Bismarck, Otto 86
Blücher, Gebhard Leberecht von 84
Born, Hendrik 136
Brandt, Willy 7, 42
Brezhnev, Leonid Ilyich 42
Ceaușescu, Nicolae 162
Chuikov, Vasily I. 31
Clausewitz, Carl von 164
Dickel, Friedrich 27
Dietze, Manfred 74
Dölling, Rudolf 23, 66
Dzierzynski, Feliks 84, 113
Ehm, Wilhelm 30
Eisenhower, Dwight D. 123
Engels, Friedrich 164
Eppelmann, Rainer 12, 32, 52, 90
Fischer, Birgit 82
Fischer, Kurt 19
Gartenschläger, Michael 72
Gneisenau, August Neidhardt von 83 f.
Gorbachev, Mikhail S. 49, 51, 53, 89, 165 f., 170, 180 f.
Grätz, Manfred 91
Gronau, Heinz 70
Grotewohl, Otto 31
Hager, Kurt 50, 181
Harmel, Pierre 44
Haußmann, Leander 125
Hitler, Adolf 9, 53, 86, 134
Hoffmann, Heinz 19 f., 24, 26, 29, 41, 49, 65, 75, 90 f., 96, 135 f., 142, 168, 205 f.
Hoffmann, Theodor 10, 52, 90, 158
Honecker, Erich 6, 13, 27, 33, 36, 41, 43, 45, 49, 51, 64 f., 73, 75, 106, 115, 137, 147, 149, 173 f.,

Kaunda, Kenneth David 172
Keßler, Heinz 90 f.
Khrushchev, Nikita S. 33, 35, 67, 118
Kleinjung, Karl 71 f.
Kocka, Jürgen 7 f., 55
Konev, Ivan S. 67
Krenz, Egon 51
Kulikov, Viktor 114
Löffler, Hans-Georg 136
Lushev, Pyotr G. 32
Maizière, Lothar de 52, 90
Malinovsky, Rodion Y. 165
Malzew, Michail M. 153
Marx, Karl 164
Maske, Henry 82
Mielke, Erich 19, 71, 73, 75, 114
Müller, Vincenz 20, 24, 27 f., 91, 136
Müntzer, Thomas 83
Neiber, Gerhard 72
Pech, Ottomar 70 f.
Peter, Erich 30, 103
Peter, Fritz 48
Pieck, Wilhelm 36
Reinhold, Wolfgang 30
Scharnhorst, Gerhard von 83 f.
Scheel, Walter 42
Stechbarth, Horst 136
Stoph, Willi 20, 26, 28, 31, 64 f., 90, 136
Strauß, Franz-Josef 84
Streletz, Fritz 42, 91, 136
Teller, Günther 107
Ulbricht, Walter 6, 13, 25, 27, 35 f., 40 f., 43, 49, 64 f., 73, 137, 149, 165, 167 f., 174, 206
Verner, Waldemar 66, 73, 90, 136, 163
Wollweber, Ernst 71
Woytiła, Karol Cardinal 47
Yakubovsky, Ivan I. 167, 205
Zaisser, Wilhelm 19
Zhukov, Georgy K. 67